And the Mirror Cracked

Also by Anneke Smelik

WOMEN'S STUDIES AND CULTURE: A Feminist Introduction
(*editor with Rosemarie Buikema*)

And the Mirror Cracked

Feminist Cinema and Film Theory

Anneke Smelik

palgrave

First edition 1998
Reprinted 2000

Published in paperback 2001 by
PALGRAVE
Houndmills, Basingstoke, Hampshire RG21 6XS and
175 Fifth Avenue, New York, N.Y. 10010
Companies and representatives throughout the world

PALGRAVE is the new global academic imprint of
St. Martin's Press LLC Scholarly and Reference Division and
Palgrave Publishers Ltd (formerly Macmillan Press Ltd).

ISBN 0–333–69324–8 hardback (*outside North America*)
ISBN 0–312–21142–2 hardback (*in North America*)
ISBN 0–333–92041–4 paperback (*worldwide*)

This book is printed on paper suitable for recycling and
made from fully managed and sustained forest sources.

A catalogue record for this book is available
from the British Library.

The Library of Congress has cataloged the hardcover edition as follows:
Smelik, Anneke.
    And the mirror cracked : feminist cinema and film theory /
Anneke Smelik.
        p. cm.
    Includes bibliographical references and index.
    ISBN 0–312–21142–2 (cloth)
    1. Feminist motion pictures. 2. Feminism and motion pictures.
    3. Women in motion pictures. 4. Motion pictures and women.
    I. Title.
PN1995.9.W6S54 1998
791.43'082—dc21
                                                    97–41547
                                                    CIP

10 9 8 7 6 5 4 3 2 1
10 09 08 07 06 05 04 03 02 01

Printed in Great Britain by Antony Rowe Ltd, Chippenham, Wiltshire

For my parents

'I have seen nothing whatsoever that is ultimately real.'

Lady Yeshe Tsogyel, Tibet, eighth century

Contents

Acknowledgements

My gratitude is due to the Netherlands Organization for Scientific Research (NWO) for subsidizing the research of this project, and to the department of Women's Studies in the Arts Faculty of Utrecht University for providing me with office space and material support.

My enduring appreciation goes to Mieke Bal whose enthusiasm in the early years of Dutch women's studies encouraged me to embark on a path of academic research. She has been a stimulating and challenging critic of my work in progress. Thomas Elsaesser's knowledgeable comments have helped to situate the text more firmly within cinema studies. I also wish to thank Teresa de Lauretis and Tania Modleski for their timely encouragements.

Renée C. Hoogland has generously read the entire manuscript with great care and an open and critical mind. Both her incisive criticism and her detailed corrections of my English have greatly improved the text. I have found wonderful readers in Bernadette van Dijck, Annette Förster and Jann Ruyters who, besides going to the movies with me, read the chapters in different stages, giving me insightful comments and intellectual sustenance.

Staff and students of the Women's Studies' graduate seminar of Utrecht University provided me with the rich intellectual and creative context in which I wrote this book: their suggestions, criticisms, and support have contributed in a vital way. I particularly want to thank my colleagues Rosemarie Buikema, Maaike Meijer and Berteke Waaldijk for many years of close cooperation and fine friendship. Finally I thank Rosi Braidotti not only for her perceptive comments which I value most highly, but also for her inexhaustible pursuit of higher goals, both in writing and in living.

An abridged version of Chapter 4 appeared in *Women's Studies International Forum*, Vol. 16, no. 4, 1993: 349–63.

Introduction

My experience of cinema is marked by a distinct event which opened my eyes to an object of study that many years later would result in this book. In 1978 I saw my first feminist film and I was shocked. My sense of shock was due to the experience that this woman's film was so very different from any film I had seen before. In a sort of gynocentric epiphany, it made me realize in ways which I had not been able to envisage nor dared to hope for as a young feminist, that it did make a significant difference whether a film was made by a woman or not.

That particular film was the debut of director Margarethe von Trotta, *Das zweite Erwachen der Christa Klages* (*The Second Awakening of Christa Klages*, Germany, 1978). Chronologically it was not the very first woman's film I had seen. I must have watched dozens of feminist documentaries on abortion, sexual violence, equal pay and other issues. I had also probably seen fiction films made by women. But this does not detract anything from that 'first time' experience, which has become part of my personal myth and memory and which initiated me into feminist cinema and film theory. For me, it has remained true ever since that the critical aims of feminist film theory must be firmly attached to both the texts of feminist cinema and to the specific forms of spectatorship they construct.

The Second Awakening of Christa Klages accomplished something new: it addressed me as a woman and it constructed me as a feminist spectator. In the historical conjunction of the second feminist wave and a new kind of cinema, an 'awakening' occurred in the practice of filmmaking which coincided with an awakening within me. Today, I think that the historical context of feminism allows both the position of the female filmmaker and that of the female spectator to become enacted and empowered as conscious and self-reflexive subject positions, and this is the thesis I will argue in this book.

The experience of my viewing pleasures in women's films also led to intellectual curiosity about the politics and pleasures that circulate in feminist cinema. It still motivates and shapes much of the present project. The object of my study is the feminist narrative film. By 'feminist' film I mean a film which represents sexual difference from a woman's point of view, displaying a critical awareness of the asymmetrical power relation between the sexes. While this open definition implies that not every film made by a woman can be called feminist, it allows for certain films made by men to fall into this category. I have avoided the term 'woman's film' because by now it contains two related risks: first, that of assuming an essentialist understanding of gendered identity; second, of suggesting an unwarranted continuity with the genre of the 'Woman's film' in classical Hollywood cinema. In this book the term 'woman's film' is reserved for the historical period of films made in the 1970s and early 1980s by, for and about women.

'Narrative' refers to films which can be distinguished from experimental cinema in that they make use of cinematic codes and conventions within a narrative plot. Let me add that experimental and narrative cinema are relative concepts which change over time. Moreover, the opposition between them is less pronounced in Europe than in the USA and had lost much of its edge anyway by the 1980s. The – mostly but not exclusively – European feminist films which I discuss in this study in fact combine elements of both genres: within a narrative structure the films privilege social and psychological characterization and foreground visual style over plot and action.

Nonetheless, I wish to stress the mainstream element here because feminist scholarship in film theory has concentrated mostly on either classical Hollywood cinema or contemporary women's avant-garde cinema. Experimental women's cinema is usually taken as a political counter-practice deconstructing the narrative and visual pleasures tailored for the male spectator of classical cinema. Let me state from the start that I find this choice of film genres too restrictive. Rather than accepting what strikes me as an unfruitful and unnecessary opposition between politics and pleasure, I am interested in films which combine visual pleasure, narrative tension and political integrity. Therefore, I focus on films which construct a feminist position through an alternative but recognizable use of traditional cinematic codes and conventions.

The hypothesis underlying my project is that feminist filmmakers represent the signs and significations of 'woman' and of 'femininity' differently from the codes and conventions of dominant cinema, while they still employ and deploy (rather than deconstruct) visual and narrative pleasure. The project consequently aims at analyzing the ways in which feminist filmmakers use and transform conventional cinematic means for communicating their non-conventional ideas. More specifically, I will look at the representation of female subjectivity in feminist cinema. The questions that frame my analyses are: how do feminist filmmakers 'make a difference' in their films?; how do they change images, narrative and representations in a positive and sex-specific manner? how do they address and construct the spectator as female?

Subjectivity is, then, central to my project. I see subjectivity as a process of continuous becoming rather than as a state of being. If subjectivity is understood as a dynamic process, it is both necessary and possible to account for change and transformation. Adopting Foucault to my purposes, I would like to add that we are not only subjected to power; we also have the potential and the power to become a subject different from the one we were socially programmed to become if only we want to, and if the social circumstances are favourable. The process of becoming-subject is taken up in a network of power relations of which sexual difference is a major constitutive factor along others like race, class, sexual preference, age. Subjectivity both constitutes and is constituted by a set of agencies and experiences as well as by external material conditions. The consciousness of sexual difference may in some cases encourage the female subject to change her own conditions and those of other women. The experience can be both productive of and conducive to political agency. This insight defines and frames my role as feminist film theorist. In the case of feminist filmmaking the question becomes how a director processes her daily experience of belonging to the social and historical gendered category of women, so as to change mainstream cultural representations of sexual difference, more specifically of female subjectivity. The equivalent question for the spectator is what kind of empowerment follows from the reception of these film texts.

In my analyses I concentrate on film form and structure: narrative, character, image, photography, framing, camera position and movement, montage, metaphors, point of view; those cinematic elements which together make up the particular cinematic style or rhetoric of a filmmaker. Rhetoric here is understood to be a productive force which enables the director to find ways of creating a feminist discourse and of representing female subjectivity. Rhetoric pertains not only to the aesthetic level, it also refers to codes of communication. It thus refers to the complex relation between the director, the film and the spectator, all of them with culturally determined codes of representation. In this respect, rhetoric negotiates between the experience of the filmmaker, represented in the film, the experience of the spectator, evoked by the film, and that of larger social and cultural codes.

Cultural representation is currently under great pressure for change from diverse directions: from political movements such as feminism, anti-racist struggle, and gay rights, but also from technological innovations such as video and computer technology. I want to suggest therefore that, in order to analyze the changing field of visual representation, film theory requires assistance from a variety of interdisciplinary sources. Accordingly, I have not confined myself to one specific theoretical school. On the contrary, in my attempt to account for the changes that feminist cinema has brought about in the field of visual representation and cinematic narration, I have sought to relate the specificity of each film to a relevant theoretical framework. The general structure of this study is thus to couple the discussion of a particular film with a critical evaluation of a particular theoretical discourse and to let the one illuminate the other. It follows that, although the chapters of the book follow more or less the chronology of the films discussed, each chapter can be read in and for itself, much like a musical variation on a theme.

The films discussed in this study have been pleasing, puzzling, moving or inspiring to me: in my critical stance, I have abstracted my located and situated experience into theory. The films do not form an exhaustive corpus of feminist cinema in the 1980s; they have been chosen because they challenge the limits of film theory. I have taken the wager of working at the interface of interpretation and theory. The pay-off is the feedback: the interpretations do not so much confirm the theory and vice versa, it is rather that the tension between them proves productive for reading film as well as reading theory.

Chapter 1, 'What Meets the Eye', gives an overview of feminist film theories from the mid 1970s to date. Feminist film theory is mostly founded upon semiotic and psychoanalytic readings of two kinds of cinema: classical Hollywood cinema, that is, American movies of the 1940s and 1950s, and experimental women's cinema, mostly of the late 1970s and early 1980s. The object of my study, the narrative feminist film, thus poses a challenge to the established parameters of feminist film theory.

In Chapters 2–6 specific theoretical issues are discussed through detailed analyses of individual feminist films.

Chapter 2, 'In Pursuit of the Author', discusses female subjectivity in relation to cinematic directorship. In the process of making and viewing a film there are at least three different kinds of subjects involved: the female filmmaker, the female character within the film, and the female spectator in the cinema. Much theoretical attention has been given to the female spectator, but little theorizing has been devoted to the other notoriously complicated category of female subjectivity:

the filmmaker or director. The issue of feminist directorship is addressed through an analysis of the German film *The Subjective Factor* (1980) by Helke Sander.

Chapter 3, 'Silent Violence', examines how female subjectivity is constructed in films about violence against women; two films by the Belgian director Marion Hänsel, *Dust* (1983) and *Cruel Embrace* (1987) are studied for this purpose. The films raise the question how an experience of violence can be represented from the point of view of the victim whose very subjectivity is destroyed by that violence. A detailed analysis of the films shows that the female characters acquire subjectivity through the construction of a cinematic point of view on a visual and narrative level. The chapter elaborates on the film narratological notion of point of view, which requires a revision of the psychoanalytic notion of the male gaze. The chapter also looks at the effects of representing female experience: the discrepancy between the destruction and construction of female subjectivity at different narratological levels produces a sense of tragedy for the spectator.

In Chapter 4, 'And the Mirror Cracked', the experience of the spectator is taken as the starting point for examining the overwhelming force of the feminist thrillers *A Question of Silence* (1982) and *Broken Mirrors* (1984), by the Dutch director Marleen Gorris. I argue that the somewhat outdated idea of experiencing or witnessing 'the truth' in these films is connected with their powerful rhetoric of grounding cinematic metaphors in realism. Thus Gorris' films can be viewed literally and figuratively at the same time, engaging the spectator in an emotional and critical viewing process. The chapter ends with an elaboration on the notion of affect as an experience of the spectator.

In Chapter 5, 'Forces of Subversion', the focus is shifted to the status of the image. This chapter looks for other ways of revisiting and transforming visual and narrative pleasure. Through a discussion of visual excess in quite different films such as *Bagdad Café* (Percy Adlon, Germany, 1988) and *Sweetie* (Jane Campion, New Zealand, 1989), the screen, or image, is proposed as a possible site of subversion in cinema. The chapter works from the hypothesis that visual excess can displace structures of voyeurism and fetishism. In *Bagdad Café* the stereotypical male gaze and female spectacle are subverted by visual excess of the image. In a different way, the excessive cinematic style of *Sweetie* privileges psychic configurations of the uncanny and the abject over and above classical visual and narrative structures. In both films the artificiality of the visual style subverts the very narrative it helps to construct.

The final chapter, 'The Navel of the Film', focuses on representations of lesbian desire and sexuality in the German film *The Virgin Machine* (Monika Treut 1988). The question is whether in challenging traditional constructions of sexual difference, *The Virgin Machine* also challenges traditional modes of representation. First an abject and uncanny fantasy is explored as a possible psychic configuration of representing female sexuality. Then a transvestite performance is analyzed in terms of a humorous lesbian masquerade and related to the representation of the feminine lesbian. The question of lesbian desire is developed within a psychoanalytic framework. The quite different strategies of abjection and humour share a similar subversive effect in that they are both forms of rejection, transgression and challenge.

My central concern in this book is with films that have sought to represent and communicate women's experiences differently. In imaging female subjectivity and addressing the spectator as female, feminist filmmakers have created films which transform and innovate cinematic codes and conventions. They also cater for a public seeking new visual and narrative pleasures. These changes are not only reflections of a changing social situation, but also transformations in representation and modes of production.

In changing dominant images and representations of 'Woman' and femininity, feminist filmmakers make powerful cultural interventions. This is how the title of my book, *And The Mirror Cracked*, is to be understood. This study traces the subversive cracks in a mirror which reflects traditional representations of female subjectivity. When the mirror cracks, splinters also hit the camera eye, introducing if not an actual breakdown in classical forms of representation at least a shake-up within them. I have been a watchful and concerned eye witness of this shake-up and of the readjustments it required in filmmakers, spectators and film theorists. As a feminist film theorist I have been looking for the potential for innovation and reconstruction in both cinema and film theory.

Feminism did crack the mirror. That gesture was necessary in order to open up the powerful camera eye to new fields of vision: to different angles, points of view, positions, images and representations. The notion that informs this book is that once the mirror has cracked, the silver screen will never look the same again.

1 What Meets the Eye: An Overview of Feminist Film Theory

Theory , Gr. Φεϖρία: A looking at, viewing, contemplation, speculation, also: a sight, a spectacle. Φεϖρός: spectator, looker on.
The Oxford English Dictionary

INTRODUCTION

Cinema is a cultural practice where myths about women and femininity, and men and masculinity, in short, myths about sexual difference
are produced, reproduced, and represented. The stakes of feminist film
theory are therefore high. In the early years of feminist film theory
Laura Mulvey wrote that women would be better off discarding patriarchal cinema altogether. Women would welcome the destruction of
'the satisfaction, pleasure and privilege' that only serves repressive
mechanisms in Hollywood cinema (Mulvey 1975/1989: 26). In the same
vein Claire Johnston wrote that if a women's cinema is to emerge it
should be 'paving the way for a radical break with conventions and
forms'; such a revolutionary strategy, however, must also embrace visual
pleasure by working through desire in the use of the entertainment
film (1973/1991: 4 and 31). From the very beginning, therefore, feminist film theory contains an inbuilt tension between politics and pleasure.
This tension has been very productive considering the tremendous development that feminist film practice and feminist film theory have
undergone in the past twenty years. In this chapter I will outline some
of the developments I consider most significant in feminist film theory.

RE-VISION

In the early 1970s, under the influence of the Women's Movement,
women started looking differently at film and film history. This 're-
visionary' approach resulted in a sort of cinema version of 'her-story',

7

that is to say an alternative historiography. This led to the rediscovery of forgotten women directors, script writers, producers and actresses and a reappraisal of female stars. Such findings would often be disseminated through women's film festivals.

This historical approach was supported by a more sociological method and by a political perspective that pursued equality and emancipation in cinema. In their books on Hollywood cinema, Molly Haskell (1987) and Marjorie Rosen (1973) analyze the historical position of women in the movies according to a tight chronological scale organized by decades which results in rather sweeping statements. These works presuppose a direct relation between film and society which is cemented by the notion of 'ideology'. Accordingly, cinema is assumed to be reflecting reality. In this sociological view, the objection to the dream factory of Hollywood is that it produces false consciousness, that films do not show 'real' women but only the stereotypical images of an ideologically laden 'femininity'. This offers a female audience no opportunities for authentic recognition, but ample room for escape into fantasy via the identification with stereotypes. The effect is alienating rather than liberating. Within this sociological perspective, the unmediated relation between cinema and reality is thought to be reversible: by showing reality as it is 'really' is, ideology and society can be changed. What a liberative women's cinema should look like in this framework can be guessed: female filmmakers have to undo the spell of a culturally dominant fantasy of the eternal feminine by showing the 'real' life of 'real' women on the silver screen. In opposition to the glamour of a Garbo, a Dietrich or a Monroe, for instance, female directors should film the everyday life of a 'normal', that is unglamorous, woman.

I believe that the struggle for equality is not yet over and the demand for authentic recognition is still heard today. Female spectators want to be able to identify with lifelike heroines without having to be annoyed by sexist clichés or transported by hyperbolical stereotypes. Whereas historical research in the field of women and film has grown stronger over the years, theoretically, however, the realist–sociological perspective was soon challenged by (post)structuralist thought.

THE MALE GAZE

In Europe, feminist analysis of cinema had been informed by the combination of Marxism and psychoanalysis which characterizes the Critical School, paying attention to films as consumer items to be sold ideologically and commercially. Ideological criticism was especially strong in the German feminist film journal *Frauen und Film*, founded by Helke Sander in 1974. The advent of (post)structuralism, introduced in the 1970s into Anglo-Saxon film as well as feminist theory by British journals such as *Screen* and *M/F*, and established as the main school in the American film journal *Camera Obscura*, definitely changed feminist film criticism. Semiotics and psychoanalysis supplied new perspectives for feminist film theory, especially for a critical analysis of classical cinema.

From semiotics, feminist film critics learned to analyze the crucial role of cinematic techniques in the representation of sexual difference. From psychoanalysis, they learned to analyze structures of desire and subjectivity. Feminist film theory shifted its focus from the critique of the ideological content of films to the analysis of the mechanisms and devices for the production of meaning in films. Film is no longer seen as reflecting meanings, but as constructing them; thus cinema as a cultural practice actively produces meanings about women and femininity. The notion of ideology is replaced by a series of new concepts which make the feminist analysis of the power of images both sharper and stronger.

Claire Johnston, one of the first feminist film critics to analyze cinema as a semiotic sign system, investigates the myth of 'Woman' in classical cinema, by defining the female character as a structure, a code or convention. The sign 'woman' represents the ideological meaning that she has for men; in relation to herself she means no-thing (1991: 25): women are negatively represented as 'not-man'; the 'woman-as-woman' is absent from the text of the film (26). Moreover, the realist convention of classical cinema, the law of verisimilitude, induces in the spectators a naive belief in the representation of the sign 'woman'. In other words, film (re)presents the constructed images of woman as natural, realistic and attractive. No wonder, then, that such images often turn into box office hits.

In her groundbreaking article 'Visual Pleasure and Narrative Cinema' (1975/1989), Laura Mulvey attempts to understand the fascination of Hollywood cinema. With the help of psychoanalysis, she has developed a theory of the male look or gaze that has become one of the dominant paradigms in feminist film theory. The fascination of cinema can be explained psychoanalytically through the notion of *scopophilia*, the desire to see, which is a fundamental drive according to Freud. Sexual in origin, like all drives, *der Schautrieb* – the curiosity to see – is what keeps us glued to the silver screen. Classical cinema, adds Mulvey, stimulates the desire to look by integrating structures of voyeurism and narcissism into the story and the image. Voyeuristic visual pleasure is produced by looking at another (character, figure, situation) as our object, whereas narcissistic visual pleasure can be derived from identification with the (figure in the) image.

Mulvey has analyzed scopophilia in classical cinema as a structure which functions on the axis of activity and passivity, a binary opposition which is gendered, that is signified, through sexual difference. The narrative structure of traditional cinema establishes the male character as active and powerful: he is the agent around whom the dramatic action unfolds and the look gets organized. In this respect, cinema has perfected a visual machinery suitable for male desire such as already structured and canonized in the tradition of western art and aesthetics. In his essay on the nude in European painting John Berger observes that: 'Men act and women appear. Men look at women. Women watch themselves being looked at' (1972: 57). More important for my purposes, the whole scene of representation is addressing an imaginary or ideal spectator who is implicitly assumed to be male. This assumption positions the woman as 'his' object.

Mulvey has disentangled the ways in which narrative and filmic techniques in cinema make voyeurism an exclusively male prerogative. Within the narrative of the film male characters direct their gaze towards female characters. The spectator in the theatre is automatically and often unconsciously made to identify with the male look, because the camera films from the optical, as well as libidinal, point of view of the male character. There are thus three levels of the cinematic gaze (camera, character and spectator) that objectify the female character and make her into a spectacle. In classical cinema, voyeurism connotes women as 'to-be-looked-at-ness' (1989: 19).

Mulvey explains narcissistic visual pleasure with Lacan's concepts of ego formation and the mirror stage. There is an analogy between the way in which the child derives pleasure from the identification with a perfect mirror image and forms its ego ideal on the basis of this idealized image, and the way in which the film spectator derives narcissistic pleasure from identifying with the perfected image of a human figure on the screen. In both cases, however, during the mirror stage and in cinema, identifications are not a lucid form of self-knowledge or awareness. They are rather based on what Lacan calls '*méconnaissance*', that is they are blinded by the very narcissistic forces that structure them in the first place (Lacan 1977: 6). Ego formation is structurally characterized by imaginary functions. And so is cinema. Even before this analogy was worked out by Christian Metz in his essays on psychoanalysis and film (1982), Mulvey argued that cinematic identifications were structured along the lines of sexual difference. Representation of 'the more perfect, more complete, more powerful ideal ego' (20) of the male hero stands in stark opposition to the distorted image of the passive and powerless female character. Hence the spectator is actively made to identify with the male rather than with the female character in film.

There are then two aspects to visual pleasure which are negotiated through sexual difference: the voyeuristic-scopophilic gaze and narcissistic identification. Both these formative structures depend for their meaning upon the controlling power of the male character as well as on the objectified representation of the female character. Moreover, according to Mulvey, in psychoanalytic terms the image of 'woman' is fundamentally ambiguous in that it combines attraction and seduction with an evocation of castration anxiety. Because her appearance also reminds the male subject of the lack of a penis, the female character is a source of much deeper fears. Classical cinema solves the threat of castration in one of two ways: via the narrative structure or through fetishism. To allay the threat of castration on the level of narrative, the female character has to be found guilty. Her 'guilt' will be sealed by either punishment or salvation and the film story is then resolved through the two traditional endings which are made available to women: she must die or marry. Either way, catharsis is at hand for the male spectator.

In the case of fetishism, classical cinema reinstates and displaces the lacking penis in the form of a fetish, that is a hyper-polished object. Fetishizing the woman deflects attention from female 'lack' and changes her from a dangerous figure into a reassuring object of flawless beauty. Fetishism in cinema confirms the reification of the female figure and thus fails to represent 'Woman' outside the phallic norm.

With Mulvey and Johnston, the notion of 'the male gaze' has become a shorthand term for the analysis of complex mechanisms in cinema that involve structures like voyeurism, narcissism and fetishism.[1] These concepts help to understand how Hollywood cinema is tailor-made for male desire. Because the structures of Hollywood cinema are analyzed as fundamentally patriarchal, these early feminist theorists declared that a feminist film should shun traditional narrative and cinematic techniques and engage in experimental practice: thus, feminist cinema should be a counter-cinema.

Although I appreciate the motives behind this move, I feel a certain ambivalence about it. At times experimental feminist films are overpraised for their subversive powers whereas realist women's films are over-

criticized for their illusionism (cf Kuhn 1982). The effects on scholarship are even more problematic: the suspicion of collusion cast on
realist or narrative film has resulted in either a concentration of critical efforts on classical Hollywood cinema or in largely unjustified acclaim of experimental women's cinema among the elected few who
get to see it. This has resulted in what I consider a paradoxical neglect
of contemporary popular films made by women for a wider audience;
a lack of academic attention which continued long into the 1980s and
even 1990s.[2] The paradox here lies in the deconstruction of visual pleasure
in experimental film practice, the very same pleasure that had always
been denied to women in classical cinema, and that was in some ways
redeemed in feminist narrative cinema. It consequently asks for women
to relinquish what they never had in the first place: their own visual
pleasure. E. Ann Kaplan (1983) has attempted a compromise by reap-
praising realism in feminist film. She argues that the narrative realist
film entails more complexity and heterogeneity than feminists have
granted. In her opinion, feminist cinema should appropriate and use
traditional means of representation for its own ends.

As I see no point in getting entangled in an opposition between
experimental and realist cinema, I have deliberately selected films which
are narrative with a vengeance, in that they combine visual and narrative pleasure with an alternative use of cinematic codes and conventions. Throughout this book, I will discuss the notion of the male gaze
in relation to specific films from several angles.

THE FEMALE SPECTATOR

Early feminist analyses may have explained Hollywood's fascination
for the male spectator, but what about the female spectator? Mulvey
was much criticized for this omission. In a later essay (1981/1989),
she addressed the vicissitudes surrounding the female spectator in classical
cinema. Mulvey suggests that the female spectator may not only identify with the slot of passive femininity which has been programmed
for her, but she is also likely to enjoy adopting the masculine point of
view, even if she remains 'restless in its transvestite clothes' (37).

Mary Ann Doane (1982/1991) also understands female spectatorship
in terms of a masquerade. Voyeurism presupposes distance, a distance
that woman in cinema necessarily lacks because she *is* the image.
Therefore the female look does not rest on the necessary gap between
subject and object in so far as woman is never quite a subject. Fem-

ininity is constructed as closeness, as 'an overwhelming presence-to-itself of the female body' (22). This can be avoided by wearing femininity as a mask which allows the female subject to create a difference between herself and the represented femininity. Thus she can keep femininity at a distance. However, Doane maintains that masquerade is not a viable strategy for the female spectator to subvert the masculine structure of the look. In addition to a transvestite adoption of the masculine position, the female spectator can therefore also adopt 'the masochism of over-identification' or 'the narcissism entailed in be coming one's own object of desire' (31–2). Doane argues that the female spectator is consumed by the image rather than consuming it.

In her book on the Hollywood woman's film in the forties, Doane (1987) comes to the conclusion that female identification and subjectivity are negatively signified in emotional processes such as masochism, paranoia, narcissism and hysteria. The woman's film, in spite of its focus on a female main character perpetuates these processes and thus confirms stereotypes about the female psyche. The emotional investments lead to overidentification, destroying the distance to the desired object and turning the active desire of both the female character and the female spectator into the passive desire to be the desired object. Mere 'desire to desire' seems to be, then, the only option for women.

Such fundamental denials of the female look make Kaplan wonder whether the gaze is necessarily male or whether female voyeurism is at all possible. Female characters can possess the look (for example in Hollywood woman's films of the 1970s and 1980s) and can make the male character the object of her gaze, but 'the problem is that, as female, her desire has no power' (Kaplan 1983: 29). The reversal of roles keeps the underlying structures of dominance and submission intact. The gaze is therefore not essentially male, 'but to own and activate the gaze, given our language and the structure of the unconscious, is to be in the "masculine" position' (30).

The difficulties in theorizing the female spectator have led Jackie Stacey (1987) to exclaim that feminist film critics have written the darkest scenario possible for the female look as being male, masochist or marginal. Gertrud Koch (1980) is one of the few feminists who in an early stage recognized that women could also enjoy the image of female beauty on the screen, that is, the vamp, an image exported from Europe and integrated into Hollywood cinema. The vamp provides the female spectator with an image of autonomous femininity. Koch argues that in women's pyschic life, the mother functions as a love object in their early childhood and that cinema can revive this image and appeal to the pleasurable experience. The sexual ambivalence of the vamp, of for example Greta Garbo and Marlene Dietrich, allows for a female homo-erotic pleasure which is not exclusively negotiated through the eyes of men. The vamp's ambiguity can therefore be a source of visual pleasure for the female spectator. Koch argues that the vamp is a phallic woman rather than a fetishized woman, as she offers contradictory images of femininity which go beyond the reifying gaze. The disappearance of the vamp in cinema, therefore, means a great loss of possible identifications and visual pleasure for the female audience.

A similar focus on the pre-oedipal phase and on the mother as love object and potential source of visual pleasure has been developed by Gaylyn Studlar (1988), though from a very different angle. Studlar formulates an extensive critique of the dominant psychoanalytic premises of feminist film theory. Analyzing films made by Josef von Sternberg starring Marlene Dietrich, she investigates the Deleuzian notion of masochism, arguing that visual pleasure in cinema resembles more the psychic processes of masochism than of sadism.[3] Stressing the positivity of desire rather than its lack, Studlar postulates on the one hand a position for the male spectator that is not based on castration fear, oedipal desire and sadistic voyeurism, and on the other hand theorizes an eroticized position for the female spectator that is based on fetishism and scopophilia. Cinema evokes the desire of the spectator to return to the pre-oedipal phase of unity with the mother and of bisexuality. The female spectator can thus identify with and draw pleasure from the powerful *femme fatale* in cinema. This is a sort of re-enactment of the symbiosis through which the spectator wishes to subject her- or himself to the powerful mother image. The condition of this active masochistic desire is that it be suspended, which is achieved by means of performance and masquerade on the part of the female character. These ritualizations of fantasy keep desire under control. For Studlar the masquerade serves as a defensive strategy for women, by which they deflect and confuse the male gaze. In her brilliant shift of psychoanalytic terms, Studlar has deconstructed the male gaze and created a place for the pleasure and desire of the female subject–spectator, albeit the pleasurable pain of desire.

Studlar's study, however, is rather the exception; generally, the prospects for the female spectator are quite sombre from a feminist psychoanalytic perspective. Are visual pleasures then illicit or politically incorrect? In order to redeem the pleasures of the female audience in the movies, feminist film theorists borrow the concept of the 'resisting reader' who 'reads against the grain' from feminist literary theory (cf Fetterley 1978). Feminist film theorists become intrigued by Hollywood genres that feature strong sexual female characters (such as the *femme fatale* in film noir), focus on women's issues, or that explicitly address a female audience (as in melodrama and the woman's film) (cf Kaplan 1980, Doane 1987 and Gledhill 1987). In reading these films against the grain critics reveal the complexities and ambivalences of Hollywood films that acutely represent woman's plight in a sexist society. Such interpretations highlight moments in the film that are possibly subversive to repressive Hollywood representations of women. Some critics go as far as to view Hollywood cinema as potentially progressive and even deconstructive (cf Erens 1990: xxii).

In her book on Hitchcock, Tania Modleski points to a loss of accountability in such an approach. She does not wish to redeem Hitchcock for feminism and refuses to see his films as a self-conscious critique of male voyeurism, fetishism and sadism. Instead she points to man's accountability for his oppressive behaviour. Hitchcock is neither 'utterly misogynistic' nor 'largely sympathetic to women and their plight in patriarchy', but his work is shot through by a deep 'ambivalence about femininity' (Modleski 1988: 3). Hitchcock's films may compel and intrigue feminists, not in the least because this ambivalence about women entails an equally fundamental insecurity and uncertainty about masculine identity, which results more often than not in lethal aggression towards women.

The discussion on the complexity of female spectatorship is still in full swing. The journal *Camera Obscura* has dedicated a special issue to 'The Spectatrix'.[4] The editors Janet Bergstrom and Mary Ann Doane state that the concern with spectatorship emerged from a theoretical matrix within semiotics and psychoanalysis. New roads in scholarship on female spectatorship have been opened up by cultural studies and ethnographic approaches. Some scholars have been engaged in analyzing spectatorship in terms of race and ethnicity and their intersection with gender (cf hooks 1992, Dyer 1993, Mayne 1993). Others have combined theoretical insights with ethnographic research (cf Bobo 1993, 1995; Stacey 1994).[5] As Bergstrom and Doane point out, differences cannot be flattened out: a semiotic and psychoanalytic approach differs profoundly from ethnography in media studies in its epistemological premises and theories of subjectivity. In ethnographic studies, for instance, 'the unconscious is not a pertinent factor' (1989: 12), a criticism that is also voiced by Modleski (1991, see later). The diversity in meanings, theories and questions of spectatorship, lead Bergstrom and

Doane to claim that 'the female spectator has become a fractured concept, activating a host of conflicting and incompatible epistemological frameworks' (12).

Although at several points in this book I will examine possible effects of a film on the potential spectator, I do not concentrate on female spectatorship as a theoretical concept. On the contrary, in Chapter 2 I will turn my attention away from it to a much less theorized category: that of the female author.

NARRATIVE AND SUBJECTIVITY

The question of female subjectivity has been explored in relation not only to female spectatorship, but also the structure of narrative in film. One of the key figures in this field is Teresa de Lauretis, who examines the relationship between historical women and representations of 'woman' in cinema from a semiotic and psychoanalytic perspective (1984, 1987). In western culture 'woman' is represented as the other, as different from man. This 'woman' is a fiction, a representation, and differs fundamentally from 'women', real referents living in a socio-historical context (1984: 5). The position of the female subject is an impossible one: 'woman' finds herself in a meaningless nowhere where women cannot represent themselves, caught between masculine representation and the specular image of femininity it produces.

In *Alice Doesn't* (1984), de Lauretis emphasizes that subjectivity is not a fixed entity but a constant process of self-production. Narration is one of the ways of reproducing subjectivity; each story derives its structure from the subject's desire and from its inscription in socio-cultural codes. Narrative structures are defined by oedipal desire, which is understood by de Lauretis as both a socio-political economy dominated by men's control of the women and as a way of emphasizing the sexual origin of subjectivity. Sexual desire is intimately bound up with the desire for knowledge, that is, the quest for truth. The desire to solve riddles is a male desire *par excellence*, because the female subject is herself the mystery. 'Woman' *is* the question ('what does woman want?') and can hence not ask the question nor make her desire intelligible. According to de Lauretis, it is a function of narrative to construct differences, and specifically to map sexual difference onto each text.[6] Narrative is therefore fully oedipal, because it constructs male or female readers according to a dualistic opposition that empowers the male as agent and disempowers the female as outsider. Narrative is not oedipal in content but in structure, by distributing roles and differences, and thus power and positions.

One of the functions of narrative, de Lauretis argues, is to 'seduce' women into femininity with or without their consent. This is a cruel and often coercive form of seduction. The female subject is made to desire femininity. Here de Lauretis turns Mulvey's famous phrase around: not only does a story demand sadism, sadism demands a story. Desire in narrative is intimately bound up with violence against women and the techniques of cinematic narration both reflect and sustain social forms of oppression of women. Representation is power by another name.

De Lauretis is hardly more optimistic than Mulvey about the female spectator. Not that she assumes identification to be single or simple; femininity and masculinity are identifications that the subject takes up in a changing relation to desire. In cinema de Lauretis distinguishes two different processes of identification. The first set consists of a masculine, active identification with the gaze and a passive, feminine identification with the image. The second set 'consists of the double identification with the figure of narrative movement, the mythical subject, and with the figure of narrative closure, the narrative image' (144). Whereas the first set is an oscillating either/or identification, the second set of figural identifications enables the female spectator to take up simultaneously the active and passive positions of desire: 'Desire for the other, and desire to be desired by the other' (143). This double identification may yield a surplus of pleasure, which for de Lauretis, however, is an operation by which 'narrative and cinema solicit the spectators' consent and seduce women into femininity' (143). Women know too well that in patriarchy and its culture of sexual violence, neither consent nor seduction are innocent words.

The notion of 'the female subject', then, seems to be a contradiction in terms, so much so that in later work de Lauretis refers to the female subject as a 'non-subject' (1985: 36), which is fundamentally unrepresentable as subject of desire, that is to say 'woman' can only be represented as representation (1987: 20). Feminist theory is built on the very contradiction between the unrepresentability of woman as subject of desire and historical women who know themselves to be subjects. According to de Lauretis, psychoanalysis is not able to address the complex and contradictory relation between 'Woman' and 'women'. In order to understand the process of female subjectivity, she suggests theorizing experience semiotically. It is through experience that women learn to be female. Experience is not only personal, it is also social: to know you are a woman is to know you belong to a group or class, that is to a gender. The female subject is the effect of a certain habitual experience of sexuality, both within herself and in relation to the outer world: to change the female subject is to change experience – in other words to change habit. As feminism is engaged in the process of bringing about a change through the invention of new signs, new strategies and new narratives, it has produced the new social subject of women. For de Lauretis, the self-conscious experience of being both 'woman' and 'women' is the productive contradiction of feminism: 'This is neither an illusion nor a paradox. It is a real contradiction – women continue to become woman' (186). In her recent work de Lauretis explores this paradox in her analysis of the radical break from 'normal' female desire, which is lesbian sexuality. More on this later.

De Lauretis' feminist semiotics gives insight into the ways in which narrative structures construct and represent subjectivity and also point to a potential change of those structures. As this is useful for my analysis of new representations of female subjectivity, I will focus on a semiotic analysis of new signs, strategies and narratives in feminist films, as well as on the notion of experience, in later chapters.

FEMALE DESIRE

Before discussing dissenting views that contest the dominance of psychoanalysis in feminist film theory, I want first to turn my attention to a major feminist critic who has approached the question of female desire in an innovative manner within psychoanalytic discourse. In *The Acoustic Mirror* (1988), Kaja Silverman shifts the focus from the gaze to the voice, which allows for an original perspective on the female subject in feminist film theory.

Following Lacanian psychoanalysis, Silverman argues that each and every subject is structured by lack or symbolic castration. As we saw earlier, however, it is the female subject who is made to bear the burden of castration in order to provide the male subject with the illusion of wholeness and unity. Silverman suggests that in cinema this displacement is enacted not only through the gaze and the image but also through the auditory register and apparatus. Contrary to the more frequent disembodiment of the male voice in cinema, the female voice is restricted to the realm of the body which amounts to keeping it outside discourse. In this way the female voice can hardly reach a signifying position in language, meaning or power and is hence all too easily reduced to screams, babble or silence in dominant cinema.

Silverman proceeds to discuss the cultural fantasy of the maternal voice that surrounds the infant like an acoustic blanket. This fantasy negatively signifies the fear of being swallowed up by the mother, whereas it positively signifies a regression to the state of harmony and abundance when mother and child are still one. In a well-founded critique of Julia Kristeva's work on motherhood, Silverman argues that both these fantasies equate the maternal voice to pure sound and deny the mother any cultural role as a discursive agent. She then rereads psychoanalysis so as to make room for the mother and for female desire within the symbolic order.

Reinterpreting Freud's account of the psychological development of the little girl, Silverman puts great emphasis on the signifying role of the mother in early childhood. The entry into language means the end of the unity between mother and child as well as of an unmediated access to reality. Silverman argues that the loss and separation entailed by the acquisition of language lead the child to desire the mother. The girl redirects her desire to the mother in what is called the negative Oedipus complex. This can only happen after the pre-oedipal stage, because distance from the mother is necessary for her to be constructed as an erotic object for the daughter. Silverman thus recuperates female desire for the mother as fully oedipal, that is within the symbolic order, within language and signification.

It is only after the event of the castration crisis, the dramatic onset of sexual difference, that the girl enters the positive Oedipus complex and learns to direct her desire to the father. For the rest of her life the female subject remains split between desire for the mother and for the father. The two desires are the site of a constitutive contradiction and are consequently irreconcilable. For Silverman, the daughter's erotic investment in the mother can be a subversive force for 'libidinal politics' because it is opposed to the normative desire for the father. Silverman emphasizes the negativity of the female negative Oedipus complex as a political potential and argues that for feminism it is paramount to draw on the libidinal resources of the 'homosexual-maternal fantasmatic' (125).

Silverman also revises the traditional view on the divergence of identification and desire. She argues that these two psychic paradigms are not always mutually exclusive in Freudian psychoanalysis and can actually coalesce. In the negative Oedipus complex the girl both identifies with and desires the mother, while the father figures as an object neither of desire nor of identification: for the girl he is merely 'a troublesome rival' (Freud quoted in Silverman: 153). The girl in this stage forms

her identity through the incorporation of the mother's imago; she both
wishes to possess and to be the mother. There is then a conjunction of
identification and eroticism which Silverman believes to have a vital
relation to female narcissism. According to her, feminism's libidinal
struggle against the phallus lies at the intersection of desire for and
identification with the mother. In more recent work, Silverman has
turned away from the issue of female desire to the representation of
non-classical masculinity (1992), and – intriguingly – to the development of a theory of 'the active gift of love' from a Lacanian perspective (1996).

LESBIAN FILM STUDIES

So far I have given ample space to what is generally perceived as the
dominant school in feminist film theory: theory that is informed by
psychoanalysis and semiotics.[7] Once psychoanalysis became the dominant discourse in Anglo-Saxon feminist film theory, however, the exclusive attention on sexual difference had some constraining effects.
One major point of criticism which has been raised is the tendency to
essentialize and universalize categories of 'man' and 'woman' and
'masculinity' and 'femininity'. As long as the female subject cannot
be conceived outside the straitjacket of sexual difference it remains
impossible to differentially theorize female desire or pleasure. The
exclusive focus on sexual difference within psychoanalytic film theory
accounts for its failure to theorize other differences such as class, race,
age and sexual preference.

Lesbian feminists were among the first to raise objections to the
heterosexual bias of psychoanalytic feminist film theory. Indeed, feminist film theory – not unlike the Hollywood cinema it criticized so
fiercely – seemed unable to conceive of representation outside heterosexuality. The journal *Jump Cut* wrote in its special issue 'Lesbians
and Film' (1981, no. 24/25): 'It sometimes seems to us that lesbianism is the hole in the heart of feminist film criticism' (p. 17). Almost
ten years later matters had, apparently, improved very little, as Judith
Mayne (1990, 1994) complains that the denial of the lesbian identity
of Hollywood director Dorothy Arzner points to a curious gap in feminist
film theory, indeed to the 'structuring absence' of lesbianism (1994:
107). As Patricia White (1991) aptly remarks, the 'ghostly presence of
lesbianism' haunts not only Hollywood gothics but also feminist film
theory.

In spite of the increasing focus on female spectatorship in feminist scholarship, the homosexual pleasures of the female spectator were largely ignored, although the lesbian appeal of female Hollywood stars has been widely recognized (see Weiss 1992). In breaking open the restrictive dichotomies of feminist film theory, Stacey (1987) tries to create a space for the homosexual pleasures of spectatorship. A more complex model of cinematic spectatorship is needed so as to avoid a facile binarism that maps homosexuality as an opposition of masculinity and femininity. Stacey suggests we 'separate gender identification from sexuality, too often conflated in the name of sexual difference' (1987: 53). When difference is no longer reduced to sexual difference but is also understood as difference among women, representation of an active female desire becomes possible, even in Hollywood films. In films such as *All About Eve* (USA, 1950) or *Desperately Seeking Susan* (USA, 1984) narrative desire is produced by the difference between two women; by women wanting to become the idealized other. An interplay of difference and otherness prevents the collapse of that desire into identification, prompting Stacey – as Silverman will a year later – to conclude that the rigid psychoanalytic distinction between desire and identification fails to address different constructions of desire.

De Lauretis (1988) has also drawn attention to the difficulties of imagining lesbian desire within a psychoanalytic discourse that predicates sexual difference on sexual *in*difference. She here follows Luce Irigaray's notion of the symbolic law representing only one and not two sexes: patriarchy is deeply 'hommo-sexual' as it erects the masculine to the one and only norm. Discussing the same problem in a later essay, de Lauretis (1991) observes that the institution of heterosexuality defines all sexuality to such an extent that 'the effort to represent a homosexual-lesbian desire is a subtle and difficult one' (252). She criticizes both Stacey and Silverman for conceiving of desire between women as 'woman-identified female bonding' and failing to see it as sexual. Here, and more extensively in her later book *The Practice of Love* (1994), de Lauretis returns to Freudian theory to account for the specificity of lesbian desire in terms of fetishism. In Chapter 6 I will return to these theories in my discussion of *The Virgin Machine*.

In answer to de Lauretis' criticism Stacey (1994) argues in her study of female spectatorship that she is not concerned with a specifically lesbian audience but with a possible homo-eroticism for all women in the audience. Her aim is to eroticize identification rather than de-eroticize desire. The female spectator is quite likely to encompass erotic components in her desiring look, while at the same time identifying with the woman-as-spectacle.

While these discussions of lesbian spectatorship are part of a wider movement in film studies to include the heterogeneity of the spectatorial situation, most discussions of spectatorship have been about white audiences. De Lauretis was criticized for not taking into account racial dynamics in the lesbian film *She Must Be Seeing Things* (USA, 1987) (see the discussion following de Lauretis' 1991 article). Little research is available about black audiences; although some critics have examined black female spectatorship in popular culture (e.g. Bobo 1995), the issue of black lesbian spectatorship has hardly been raised. The collection *Queer Looks* (Gever *et al.*, 1993) addresses the combination of racial difference and homosexuality, but it focuses more on gay and lesbian filmmaking than on spectatorship as such.

A BLACK PERSPECTIVE

Persistent critique of psychoanalytic film theory has come from black feminism for its failure to deal with racial difference. Jane Gaines (1988) is one of the first feminist film critics to point to the erasure of race in theories that are based on the psychoanalytic concept of sexual difference. She pleads for an inclusion of black feminist theory and an historical approach in feminist film theory to understand how gender intersects with race and class in cinema.

White film critics have universalized their theories of representations of women, while black women have been excluded from those very forms of representation. The signification of the black female as non-human makes black female sexuality the great unknown in white patriarchy, that which is 'unfathomed and uncodified' and yet 'worked over again and again in mainstream culture because of its apparent elusiveness' (Gaines 1988: 26). The eruptive point of resistance presents black women's sexuality as an even greater threat to the male unconscious than that of white female sexuality.

The category of race also problematizes the paradigm of the male gaze possessing the female image. The male gaze is not a universal given but it is rather negotiated via whiteness: the black man's sexual gaze is socially prohibited. Racial hierarchies in ways of looking have created visual taboos, the neglect of which reflects back on film theory, which fails to account for the ways in which some social groups have the licence to look openly, while others can only 'look' illicitly. The racial structures of looking also have repercussions for structures of narrative. Gaines discusses the construction of the black man as rapist, while in times of slavery and long after, it was the white man who raped black women. The historical scenario of interracial rape explains much of the penalty of sexual looking by the black man, who was actually (rather than symbolically) castrated or lynched by white men. For Gaines this scenario of sexual violence, repression and displacements rivals the oedipal myth. In Chapter 3 I will discuss such a configuration of racialized sexuality as depicted in the film *Dust*.

Interventions such as Gaines' show that the category of race reveals the untenability of many one-sided beliefs within feminist film theory, and points to the necessity of contextualizing and historicizing sexual difference. Thus, Lola Young (1996) examines the representation of black female sexuality by situating films in their historical and social context. Intersecting theories of sexual difference with those of differences of race and sexual preference, along with ethnicity and class, will eventually make other forms of representation thinkable, although Young argues convincingly that white and black filmmakers find it hard to challenge stereotypical images of black women.

As the work of such black feminist critics as bell hooks (1990, 1992 and 1994) and Michele Wallace (1990, 1993) shows, a multicultural perspective will also engender a more diversified theory of female desires and subjectivities, and of female spectatorship. For bell hooks, black female spectators do not necessarily identify with either the phallocentric gaze or white womanhood as lack, but they rather 'construct a theory of looking relations where cinematic visual delight is the pleasure of interrogation' (1992: 126). For hooks this is a radical departure from the 'totalizing agenda' of feminist film criticism, and the beginning of an 'oppositional' spectatorship for black women. From the experience of black women as resistant spectators, Wallace (1993) also seeks to expand the notion of spectatorship 'not only as potentially bisexual but also [as] multiracial and multiethnic' (1993: 264).

THE TURN TO CULTURAL STUDIES

In the early 1990s, the exclusive focus on Hollywood cinema shifted to more genealogical studies on women's cinema. Lucy Fischer (1989), Judith Mayne (1990) and Sandy Flitterman-Lewis (1990) place women's films in relation to cinematic traditions. These studies shed a new light on the ways in which female filmmakers use aesthetic conventions for different ends. For example, many feminist directors self-consciously play on the tradition that has made women into a visual object. In their films they thematize the screen by using mirrors, pictures, painting or video images within the cinematic screen (cf Mayne 1990). More recently, Foucault-inspired genealogical studies explore the relation between women and early film (Bruno 1993). In Chapter 5 I explore the cinematic image as a possible strategy for representations of female subjectivity.

The issues of the female spectator and her viewing pleasure continue to dominate most of the agenda of feminist film theory, even though some major shifts in theoretical paradigms occurred towards the end of the 1980s. Two collections that are dedicated to the pleasures of the female audience, *The Female Gaze* (Gamman and Marshment 1988) and *Female Spectators* (Pribram 1988), are indicative of the turn away from psychoanalysis towards cultural studies. Both books contest the dominance of psychoanalysis in feminist film theory for the same reasons as the lesbian and black critics discussed earlier: the neglect of differences among women, especially those of class, race, (homo)sexuality and generation.

In this view, psychoanalytic film theory leads to a universalist and reductionist approach to subjectivity. It conceives of ideology as monolithic, leaving no room for contradictions in cinematic practices. One of the main omissions of such a transhistorical approach, argues Pribram, is the disregard for the socio-historical context in which female spectators actually watch movies or television.

This criticism revives the tension between politics and pleasure I mentioned earlier. The neglect of the female spectator, as individual or as a social group, has resulted in a feminist endorsement of alternative cinema and, simultaneously, in a dismissal of mainstream cinema. Gamman and Marshment and Pribram argue that these normative views reinforce women's exclusion from cultural production and reception and are therefore politically unproductive. Instead, they are interested in feminist interventions in mainstream culture and in empowering women's presence in popular culture and, accordingly, address the issue of female audience as an historical participant in popular culture.

These two collections adopt a different theoretical perspective from the dominant semiotic-psychoanalytic school in feminist film theory, and that is cultural studies, influenced mainly by the British Birmingham school.[8] These cultural critics do not come from the humanities, as do most film critics, but from sociological backgrounds. The analysis of media is directed at several levels: production and economy; textual analysis; and audience reception. Their approach to mass culture is therefore more informed by ethnographic research than by an exclusive focus on the text. Early examples of such an approach to popular culture from a feminist perspective are Janice Radway (1984) and Ien Ang (1985), who based their readings of respectively Harlequin romances and the soap opera *Dallas* on interviews and viewers' responses. A more recent example is Stacey's (1994) work on female fans of female Hollywood stars.

The history of cultural studies in the USA is somewhat different as it developed out of the necessity for interdisciplinary work on contemporary culture and is consequently more related to issues of postmodern culture than is the case in Britain. Because Andrew Ross quite rightfully remarks that 'postmodernism means many things to many people' (1988: vii), I am careful to define postmodernism here as a historical condition: it is the complex and often contradictory culture of postindustrial society. Hal Foster (1983) distinguishes a postmodernism of resistance which tries to deconstruct modernism and a postmodernism of reaction which returns to traditional values. For Kaplan (1988) this distinction between progressive resistance and conservative reaction is in itself too modernist. She argues that two postmodern cultural practices coexist: a utopian postmodernism developed from feminist and poststructuralist theory, and a commercial or annexated postmodernism, closely linked to hi-tech capitalism.[9] What both postmodern practices have in common is a tendency to transcend the western tradition of binary thought. They also share the emphasis on the decline of the unified subject. The deconstruction of oppositions, and the deconstruction of a universal subject, i.e. the white middle-class heterosexual male, together form the utopian aspect of postmodernism for feminist and anti-racist theory.

E. Ann Kaplan's book on MTV (1987) is an example of feminist research on popular culture that is still influenced by semiotics and psychoanalysis, but that in its analysis of postmodern cultural practices goes beyond the confines of those disciplines. In a later collection, Kaplan (1988) places work on popular culture within the framework of postmodernism. A collection from the journal *Camera Obscura*, on the popular genre of science-fiction films, also shows this postmodern trend of working through and hence beyond psychoanalysis into a broader approach to cultural criticism (Penley *et al.* 1991). More recently, lesbian film studies has also moved to popular culture and to the question of postmodernity (Doan 1994, Hamer and Budge 1994, Wilton 1995, Hoogland 1997).

Despite different genealogies, American cultural studies dedicate the same attention to notions of multiple difference as feminist film and cultural critics elsewhere. Cultural studies maintain close links to women's studies, black studies and gay and lesbian studies, where, as bell hooks puts it: 'issues of difference and otherness have long been a part of the discourse' (1990: 125). She sees cultural studies within academia as one of the few locations in the academy where there is the possibility of interracial and crosscultural discussion.

It seems then that the debates around the issue of 'difference' and of diversity have led feminist film theory to open up to discourses outside the paradigms of semiotics and psychoanalysis. In her latest book Modleski (1991) politicizes feminist debates about popular culture. Being one of the very first feminist critics to work on popular culture (1984), she has consistently worked out an approach to mass culture that includes critical theory and psychoanalysis (1986). Although Modleski wants to rethink 'the articulations of popular culture and political criticism', she does not want to celebrate 'this culture as politically progressive so as to legitimate and protect one's private pleasures' (1991: ix). She criticizes ethnographic researchers for neglecting the viewer's unconscious in their zeal to undo the excesses of psychoanalytically based textual analysis. They fail to recognize for instance that female spectators (or readers) may contradict themselves, thus creating a notion of 'resistance' or 'subculture' that is devoid of inner tensions. This is analogous to the denial of self-reflexivity in ethnographic studies, which posits a big divide between the critic herself and the women she studies. Modleski argues it might be more productive for the feminist critic to acknowledge that she is caught up in contradictions and how much her fantasy life may resemble those of the women she studies. Here we are again at the crossroads of politics and pleasure, with an added emphasis on the necessity of self-reflexivity on the part of the feminist critic, of which I am ever mindful in this book.

CONCLUSION

What emerges from this overview of feminist film theories is the contested hegemony of semiotics and psychoanalysis; an hegemony that is beginning to be challenged from diverse discourses: history, ethnographic research, black studies, gay and lesbian studies, cultural studies, as well as the advent of the new electronic media. The predominance of psychoanalysis as a method has also led to certain thematic gaps in feminist research on cinema: in my view one of the most notable has been the neglect of contemporary and mainstream feminist films, which is the main reason why I chose to focus on them.

Another methodological approach which in my opinion has received little attention in the past few years is a close and detailed analysis of the specifically cinematic aspects of the medium of film. In my study I therefore examine the following elements of film rhetoric: the question of authorship, point of view, metaphor, and the cinematic image. In the final chapter I concentrate on feminist forms of representation which are not specific to cinema: abjection and humour. In my readings of feminist cinema I will pick up and elaborate on some threads out of the large fabric of feminist film theory, adding new material and new colours and reweaving them into a different pattern. First and foremost, however, I turn my attention to the films themselves.

2 In Pursuit of the Author: On Cinematic Directorship

If you know a film is by a woman, don't ignore that knowledge. Saying that the work stands by itself so look at the text was useful now it is bullshit. Use what you know.

Barbara Halpern Martineau[1]

Although Romantic notions of authorial creativity cannot be returned to the central role they once played in criticism and interpretation, the question of agency in cultural practices that contest the canon and its cultural dominance suggests that it really *does* matter who is speaking.

Kobena Mercer[2]

INTRODUCTION

As stated earlier my focus is on questions of female subjectivity in feminist cinema. In this chapter I will explore this issue in relation to cinematic authorship through an analysis of the German feminist film *Der subjektive Faktor* (*The Subjective Factor*, 1980) by Helke Sander. I will argue that for both political and theoretical reasons it is of vital importance for feminism to maintain that the gender of a filmmaker makes a difference and is theoretically significant.[3] A first reason for acknowledging differentiation by gender lies in the need to hold a filmmaker accountable for her or his sexual politics, that is, for the representations of sex and gender in a given film. A second reason is more epistemological and leads to the question of gender-specific representation. I will focus on the question of how the gender of the filmmaker makes a difference for the representability and representations of female subjectivity.

The vast corpus of films made by women in the past twenty years is evidence of the many ways in which women filmmakers posit themselves as social and historical subjects. In their work they have created diverse ways of representing female subjectivity. This evidence stands in stark contrast to the tendency to negate female cinematic subjectivity in earlier feminist film theories. In the previous chapter I described how the emphasis on Hollywood cinema brought feminist film theorists to conceive of female subjectivity within cinematic discourse and representation in predominantly negative terms or even as an impossibility; the female subject is postulated as masculine (Mulvey), marginal (Kaplan), masochistic (Doane) or as a non-subject (de Lauretis). Experimental cinema by women directors has inspired some theorists to reflect on female subjectivity within the film but usually not explicitly in relation to authorship. Invariably the female subject is described in poststructuralist terms as a subject-in-process, allowing room for ambiguities, contradictions and fragmentation in the representation of female subjectivity (cf de Lauretis 1987).

I believe that in addition to the obvious presence of women as spectators, the factual existence of feminist directors and their corpus of films demands a reconsideration of female subjectivity in cinema. As Mayne rightly observes: 'The notion of female authorship is not simply a useful political strategy; it is crucial to the reinvention of the cinema that has been undertaken by women filmmakers and feminist spectators' (1990: 97). In the present chapter I therefore undertake to defend the woman director as subject, and more specifically, the feminist director as a female and feminist subject.

Two relevant theoretical contexts complicate the conception of female authorship in cinema: the school of *auteurism* in film studies, and the debate around 'the death of the author' in poststructuralism. In what follows I will first relate questions of female subjectivity to three relevant points of reference: to the notion of the director as *auteur*, to explorations of the female author in a poststructuralist context, and to feminist theories of female subjectivity. After a first analysis of the film *The Subjective Factor* I will turn to a psychoanalytic theory of authorial libidinal coherence and finally to authorship in film narratology.

THE FEMALE AUTHOR IN *AUTEURISM*

Between 1954 and 1970 a critical practice came into existence that postulated the director as the individual 'author' of a film (cf Caughie 1981).[4] The *auteur* school characterized a film as the sole production of its director: it was to be seen as the expression of his individual personality and as containing a meaningful coherence. A director's particular style or themes could be found in all of his work. These *auteurist* ideas reveal the notion of the romantic artist in the tradition of 19th-century art criticism, with its emphasis on the artist's individuality, originality and creativity and the art's work of unity, coherence and wholeness.

With its focus on the individual genius the concept of the film *auteur* is an implicitly masculine one. I believe that the idea of genius is overdetermined by such categories as gender, race and class since it creates an illusory idea that only the white, bourgeois male can be a true artist (cf Cook in Caughie 1981). Hence the *auteur* school precludes any conceptualization of female authorship in cinema as well as the actual presence of women directors. Significantly, within the texts canonized by the *cinéma des auteurs* there is not one female director who counts as author, contrary to literary studies where at least some women writers made it into the canon.

Auteurism privileges individualism and personal expression in avant-garde cinema. This particular aspect of *auteurism* is paradoxically close to a fundamental feminist belief in the importance of self-expression and 'its emphasis on the personal, the intimate, and the domestic' (Cook 1981: 272). This similarity does not, however, qualify women's cinema as an example of *auteurism*, as will become clear below in the analysis of New German Cinema.

The bias towards masculinism fuelled feminist attacks on *auteurism*. Johnston reproaches Sarris for the 'derogatory treatment of women directors' in his work and quotes the editors of *Women and Film* who describe *auteurism* as 'an oppressive theory making the director a superstar as if film-making were a one-man show' (1991: 26). Yet, Johnston also defends *auteurism* for the new insight it produces and more especially for its elevation of Hollywood cinema to the same status as art cinema. On the whole, feminist interventions in film theories of authorship have been rare, an omission that has only recently been addressed. Silverman (1988) and Mayne (1990) point to the neglect of both the category of the author and to women directors within feminist film theory.

THE FEMALE AUTHOR IN POSTSTRUCTURALISM

No sooner is *auteurism* being itemized by feminist analyses than poststructuralism announces the death of the author. Attention shifts away from the 'author' to the 'text' and new categories of analysis are introduced.[5] Because the act of decoding the signs of the film text is performed by the viewer, much emphasis is now placed on subjectivity as it is constructed in the film and reconstructed by the spectator in the process of viewing. Poststructuralist film theory here follows Roland Barthes who declared that 'the birth of the reader must be at the cost of the death of the author' (1977: 148).

The debate on the 'death of the author' takes place in the more general context of the poststructuralist crisis of the subject. Feminist theorists have not failed to point out that the 'death of the subject' occurs at the historical moment when disenfranchised subjects – labourers, women, blacks, gays – claim their subjectivity. Alice Jardine (1985) and Rosi Braidotti (1991) both pointed to this curious coincidence. The same can be observed in film theory. At a time in the mid 1970s when women filmmakers started making movies and female subjectivity became an issue for feminists, poststructuralist film theory declared it *passé* to theorize the author/subject.

Both the glorification of the *auteur* and the death of the author/subject leave little leeway for female authors as subjects. In this sense, these dramatic shifts in paradigm make little difference to the continuing exclusion of women. It makes one wonder whether the 'artist as genius' and the 'death of the subject' are not two sides of the same coin; Andreas Huyssen seems to suggest as much (in Miller 1986: 106–7). With different arguments, alternative subjectivities are either ignored or declared null and void, even before they actually get the chance of expressing themselves (see Miller 1986, Schor 1987).

Barthes (1975) and the other poststructuralists were not altogether right when they predicted that the 'death of the Father' would take pleasure away from the text. I rather think that, if anything, women's cinema has triumphantly and with some malicious pleasure embraced the death of the Father as a great liberation and an opportunity to tell stories of female subjectivity with a renewed sense of purpose and destination.

THE FEMALE SUBJECT IN FEMINISM

Despite the negative implications that both *auteurism* and post-structuralism have for female subjectivity, I share some basic assumptions with these theoretical schools. I prefer to speak of authorship in cinematic terms, that is, instead of the 'author' I will use the term director (except when I discuss theories which explicitly use the term 'author'). The differences are significant. Unlike the author in literature, the film director is assisted by a large crew in making a film. Filmmaking is therefore much more of a joint effort than creative work in other arts. Moreover, I question the usefulness of literary methods for film analysis.

As is often the case for feminists, my position is made of a series of balancing acts: on the one hand, I agree with the emphasis that *auteurism* places on the director as filmmaker, because this allows me to hold her/

him accountable for the representation of sexual difference s/he enacts. However, I find it more useful to redefine the notion of authorship with poststructuralism, thus linking it to subjectivity. I do hold, however, to my objection with the premature dismissal of female subjectivity in poststructuralist theory. As an alternative to these pitfalls, I would like to propose the idea of a female subject as gendered, racialized and politicized. A subject has agency and volition, but also desire. I therefore want to distinguish and recognize these two registers in female subjectivity that can mutually inform and reinforce each other: of desire and fantasy on the one hand and of will and agency on the other.

Many feminist theorists have placed the issue of female subjectivity in the foreground; of, that is, what it means to be a subject that is both a woman and a feminist. Braidotti (1994a) gives a lucid account of the many developments in feminist theories on female subjectivity, showing that 'the female subject' is by no means a monolithic category. Feminist criticism has come a long way from theorizing the female subject as 'lack' and 'negativity' to an understanding of female subjectivity as an embodied, multilayered and inclusive entity, which is as bound to unconscious processes as to political agency. The challenge is to maintain the many different levels and to achieve coherence, while also avoiding the monolith of an abstract female subject. I will try to integrate a multilayered concept of female subjectivity in my analyses of women's films. I propose a framework of analysis based on three interconnected levels of female subjectivity:

1. The subject as a social agent requiring self-determination. This is the level of will, agency and history.
2. The subject of the unconscious, with desires that are structured in a relational link to another or to others. This is the level of the fantasmatic.
3. The subject of feminist consciousness, understood here as a process that structures relations between director, film text and spectator. This is the level of film form, strategies and rhetoric.

I will now apply this scheme to my reading of *The Subjective Factor*, a feminist film that leads into the heart of the matter: the representation of female subjectivity in women's cinema.

SUBJECTIVE FACTORS

In *The Subjective Factor* filmmaker Helke Sander narrates the rise of the Women's Movement in West Germany at the end of the 1960s. The most important feature of the film is its breakdown of traditional genre distinctions: within a fictional narrative about main character Anni who lives in a particular time (1967–70) and in a particular place (Berlin), Sander has included many documentary images such as pictures, pamphlets, posters, newspapers, newsreel and film footage of those years. The soundtrack, too, contains authentic material from that period: music, radio, lectures, happenings. Sander's film shares this characteristic of mixing genres, of combining fiction and documentary, with other feminist films (see Knight 1992).

Contrary to classical cinema, the opening scene of *The Subjective Factor* does not introduce the rest of the film as a flashback, but introduces the complex issue of writing history, or better, filming her/story. Annette Förster (1982) stresses that Sander's mixture of fact and fiction in the opening sequence makes the viewer aware that the documentary images are not 'objective facts' but have a function within Anni's story, within her experience and her memory of the events. Although the images are presented from the subjective point of view of women, particularly that of Anni, the juxtaposition of different levels of historical events, fiction and commentary complicates her subjectivity. Thomas Elsaesser (1989) draws attention to the 'traumatic' nature of Anni's experience of her confrontation with her past, or rather with the multilayered time sequences that make up her life.

What is striking about *The Subjective Factor* is the extent to which the questions of female subjectivity determine the cinematic form and vice versa. For Roswitha Mueller (1983) this film actually portrays the experience of the female director. This is reflected both in the blurring of the genres – the mixture of documentary and fiction – and in the breakdown of the distinction between the character and the filmmaker. The director's motivation becomes therefore a very important issue. According to Knight (1992), one of Sander's main motivations in making this film was to supply the Women's Movement with an historical record of the period of its beginning, so as to save it from the oblivion that struck earlier 'waves' of feminism. For Richard McCormick, Sander aims at countering 'conservative and/or primarily male-oriented histories of the student movement' (1991: 208). Yet, the film is explicitly neither a documentary about the Women's Movement nor about the student movement. With such high aims, it is no wonder that the director could not fulfil all expectations.

Sander was criticized by some spectators for not giving the historical account they had expected, but trying instead to make a film that tells her own subjective story. I believe rather that in filming her/story she wanted to account for the process of writing history. In a lecture about her film Sander phrases it as follows:

> A recurring angry attack on the film often starts with the words: 'But for *me* it was all quite different'. Indeed. That's my point. I want to hack at that again and again until the meaning of this sentence is finally understood. I tie this up with the question of how we learn history and what we learn from it.
>
> (Sander 1981: 5; translation AS)[6]

I tend to see this position as (self-)consciously subjective, in the sense that it questions and interrogates the very form of subjectivity which it portrays. Consequently, Sander has chosen not to subordinate the fictional level to any form of documentary report. By intercutting authentic material into staged scenes she indicates that *The Subjective Factor* is not an imitation of historical events but a specific representation of those events.

The Subjective Factor is generally situated within the context of a return to history in German cinema and literature of the late 1970s and early 1980s, a cultural-political situation also known as 'New Subjectivity' or 'New Sensitivity' (see Mueller 1983, McCormick 1991). Such a trend to question and confront history was merged with earlier trends that sought to emphasize subjectivity and interiority. *The Subjective Factor* then is a film that refuses to be a reconstruction of a particular time in history; it actively questions and confronts personal memories and historical discourses about the beginning of the Women's Movement, splitting open our understanding of history.

Feminism is another major context that feeds into the project of Sander's film and accounts for the forceful way in which she puts both history and subjectivity at stake. Feminism, with its questioning of female identity, the emphasis on 'the personal is the political' and the desire to empower the presence of women in history, informs the very structure of *The Subjective Factor*. The cinematic form respects the complexities and even the contradictions of the women involved in this process. Sander's film gives ample space to gaps, omissions and silences, thereby suggesting as much as portraying the efforts of women groping to understand their position in society, at a time when that society is coming apart at its bourgeois seams. *The Subjective Factor* constructs and supports the women's struggle with themselves and with their surroundings, in their double conflict with both middle-class values and the left-wing students' movement. In some ways it is the journal of a crisis. For Sander, subjectivity (as referred to in the film title) is not a certain degree of autobiography, but rather a process of experience, which is privileged over story, just as narrativity is privileged over the finished product of narrative. As Sander writes herself, the subjective factor can be found 'in the connection of images and sound, in my rhythm, in my way of presenting, in the *form* of how images relate to other images through montage' (1980: 2). Narrativity in *The Subjective Factor* is at the forefront of Sander's style of montage which juxtaposes scenes in a non-hierarchichal way where each scene relates to another or others, leaving many possible meanings open without ever reaching closure. Förster writes that Sander's films are like puzzles with some of the pieces missing, representative of the complexity of reality (1985: 82). The subjective factor is constructed not as an essence but as something in between: 'the subjective factor can be found between subjectivity and objectivity, between documentary and fiction, between factual events and narrated events, between images and representations' (Förster 1982: 11). This in between-ness represents female subjectivity in terms of process rather than in essentialist terms.

Sander's cinematic style in *The Subjective Factor* is reminiscent of the Russian filmmaker Sergej Eisenstein's concept of intellectual montage that he describes as a conflictual combination of several intellectual effects simultaneously (1987: 193). Sander herself regularly refers to the notion of conflict, which she translates into non-hierarchichal juxtapositions by confronting documentary with fiction, thus giving space to ambiguities and the simultaneity of many potentially contradictory events. The effect of this particular style of montage is that the actual combination of the events strikes the spectator experientially, rather than being acted out by the characters. The juxtaposition of the cinematic material produces a puzzle-like effect which, in my reading, mirrors the discontinuous and contradictory forces of history. Sander's film therefore mimes, rather than merely represents, the process by which the Women's Movement emerged in West Germany. Moreover, in the continual crossrelation of ideas to everyday life, *The Subjective Factor* shows how the intellectual foundations of feminism are firmly rooted in experience.

In its intellectual montage *The Subjective Factor* brings together several meanings of 'history'. First, the film deals with the Marxist understanding of history as a revolutionary process that would call for new forms of representing a collective subject, i.e. the working class. Second, it portrays the feminist challenge to this Marxist premise in the name of a collective subject that has historically been *un*represented, thus raising the issue whether women form a 'class'. Third, it points to history as the promise of the future, giving a glimpse of a utopian belief, of a tomorrow that allows women to postulate a new subject: the female, feminist subject. At the same time, the intricate temporality of the film makes the spectator aware of what has become of that utopian hope some thirteen years later, the year the film was made. This does not necessarily point to a disappointment, but rather to a sense of continuity, of what has been achieved and of what still needs to be achieved. In that sense, I think that the film succeeds in creating a genealogy for women, of writing women's history.

In view of the many-layered notion of 'history', the irony of Sander's film title can be made apparent. As Mueller writes, the title *The Subjective Factor* 'cleverly refers both to the Marxian notion of the human subject in the historical process and to the insistence on identifying the film voice or point of view as a subjective one: a part of women's history is thematized discursively' (1983: 5). The film is thus the perfect answer to the question asked by Rudi Dutschke:[7] 'How and under what conditions can the subjective factor inscribe itself as an objective factor in the historical process?'[8] For example, in a discussion between Anni and her friend Uwe, Anni admits that she is shocked to discover that Marxist scientists have simply forgotten millions of housewives in their analysis of society. They even account for the few remaining chimney sweeps and blacksmiths, while the housewives remain conspicuously absent. Anni accuses socialism of abstracting from the personal and the domestic; in spite of its proclaimed interest in 'subjectivity', socialism explains away the subjective factor.

The female subject that emerges from my reading of *The Subjective Factor* is very much a social agent, referring to the first level of will, agency and history in my proposed analytic framework. But she is also the subject of her memories, desires and fantasies; moreover, Anni's attempts at self-determination are presented as the process of acquiring feminist consciousness.

PAST/PASSED AUTHORS

The case of the complex subjectivity structure in *The Subjective Factor*, and of the consequences for the role of the director is relevant to the discussion of *auteurism* in film theory. It is important to note that the

New German Cinema, also known as *Autorenkino*, is the perfect example of *auteurist* criticism, with star directors like Fassbinder, Herzog and Wenders in the role of creative geniuses. Elsaesser (1989) argues that the notion of *auteurism* was present as early as the 1962 Oberhausen Manifesto and developed into the dominant tradition in film criticism.[9]

A distinctive trait of the New German Cinema is personal expression; Elsaesser calls it a 'cinema of experience' and he stresses that women's cinema is in some respects the best example of this because it combines personal self-expression with social responsiveness (1989: 183). As such, women's cinema could qualify as a perfect example of *auteurism*. This, however, is not the case. Knight (1992) argues that the characterization of New German Cinema as an *auteur* cinema has resulted instead in a marginalization of women's films. This is partly due to an implicit norm of masculinity behind the idea of a creative individual. Knight shows how film critics discussed women directors in terms of 'followers' and 'adapters' rather than as 'originators' (62–3). Where in the case of male directors all the emphasis is focused on the individual filmmakers, in the case of women they all get lumped together. Directors as diverse as Ulrike Ottinger, Helke Sander and Margarethe von Trotta are subsumed by the same, nondescript title of 'women's cinema'. The specific structural, stylistic and thematic features of their respective films tend to be assessed within the narrow confines of this spurious genre, to the detriment of their individual characteristics. Moreover, as Knight also points out, German critics tend to classify all female filmmakers under feminism, thus flattening out their singularity even further. Even more puzzling are the idiosyncrasies as well as the nature of the critical evaluation of personal expression in the New German Cinema. Whereas in the case of celebrated male authors like Fassbinder, self-expression was taken as a sign of genius, when it came to women directors like Sanders, the representation of personal experiences was seen as a sign of lack of inspiration which gets compensated for by references to lived experience or reality.

Knight ventures no speculation for these contradictory trends in film criticism and for the gender-laden oppositions they create. For me, however, this is a rather blatant example of familiar double standards to the detriment of women filmmakers, due to the culturally induced bias that equates genius with men and acts accordingly in the realm of canon formation. Ignorance also plays a part: the critical reception suggests that the most innovative elements in feminist filmmaking, a shift in consciousness and the redefinition of subjectivity, are being missed or misunderstood.[10] It is in such a framework that *auteurism* inflicts the final blow to the emerging subjectivity of women filmmakers and inhibits serious consideration of their work. Being denied access to authorship, it is equally difficult for women filmmakers to acquire a position of authority.

THE AUTHOR IN CINE-STRUCTURALISM

In this section I want to examine whether the poststructuralist redefinition of authorship, sometimes referred to as 'cine-structuralism' (Caughie 1981), might yield other ways of understanding female directorship. My argument is two-pronged: on the one hand I shall not mourn the demise of a male-centred theory of *auteurism*. On the other hand, however, I shall express some reservations about the terms that have come to replace it. The emphasis shifts first towards anonymous textual structures and then towards the agency of spectatorship. I will both explain and evaluate these in the light of feminist cinema.

Auteur theory came under attack, mostly in British Marxist structuralist circles around the journal *Screen*, for the romantic idealism of its definition of the author and its lack of solid theoretical foundations. Peter Wollen is among the first to reformulate *auteurism* by invoking structuralism in his widely read *Signs and Meaning in the Cinema* (1972). Relying on Lévi-Strauss, Wollen applies structural analysis to the study of film as myth, that is to say as an artifice that is carefully structured according to accountable cultural codes. Wollen also introduces the psychoanalytic notion of the unconscious and defines film as a dream with a latent meaning which must be made manifest. According to both Caughie (1981) and Silverman (1988), Wollen makes a significant shift by taking the source of coherence and meaning away from the *auteur* and placing it in the spectator; it is her/his responsibility to unveil the meaning of the text.

From that moment there is a snowballing: first *auteurism* goes, then the notion of the author as agent of meaning is disputed. Last but not least, the whole idea of the unified subject comes under attack as an ideological construct needing deconstruction. As Stephen Heath (1981/ 1973) put it, by the mid 1970s, a new object of reflection emerges: 'the subject', which involves a collapse of the concept of cinematic authorship. The Foucauldian critique of discourse completes the picture; the subject is seen as an effect of discursive practice (Foucault 1977). The authorial subject in particular must be stripped of its aura of mastery and intentionality and be analyzed instead 'as a complex and variable function of discourse (138)'. The result is a renewed emphasis on the role of the spectator as producer of meaning.

Christian Metz (1982) applies the notion of discourse to cinema and film theory. He borrows from Benveniste the distinction between story and discourse (the utterance, and the object of the utterance respectively) and relates it to the position of the subject. The subject is now analyzed in terms of enunciation (the utterance of a speaking subject) and the enunciated (the statement which contains a subject of speech). Although both discourse and story are forms of enunciation, the speaking subject is positioned differently within them. In the former the subject is present, whereas in the latter, s/he is masked. Although Metz identifies traditional cinema as pure story, he immediately qualifies this statement by adding that cinema is indeed discourse, if the filmmaker's intentions are taken into account. However, the basic characteristic of cinematic discourse is that it masks all traces of the enunciation. In other words, cinema is a discourse that passes itself off as story (1982: 91). The bracketing of authorship has a counterpoint in a shift where the spectator becomes the subject of enunciation. According to Metz, the spectator identifies with the source of discourse, that is, with the invisible agency of the film, through his primary identification with the focus of the camera.

The result of this view is an obliteration of authorship. In the analysis of film as discourse, the subject of enunciation is the cinematic apparatus as a whole – camera movement, montage, point of view, composition, soundtrack, etc. (Nowell-Smith 1981: 235; Silverman 1983b: 46). More especially, it has been identified with the camera, that is, the camera's look (Silverman 1988: 200–1). This results in a general bracketing of the author/subject in semiotic film studies.

I think that the insight of psychoanalysis allowed film theory to develop a more dynamic view of a sexual and divided subject than the reductive formalism of semiotic theories of the textual subject. It also raised questions of desire and pleasure (Caughie 1981: 206). Jean-Pierre Oudart (1981) attempts a compromise: while stating that the author is an 'empty field', he also speaks of the authorial inscription of desire (mostly repressed or foreclosed in the film text), which can be decoded by the spectator through the characters or the style.[11]

As I said earlier, the methodological changes that came about with the shift from *auteurism* to poststructuralism resulted in an emphasis on textual analysis. Such text-immanent methodology determined not only the approach to (authorial) enunciation, but also to the spectator, who was understood to be an effect of the film text. Although lip service was paid to cultural and social determinations, context and history are usually abstracted from semiotic and psychoanalytic film theories.

A QUESTION OF SUBJECTIVITY

The question for me is whether cine-structuralism can be productive for analyzing the subjectivity of the female director in *The Subjective Factor*. Let us pick up the argument where I left it earlier, on the point about 'personal expression' in *auteurism*, and see how it can be reformulated in poststructuralist terms.

Elsaesser remarked that the formal complexity of autobiographical women's films reflects a filmic problem, that is: 'How to give the female character in the fiction film a coherent identity, when the very thing that makes her a woman is the constant struggle and failure to cohere' (1989: 61). The issue here is indeed the question of enunciation and the related problems of subjectivity. The multilayeredness of subjectivity comes to the fore in a particular, and much discussed, scene in Sander's film. Sander was criticized by the influential German film critic Norbert Jochum for making a film of ideas after the principles of Eisensteinian montage, which he suggests is today obsolete (Sander 1981: 25–6). He refers to a scene where filmmaker Sander appears on the screen while she watches film footage of herself giving a speech at a student congress thirteen years earlier. This speech is historic in the sense that it 'is generally taken to mark the birth of the new women's movement in West Germany' (Knight 1992: 74).

Within the fictional story the scene is related to Anni; both the woman in the present and the one in the past are supposed to be her. Jochum claims that this scene cannot be understood because most spectators would not recognize Sander either in the images of the present or of the past. Although this last point is true (I have never been able to identify Sander in either footage) Jochum's response is beside the point. Whether spectators actually recognize Sander, or think it is Anni, or maybe that one is Sander and the other Anni does not really matter, because in any of these cases the scene raises issues of time and history and of authentic versus fictional self: that is, it raises the question of subjectivity. As Sander puts it: 'In my view it is more than enough for an understanding, when the spectator grasps that this scene was "then" and that this is put in relation to "now"'(Sander 1981: 25; translation AS). This quote strikingly parallels the way in which Nowell-Smith explains discourse in terms of 'here and now' and story in terms of 'there and then' (1981: 234). What Sander does here, by inserting herself into the cinematic image as the subject of enunciation, is to present intentionally history as a form of discourse. Instead of disembodying authorial subjectivity as is mostly the case in classical cinema, Sander effectively unmasks the enunciative level. As a consequence, the historical 'there and then' can only be understood from the perspective of the 'here and now'.

Sander herself acknowledges that 'this sequence is fairly sophisticated', but in its confrontation of past and present, of fictional and authentic material, and not least, by underscoring the act of enunciation, it is exemplary for the narrative structure of the film as a whole. The scene is technically even more intricate than Jochum seems to realize. Since there was no visual recording of that historical speech – the camera and microphones were switched off when Sander mounted the stage – she had to use a sound recording of her speech that some friends had made and superimpose it on film footage from another speech. However, this information (that the spectator does not actually have) is not necessary to prompt a reflection on the relation between history and discourse, between past and present, and by extension, on female subjectivity.

The memory I have of my first viewing of the film confirms this. I remember seeing *The Subjective Factor* for the first time in the early 1980s with a few friends; we had formed a small group of film students interested in 'women and film' and were doing research on women's films in the Netherlands at the time. We were moved by *The Subjective Factor*, a film which we understood to be a representation of how the Women's Movement must have been at a time when we were still too young to be part of it. For feminist film students in the beginning of the 1980s, this film about the emergence of the Women's Movement came across as fully 'authentic'. Our appreciation of the film was due partly to the fact that so many scenes of male derision, of women not being taken seriously in their demands and desires, of jokes and laughter at their expense, were still only too recognizable for us.

Recognition of our lived reality was, however, not the only effect the film produced. More important was the recognition of an historical process, in that the film made us aware of a women's history, discontinuous, full of fits and starts, but to which we ourselves belonged. Apparently, it did not matter for us not to recognize Helke Sander in that particular scene (nor at the end of the film where she makes another appearance), nor did it matter that we lacked 'inside' information about the historical details of so many other scenes. The film's emphasis on its enunciation made very clear that the writing of history is a subjective process. In the juxtaposition of 'then' and 'now' the film made us realize what feminists had achieved some fifteen years later and what remained to be done. *The Subjective Factor* presented us with an historical, yet subjective reflection on 'how it all started'. We got the point that making a film about women's history involves difficulties because so little is actually recorded or preserved. Paradoxically, the emphasis on historical discontinuities gave us a sense of continuity.

What this memory shows is the importance of films that evoke experience. *The Subjective Factor* manages to capture the experiences of women in the early stages of the second wave of feminism and presents spectators with a strong representation of the making of feminist consciousness through a variety of devices, not the least of which is its self-conscious appeal to feminist viewers to recognize the immediacy of certain experiences – some negative (male derision), some positive (women's self-assertion). This process of recognition crosses time barriers and shifts the debate about historical authenticity to the authenticity of experience, 'at once social and personal', centred on feminist consciousness raising (de Lauretis 1984: 166). For Jochum, Sander's personal experience fails to become social, but for feminist viewers it does translate into questions of subjectivity and history.

Precisely because of its clever mix of the historical with the fictional, and of story and discourse, the scene also goes to the heart of the difficulties concerning the representation of female subjectivity. Although he did not recognize Sander watching her own historical image in this sequence either, Elsaesser provides a poignant reading of the scene. Like most spectators he identifies the woman watching the newsreel of the historical Helke Sander as the fictional Anni. For Elsaesser this confrontation of the historical with the fictional opens up questions of representation and sexual difference: it marks 'the gap where the fact that her integrity as a "person" is no longer recoverable (no image to match her voice) becomes a political one' (1989: 192).

Elsaesser alludes here to the politicization in *The Subjective Factor* of questions of women's representation; without actually showing how cameras and microphones were switched off before Sander's speech, she still makes the point in this striking scene. In the newsreel footage shown, Sander is filmed from the back with the effect that her face is not visible and the film audience cannot see her speak. The director Sander walks in front of the image and takes a position on the right side of the screen watching herself, her profile dominating the historical image. The sequence thus problematizes women's struggle to become a speaking subject. Within the narrative of the film this had already been established by showing Anni's difficulties being accepted as one of the speakers at the student congress, precisely because she is not a 'representative'. Her argument that women might form a class in the Marxist sense, and that she might represent women, is met with a roar of laughter. Her idea, presented with great uncertainty and hesitation, is considered to be truly non-Marxist and hence ridiculous. Yet Anni is allowed to speak, and Helke Sander's historical speech took place, making women rise as a class, that is: as their gender.

The intellectual montage of historical and fictional material adds to a recognition of authenticity and complicates our sense of history, whether we 'get' all the historical details or not. But, more relevant for the present discussion, the appearance of Sander points to the intricate question of authorship: the relation between the director and her film. One of the effects of the procedure by which cinematic discourse is masked as pure story in classical cinema is the absence of the director from the images and soundtrack, whereas in *The Subjective Factor* the director Sander is present both in image and in sound: she visually appears twice in the film (without speaking) and once in the historical film footage. Sander is also clearly present as the narrator of her film in accompanying the images with her voice-over.

These strategies are not uncommon to modernist cinema and many critics have indeed commented upon the modernist style of *The Subjective Factor*: Jochum links Sander's style of montage to Eisenstein; McCormick relates it to the 'Brechtian legacy' (1991: 225); and Knight points to the concept of 'defamiliarization' of the Formalists (1992, 143). In their need to find new ways for viewing and representing the world, Sander and other feminist directors have allied themselves with certain traditions of modernism. They take modernism a step further than many of their male colleagues by exploring their own subjectivity within their films. The scene I am discussing here is an example of how Sander goes beyond the modernist strategy for film editing, in her 'willingness to foreground her own position in structuring the film' (McCormick 1991: 225). The scene represents the very project of Sander's film: 'Her examination of personal memory and public record vis-à-vis the late 1960s from her vantage point in 1980' (227). In other words: Sander problematizes her cinematic authorship. In making a visual and acoustic appearance the director and narrator of the film gives up her privilege of invisibility; she exposes 'the position of the "subject of enunciation" in regard to her film' (228).

For Silverman, the third-person voice in the film reveals its enunciation, because 'it indicates both its discursive vantage and its point of address', that is, it remains 'closely identified with the point of view which structures the image track – i.e., with Anni' (1983a: 15).

This close alliance between third-person (voice-over) and first-person (Anni) narration, however, nowhere entails a complete integration of the two. Elsaesser argues that the film continuously displaces 'the question of who "speaks the image"' (193). This is not only cinematically represented by the insertion of documentary images into the fictional narrative, but also acoustically, in that Sander's voice-over 'splits' the female character Anni. McCormick writes that the use of both first- and third-person narration 'foregrounds the interplay between the fiction and the autobiography in the film, problematizing any total identification between Anni and Sander as narrator' (227). The voice-over narration clearly presents a subjective perspective. It never pretends to be omniscient but always remains tied to 'only one character's subjectivity, the one who is based on her own experience' (227). Thus, in this film the subject of enunciation is not the abstract 'Absent One' of classical cinema, but is instead grounded in the subjectivity of director Helke Sander.

From these various readings of *The Subjective Factor* I conclude that the process by which a female, feminist subjectivity is established, informs the very style and structure of the film; the third level in my framework of analysis. The very fact that film critics provide interesting and adequate readings of the scene challenges Jochum's objection to Sander's 'obsolete style'. I have attempted to show that the director's appearance in her own film is in no way gratuitous, even if that knowledge is inconsequential to a general understanding of the film. I therefore argue that Sander's interventions recreate the modernist style into a pertinent feminist questioning of female subjectivity. Rather than disposing of her style as old-fashioned, I claim it as something new and meaningful. Unlike classical cinema, Sander plays with the boundaries between absence and presence of the director. Neither an 'objective' documentary nor a 'subjective' piece of autobiography, Sander's film moves between different genres of autobiography, history, documentary and fiction. When the fictional story becomes more objective and the historical narrative more subjective, the boundaries between the two categories are challenged and an altogether new definition of the subject emerges. Her history of becoming a feminist does not claim to be the history of the Women's Movement, although there is obviously a representative communality to her/story. In *The Subjective Factor* Sander performs an important aspect of feminism: she succeeds in making the personal political, as well as the political personal.

By integrating the personal into the political, Sander establishes a successful form of feminist rhetoric. Rather than asserting an authoritative feminist voice, *The Subjective Factor* seeks simultaneously to represent and to perform women's struggle and uncertainty to speak. The precarious positioning of enunciation gives shape to the unrepresentable. Sander's cinematic style enables her to visualize female subjectivity as a (dis)continuous process; the process of women becoming feminists. My 'cine-structuralist' reading of the cinematic author in terms of enunciation, suggests that forms of filmic narration are of the utmost importance for representations of female, feminist subjectivity.

PATTERNS OF DESIRE

A cine-structuralist reading of *The Subjective Factor* does not place in the foreground questions of desire and sexuality. That is why I now wish to turn to psychoanalysis by discussing Kaja Silverman's model of female authorship in cinema (1988). Although Silverman basically agrees with the poststructuralist location of authorship within the text, she does not want to dispose so readily of the biographical author whom she designates as 'the author "outside" the text', and who is linked to Benveniste's category of enunciation (193). In her study of the female authorial voice she proposes to combine the two. Silverman agrees that the author is 'constructed in and through discourse' (209), but she also bases her model of cinematic authorship on the psychoanalytic categories of identification and desire.

The authorial subjectivity of the enunciator inscribes itself in the cinema text in several ways. First, as either an image or a voice; this is the cinematic equivalent to the first-person pronoun (Hitchcock's appearances in his own films are the best known example of this 'directional appearance'). Silverman argues that such an authorial subject can be constructed through identification: the image has to be claimed by the filmmaker who identifies it as a reflection of her or himself. However, appearances of the author in film are a cinematic construction that can undermine or idealize her or his authorial subjectivity. This is shown in all its complexity in *The Subjective Factor* where Sander's appearance throws open the issues of identification and representation.

Second, the enunciator can be inscribed in film through 'secondary identification', that is, the identification with 'another who also happens in this case to be a fictional character' (214). The system of surrogation, where the character stands in for the director/author, is the usual paradigm for dominant cinema when that character is active and male. Silverman points out that a filmmaker can depart from this paradigm through identifications which challenge authorial subjectivity by undermining its authority. Examples are Ulrike Ottinger's fascination with freaks, or Marguerite Duras' investment in the figure of the exile (215).

Helke Sander's strategy is even more complex. In two other feature films, *Die allseitig reduzierte Persönlichkeit – Redupers* (*The universally reduced personality – Redupers*, 1977) and *Der Beginn aller Schrecken ist Liebe – Eskalation* (*The beginning of each shock is love – escalation*, 1984), Sander herself plays the main female character. By so openly collapsing the boundaries between director and character she challenges the traditional paradigm of surrogation. In *The Subjective Factor* the secondary identification between Helke Sander and the fictional Anni is established by Sander's voice-over, which then gets confused when Sander makes her visual appearances in the film – once together with Anni – without clearly identifying herself as such. Overall, it is a marked feature of Sander's cinematic style to inscribe clearly the enunciator, 'the author outside the text', into her films, which raises the problems of women's autobiographical history discussed earlier.

Third, the enunciator can be identified through a formal or narrative image, by a distinctive style that marks a director. Silverman connects authorial constructions of identification to the issue of desire. She proposes a framework of analysis that focuses on authorial inscription as patterns of desire; the 'libidinal coherence' revealed by a group of films of one director (216). Silverman's framework rests on the notion of the fantasmatic as theorized by Laplanche and Pontalis: the fundamental unconscious fantasy that structures the psychic life of a subject. This fantasy is properly speaking a 'scene', that is, it is dynamic and the characters are interchangeable in a pattern of desire governed by difference and repetition. Being fluid, the fantasmatic circulates and thus provides libidinal coherence to the film. In such a '*mise-en-scène* of desire' the author occupies a subject position, which is transferred onto a fictional character; this is where identification and desire mutually shape each other (217).[12] Silverman relies on Freudian psychoanalysis to sketch the kinds of fantasies that structure the psyche. These include a limited but crucial set of scenes, which move within the range of oedipal fantasies.

Fourth and finally, Silverman suggests a possible point of entry into the libidinal economy of a film or corpus of films. This is a 'nodal point'; a point to which the film repeatedly comes back, such as a sound, image, scene, place, or action (218), though it can also be marked through a certain excess at the level of formal style. The authorial fantasmatic can thus also be found at the level of the story, in so far that Silverman believes that there is always desire in narrative.

With respect to libidinal coherence, the authorial presence in *The Subjective Factor* is problematic. McCormick notes that: 'In the film, the kitchen becomes a motif used to depict various contradictions of the public/private dichotomy' (1991: 210). The question is whether the repeated return to the kitchen can be read as the 'nodal point'. Certainly one of the most important scenes in the film takes place in the kitchen: the scene depicting the mutual recognition of Anni and her friend Annemarie as women (I will come back to this scene). The kitchen is a crucial space of interaction where gender roles are confronted; it is a space of radical consciousness raising, but it hardly functions as a 'nodal point of authorial fantasy'. That is because *The Subjective Factor* as a whole is conspicuously reticent in displaying emotion or fantasy. The film reveals a certain resistance to seduction and pleasure that may be all too understandable in view of the conventions of traditional cinema but that runs the risk of alienating the spectator. Förster (1982), for example, is irritated by the rigid and wary way in which the film deals with fantasy and emotion, though she also justifies it in the light of the horrific history that the manipulation of fantasies and emotions has in Germany. This resistance highlights for me one of the issues with which I am concerned in this book, namely the difficulties feminist filmmakers encounter in undoing the oedipal structures of the fantasmatic. I do find, however, that the puritanical withdrawal from those Freudian narratives ends up paradoxically in confirming their power.

We can, in fact, read such disavowal symptomatically. A fantasmatic scenario in *The Subjective Factor* can be found in the psycho-emotional investment in politics. This works in two ways: positively, in the passion the women invest in their political struggle; negatively, in the super-ego function the left-wing movement exercises on their personal and sexual relationships. I want to suggest that the nodal point of authorial desire in *The Subjective Factor* can be situated in the interstice between the personal and the political, subjective and historical experience, story and discourse. In these nodal points I recognize the fantasmatic at work – with a vengeance.

To evaluate the contribution of cine-structuralism and poststructuralism to the problem of female directorship in *The Subjective Factor*, I would say that both the category of enunciation and that of desire cast useful light on the issue. Silverman's model of the double authorial 'voice' inside and outside the text clarifies the question of desire and identification. It ends up, however, confirming the Freudian apparatus and consequently fails to account for feminist attempts to move beyond it. As such, their usefulness for a reading of *The Subjective Factor* is limited. I shall now turn to film narratology in the hope that the distinction it introduces between the narrator (the subject who tells the story) and the focalizer (the subject who sees, speaks or acts) may be enlightening to analyze both the author 'inside' the film text and the one 'outside'.[13]

CINEMATIC NARRATION

Film theories that are more empirically and cognitively oriented also repudiate the notion of the author, which is usually replaced by the concept of a narrator. Nick Browne (1976) who, among film narratologists stands closest to structuralism, studies filmic narration as a process that structures the relations among narrator, character, and spectator. He especially criticizes structuralist approaches, such as Oudart's theory of suture, for placing the final authority on a film's meaning in the spectator, at the expense of the authorial agency of the narrator.

Edward Branigan (1984) goes even further and dismisses the author as nothing more than a subcode of narration, an hypothesis on the part of the spectator. He postulates a narrator to replace the author; not as a person, but as a role or function, or rather as 'a symbolic activity – the activity of narration' (40). This activity cannot be framed within the boundaries of the text, and is assumed to be implicit. Branigan here comes very close to Browne's concept of the effaced narrator.[14] The term 'effaced' is equivalent to the masked process of enunciation in poststructuralist film theory.

One important implication of Branigan's position is his anthropomorphism of the term 'narrator'. Branigan seems to imply that the narrator is a more neutral and acceptable concept now that the author has become suspect. It seems to me, however, that with the concept of the narrator much of the authorial agency that was lost with the death of the author slips in again through the back door. This is how I interpret David Bordwell's warning (1985) against postulating the narrator as a central concept in theories of filmic narration. Bordwell's opposition to the anthropomorphic illusion has other theoretical implications: it also attacks the idea of cinema as a communication system. The narrational process presupposes a spectator, but not necessarily a narrator. Rather than postulating a narrator, he prefers like most cognitivists to focus on the general organization of the narrational process. In his view, it is not the narrator who creates the narration, but vice versa.

The French film narratologist François Jost (1992) notes a fundamental ambiguity in that depersonalised conception of the narrator: on the one hand the narrator is reduced to a pure logic of the text, while on the other hand it entertains a communication link with the spectator. In chasing away any anthropomorphism one can only fall back on a purely machinistic system. For Jost, anthropomorphism is not specific to film theory but part and parcel of western metaphysics, and as such, it is unavoidable. Following Genette's narratology, he postulates several levels of filmic narration, where the author invents a narrator, who tells a story about characters, who in turn tell stories (32). Branigan (1992), too, has doubts about escaping the anthropomorphism inherent in the term 'narrator' (109). He suggests that its strength is due to its psychological function: 'Perhaps these metaphors are evidence of a displacement of the human ego onto the world . . .' (110).

Since I am intent on maintaining critical categories that make an analysis of authorial agency and especially subjectivity in film possible, I must say that I do not find Bordwell's non-personified and disembodied definition of narration particularly useful. If I want to leave room for questions of accountability and gender-specific representation, I must heed the poststructuralist warning that a cinema which masquerades its discourse in the form of story, or to put it differently, that knows no author and seems to come from nowhere, allows its ideology to be naturalized and its history to be effaced (Caughie 1981: 202).

Precisely because of cinema's often effaced narration, film studies need to elaborate on the complex ways in which the medium tells its stories. I will proceed with discussing Branigan's (1992) model of filmic narration in which he distinguishes many different levels and hence different types and functions of authors, narrators and character-as-narrator. Branigan breaks down the many narrative functions of a film into a model of eight hierarchically organized levels of narration (111–12, cf also 87), which I will briefly discuss in relation to Helke Sander's *The Subjective Factor*.[15]

The *historical author* (1) refers to the biographical person, or rather the public persona of a filmmaker as it functions in a social and cultural context. In the case of Helke Sander it would entail the knowledge of her as a filmmaker, as a leading socialist feminist in West Germany, as one of the founders of the feminist film journal *Frauen und Film* and as a writer. The *implied author*[16] (2) is an anthropomorphic term that according to Branigan, here following Metz, implies a 'diffuse but fundamental set of operations' underlying the narration (94). One can think of cinematic operations of montage such as selection, arrangement, duration, exclusion and emphasis; or of camera style such as framing, angle and movement. The intellectual montage in *The Subjective Factor*, such as the juxtaposition of fiction and documentary, is a good example.

Although Branigan does not adopt Metz's linguistic assumptions, in this model he does hold on to 'author'. As I have argued before, I want to abandon the term 'author' and replace it with 'director', in order to dispel any connotations of linguistic analogies as well as any smacks of *auteurism*. The function of the implied director refers also to operations that are specific to cinema, such as montage and camera style. Therefore, I will speak of the '*historical director*' and the '*implied director*'.

The *extra-fictional narrator* (3) can, unlike the implied director, be seen or heard in the film, yet is not part of the fictional world. In *The Subjective Factor* Sander's voice-over is an expression of the extra-fictional narrator. The status of her visual appearances is more uncertain, because these refer to the biographical director, but only for the initiated spectator; otherwise they are just part of the fictional world. The ambivalence at the level of narration created by Sander can be read as a sign of triggering the misrecognition that Silverman argues to be inevitable in such images of authorial identifications.

When the extra-fictional narrator is less personalized it can be analyzed as the *non-diegetic narrator* (4) who orients the spectator towards the story world by presenting information through, for example, a title. The non-diegetic narrator, then, presents something outside the fictional world, whereas the implied director or the diegetic narrator (see below) would show something to happen within the story. The non-diegetic narrator in Sander's film appears in the written words: 'There is no truth in the false' at the beginning of the final credits and 'There is a lot of false in the truth' at the end of the credits. These words provide an aphoristic commentary on socialist or feminist truths as well as on historiography.

The *diegetic narrator* (5) is implied, that is to say invisible, and yet present within the story world. Branigan describes this level of narration as 'the pictorial equivalent of a subjunctive conditional': if a bystander had been present, he or she would have seen and would have heard what is shown in the filmic image (95). The difference between the implied director and the implied diegetic narrator is the frame of reference: in the first case the frame of reference is the entire film, while in the second it is the fictional story. This entails that a particular scene can be operating simultaneously at various narrational levels.

In *The Subjective Factor* the use of the camera within the fictional scenes is a clear indication of the diegetic narrator. As McCormick points out 'the camera in Sander's film (operated by Martin Schäfer) does seem to take on a life of its own, to become a character in its own right' (1991: 222). This particular form of diegetic narration draws the spectator into the film; at the same time in the very act of drawing attention to itself such camera movement makes the audience aware of the independent subjectivity behind the camera. In other words, it makes the implied narration quite explicit. Of course, this is a typical example of the Brechtian technique of simultaneous seduction and distancing.

So far so good. The different functions of the narrator, however, are not the only technique of filmic narration to inscribe authorial subjectivity. As Silverman argues, the 'author inside the text' can also reside in the characters. The level of cinematic characters, can be described in the narrational terms of focalization. Introduced by Gérard Genette (1980) into literary theories, focalization is a relatively new term in film studies. For Branigan, focalization in cinema is an attempt to represent the consciousness of a character in pictures rather than in words (106). It is important to note that for Branigan focalization is related exclusively to characters, so as to keep a clear distinction between narration and focalization, whereas other (literary) narratologists postulate narrators who focalize events.

The remaining four levels of narration in Branigan's model, then, are related to characters. *Non-focalized narration* (6) refers to what he calls a 'primary' level of action as a depiction of character. Within this limited context, the character is an agent who is defined by actions and events (100–101). Whereas authorial narration is to the fore in *The Subjective Factor*, in terms of the depiction of characters the narration is mostly non-focalized. I would argue that this is in itself a feminist commentary, because the actions (by men) and the (historical) events that define Anni are meant to shed significant light on her expanding feminist consciousness, especially in the first part where Anni's silence and passivity make her undergo rather than undertake actions and events. When she succeeds in gradually liberating herself, the narration becomes more focalized.

Focalization can be either external or internal, depending on camera framing and movement. In *external focalization* (7) the camera technique and montage are physically external to the character, yet are still a focalization of that character, hence external focalization is 'semi-subjective'.[17] It has the powerful effect of establishing the character as a narrational centre. External focalization in *The Subjective Factor* is related mostly to Anni. In one scene, for example, we see a group of socialist students discussing and planning their campaign against the Springer group. The camera travels back and reveals Anni sitting in the left corner patiently waiting for her turn to speak. The narrational commentary through the camera work makes the exclusion of the woman's point of view quite explicit.

Internal focalization (8) is 'more fully private and subjective' (103). Internal focalization can take place at the 'surface', for example through perception or impressions (usually rendered via the point-of-view shot that I will discuss in detail in the next chapter). It can also render visible the deeper thoughts of a character through dreams, desires, fantasies or memories. It is the most subjective form of representation in film and according to Branigan invites the spectator to identify with the character. The final category of narration in Branigan's model, internal depth focalization, does not occur at all in *The Subjective Factor*, as I noted earlier in the film's unwillingness to deal with questions of desire and fantasy. There is, however, one striking occurrence of internal surface focalization, in a scene that is generally recognized as the turning point of the film (Förster 1982: 15–16; McCormick 1991: 209–11). In this scene Anni proposes using pamphlets about the representation of women as pin-ups in the anti-Springer campaign. The students do not consider her proposal and tell her to go the kitchen where she may find Annemarie who is interested in similar subjects.

Anni hesitates before the glass door and looks into the kitchen. In several internal focalization shots, the camera films Anni looking at Annemarie who sits at the kitchen table under a poster of Che Guevara, and Annemarie looking at Anni behind the kitchen door. Then the camera cuts back to Anni's face in close-up. This is the very first frontal close-up of Anni in the entire film, one-third of the way through. This shot is followed by a close-up of Annemarie staring at Anni. Anni opens the door and in another internal focalization shot, the camera pans slowly through the whole kitchen, as if Anni wants to take in very slowly the full impact of what is happening then and there. Other close-ups follow in which the two women look silently at each other while a smile starts to play on their faces. When the women sit down to talk, the camera moves outside through the window and travels vertically along several kitchens in apartment buildings, one above the other, while we hear Anni's voice saying: 'Maybe we are not stupid, maybe we are just different. Maybe there are many people like us in many kitchens. Maybe we are strong'. A cut-back to the kitchen shows us how the two women have changed the table into a platform for political action, surrounded by books and political posters as well as by food, stoves and refrigerators. As Silverman mentions, the 'moral' of the scene is clear: the socialist students refuse to integrate questions of the domestic sphere and of personal relationships into their politics, whereas the women show that 'political inquiry not only coexists comfortably with domestic labor, but is a necessary extension of it' (1983a: 21–2).

Internal focalization in *The Subjective Factor* is, then, directly connected to the representation of the dawning of feminist consciousness, of the birth of women's solidarity. The narrational code of focalization coincides with the female characters' acquisition of feminist subjectivity and is hence explicitly used as a means of giving the women a higher degree of awareness. The spare use of this technique in the film makes this scene even more pregnant with meaning.

I think that Branigan's framework of filmic narration introduces a range of narrational forms that breaks down authorial subjectivity into different shades of directorship, thus showing the complex and often ambiguous representations of the 'author outside' and the 'author inside' the medium of film and the interrelations between them. In my view, the complexity of the representation of cinematic directorship is connected to the ambiguous status of the visual moving image, where so many cinematic techniques, such as montage, camera style, directional appearances, titles, and focalization can be read as inscriptions of authorial subjectivity, or enunciation. Focalization, as Branigan understands it in the context of character experience, may at first sight be related not to authorial subjectivity but rather to character subjectivity. Yet, from my short analysis of focalization in *The Subjective Factor*, the process appears as a major cinematic code for inscribing desire into a film, and can therefore be directly related to Silverman's psychoanalytic notion of libidinal coherence.

It seems to me therefore that the poststructuralist notion of enunciation and the cognitive model of narration, far from necessarily excluding one another, instead complement and enhance. In my assessment, the poststructuralist question of cinematic authorship, refocused by Silverman along the lines of enunciation and desire, needs to be asked *a priori* in order to take seriously the issue of female directorship. Yet, as we have seen, Silverman's model of libidinal coherence does not address the specific engagement with cinematic directorship of a feminist film like *The Subjective Factor*. I have therefore complemented her approach with the cognitive model of narration. In itself, Branigan's model of cinematic narration, however, remains too limited and technical for dealing with any questions of ideology. Yet, when we consider how the concept of masked enunciation in cinema has tended to neglect the question of authorial agency as it has become central in poststructuralist film theory, it becomes clear that the categories of cinematic narration distinguished by Branigan can help us to understand more systematically the many ways in which enunciation and desire, or the 'author outside' and the 'author inside', are actually inscribed in film. Branigan's narratological model is therefore useful in analyzing the poststructuralist notions of enunciation and desire in more specifically cinematic terms.

CONCLUSION

In this chapter I have claimed that there are strong political and theoretical reasons for spotlighting the female, feminist director. Although I have taken a firm stand against the implicitly anti-feminist propositions in film theories, such as 'the artist as genius' in *auteurism* and 'the death of the subject' in poststructuralism, I have followed the *auteur* school in postulating the director as the filmmaker who can be held accountable for the representation of sexual difference in her or his film, and I have adopted ideas from poststructuralist film theory to conceive of directorship in terms of subjectivity.

The introduction of semiotics and psychoanalysis into film theory has resulted in an important shift away from the cinematic author to the film text and to the spectator. Attempts to rethink cinematic authorship in semiotic terms of discourse and enunciation, or psychoanalytic terms of desire and the fantasmatic, have not always proved equally successful in my search for a female authorial voice. A cognitive model of filmic narration here appears to be a necessary addition for analyzing more systematically the director's many manifestations within her or his film.

In my analysis of female directorship in *The Subjective Factor* I have paid attention to three interconnected layers of female subjectivity: those of agency, desire and rhetoric. In the case of Helke Sander's film, authorial agency and feminist politics are emphasized at the expense of representations of desire and fantasy. The spare use of character focalization in *The Subjective Factor* stands in sharp contrast to the manifestations as director or narrator by which Sander plays out her authorial agency: the historical director outside the film who, as an intellectual woman, writes and lectures about her own work; the implied director who is responsible for the intellectual montage; her appearances within the film as an extra-fictional narrator; the non-diegetic narrator who gives written commentaries within the credits; and as the diegetic narrator in the marked camera style. In a double shift, Sander simultaneously establishes and questions the status of her own cinematic directorship. The way in which the film structures the relation between director, film text, and spectator shows the significant relation between the filmmaker's gender and the representation, or better, representability of female subjectivity.

3 Silent Violence: On Point of View

Tried always and condemned by thee
Permit me this reprieve
That dying I may earn the look
For which I cease to live—.
                    Emily Dickinson[1]

INTRODUCTION

A white woman in a black dress looks into a vast barren landscape, her back turned to the camera. A female voice-over says slowly and monotonously:

> To my father I have been an absence all my life. Sundown after sundown we sat facing each other over the mutton, the potatoes, the pumpkin. We must have confronted each other in silence. Is it possible that we spoke? No.

The woman winds a long-case clock and then serves her father dinner, in silence. She looks out of the window into the dry, dusty land while the voice-over says: 'Since I found no enemy outside I made an enemy of myself'. A sound like an approaching storm increases and the woman grabs her head with both hands. Next morning she serves her father breakfast, still in silence. While father and daughter sit on the porch next to each other, silently looking into the distance, the opening credits of the film *Dust* roll on. The film by Marion Hänsel is dedicated 'to my fathers'.

In this chapter I will focus on representations of female subjectivity residing in the cinematic character. The two films by Hänsel that I will discuss, *Dust* (1983) and *Les Noces Barbares* (literally 'the barbaric wedding', English release title, *Cruel Embrace*, 1987), do not spotlight the filmmaker in any way like the films of Helke Sander do. The dedication 'to my fathers' in *Dust* is the only direct reference to the historical director. Hänsel's authorial agency can be traced in

56

manifestations of the implied director, through her marked cinematic style of artful framing and camera work, and ambigous narration. I take the authorial agency to be the subject of a feminist consciousness that establishes a specific film rhetoric structuring the relation between director, character and spectator. However, I am also concerned here with female subjectivity in terms of desire and fantasy (the second level in the framework outlined in Chapter 2). As the previous chapter warranted the conclusion that an analysis of point of view may yield insight into questions of desire and fantasy, I will approach the question of female subjectivity in these films through an analysis of point of view.

Dust and *Cruel Embrace* tell tragic stories of women who are unloved and hence incapable of love themselves, women who are violated and humiliated; tragic stories of the impossibility of female subjectivity in masculinist society. Later in the chapter I will explore the films' effect as an experience of the spectator, but first I will concentrate on representations of the suffering female characters in both *Dust* and *Cruel Embrace*.

BREAKING WINDOWS

The Belgian/French filmmaker Marion Hänsel based the script for her fiction film *Dust* on the novel *In the Heart of the Country* by J. M. Coetzee. The story centres on a white middle-aged woman who lives with her old father and their black servants on an isolated farm in South Africa during the first half of this century. The film explores what Toni Morrison, in one of her elegant essays on American literature, has described as 'an almost completely buried subject: the interdependent working of power, race, and sexuality in a white woman's battle for coherence' (1992: 20). The difficulties of telling such a hidden story are reflected in the visual style of *Dust*, which is filmed in a slow rhythm, with little dialogue and little film music, giving the spectator a feeling of the emptiness and loneliness of both the vast African land and the characters' lives.

The story is told from the perspective of the white woman, Magda, who yearns for the love of her widowed father, the 'Baas'. The unloving father, however, can feel only contempt for his daughter. She goes about the house silently cooking his food, taking off his boots, cutting his hair, heating water for his bath, but in return for all her subservience she receives only an occasional grunt while he is eating. The father's only verbal expressions consist of orders shouted at his black

servants. *Dust* carefully traces the effects of the father's cruel indifference on Magda in short fantasmatic visions which show her frustrated
desire. Her fantasies[2] are accompanied by a soundtrack that is a mixture of both ethereal and threatening sounds like screeching crickets,
an African flute, a heartbeat, a sandstorm. The sounds swell during
each fantasy and abruptly stop when the scene is over.

In the first short fantasy scene (at the very beginning of the film),
Magda watches from the window as her father arrives in an open car-
riage with his bride. When he and the woman are asleep Magda kills
him with an axe crying out 'father!', blood splattering all over them.
Because this is the first fantasy scene the spectator watches within the
film, it is only when s/he sees Magda sitting with her father on the
porch in the next shot that s/he realizes the previous scene must have
been fantasmatic. The spectator has yet to 'learn' that the peculiar
soundtrack is not only creating a certain atmosphere and underlining
Magda's psychological state, but is also a cue for a hallucinatory scene.
After the fantasy scene Magda tells us in voice-over that 'he does not
die so easily after all'.

As if Magda's nightmarish fantasy were a premonition of things to
come, in the following scene the black servant Henrik brings home his
wife Anna on a cart. The white Baas soon tries to seduce the young
black woman, much to Magda's and Henrik's distress. After having
served her father his dinner one night, Magda stands in front of the
dark window, reflecting her image. While she rubs her wrists against
the glass harder and harder, her voice-over speaks the following words:

> I must not fall asleep at the halfway point of my life. I have my
> senses, but I don't know them. I inhabit a body that inhabits a house.
> I know of no act that can open me to the world.

Then the window breaks. From the outside and in slow motion for a
split second we see the glass cutting into Magda's face and wrists,
glass and blood shattering, intermingled. The soundtrack stops abruptly
and we see Magda again from the previous camera position in the
back, now leaning her head against the unbroken window pane and
slowly letting her arms fall down along her body.

It is through such fantasy scenes that *Dust* brings about a deep sense
of sympathy in the viewer for the plight of the female character en-
trapped in her rough and isolated world. The film represents a closed
microcosm of white patriarchy in which the complexities of power
pertaining both to gender and race are effectively laid out. *Dust* ex-

plores these power relations by focusing on the physical and mental suffering of the white woman in her relationship both to her father and to the black servants. Such consistent focus on the figure of Magda helps to construct her as a subject, that is, into someone who has (repressed) desires and acts on them. The film rests on a paradox: through narrative means and cinematic devices the implied director constructs the very subjectivity that the story itself denies Magda, both in relation to her father and to her servants. Within the terms of the framework of interrelated layers of female subjectivity set out above, the feminist rhetoric in *Dust* points to a tension between female desire and a society that grants no agency to the female subject. One might even say that because Magda's struggle for social agency and self-determination is doomed, she retreats into a life of frustrated desire and fearful fantasies. In the following section I will analyze how the film represents Magda's wounded subjectivity through a careful construction of point of view.

Point of View in Cinematic Narration

As mentioned earlier, *Dust* is told from Magda's perspective. Her perspective or point of view takes shape on three levels: the optical point of view within the story (we see what the character Magda sees); the mental point of view within the story (we learn the vision of character – narrator Magda); and the metaphorical point of view on Magda within the cinematic discourse (the vision of the diegetic narrator). These three levels together create a subjective point of view both of and on Magda. Point of view then is one of the strongest cinematic means by which *Dust* seeks to produce the subjectivity of its main female character. Point of view (like perspective) is a term that has come to mean many things in film narratology. As Francesco Casetti remarks, the term in itself incorporates the 'polysemic' points of seeing, showing and observing (1990: 129, note 4). And in his book on filmic narration, Nick Browne has pointed to the importance 'of narrative theory to examine and explain the linkages between different orders of seeing integrated within a film: "shot," "point-of-view-shot," "character's point of view," and "narrative point of view"' (Browne 1976: 58). I think it necessary therefore to unravel the meaning of the term and propose some alterations and distinctions relevant for my analysis of *Dust*.

The term 'point of view' is usually reserved for the optical point-of-view-shot, conventionally abbreviated as POV. The POV shot is described as a subjective shot presenting the character's vision (Monaco 1981: 170; Bordwell and Thompson 1986: 196–7). The POV shot always consists of two shots: the character looking and the object looked at (the order can be reversed) (Branigan 1984: 103). Bordwell (1985) uses the term point of view as synonymous with the optically subjective shot, with cinematic techniques like mobile framing, close-ups and camera movement, which are opposed to the more objective approach of long shots, deep focus and static camera.

Dust employs a filmic style that is much closer to art house cinema than to Hollywood realism. The diegetic narrator keeps the camera at some distance from Magda, as in the medium shot of the opening scene where the camera is situated behind her looking into the landscape. Still, the film has some optical POV shots, for example in the scenes in which Magda looks through the window or in the mirror. Of the subjective cinematic techniques only the close-up is used frequently. Camera movement is scarce in *Dust* because the cinematic style in general is quite composed, creating the earlier mentioned effect of stillness and loneliness. The same holds for the relative absence of mobile framing; Magda is often framed in a still shot without movement or change in framing. Rather, many shots in the film actually 'frame' Magda, holding her captive within the image, such as mirrors or windows. In the recurring shot of her winding the long-case clock at the end of a corridor, for example, the effect of framing is enhanced by many vertical lines of doorways, jambs and walls. Such découpage not only creates artful images, but also metaphorically suggests Magda's imprisonment in the house.

Yet, in spite of the relative lack of conventional subjective cinematic techniques, the film consistently constructs Magda's point of view. There is no scene which is not shown through Magda's eyes or presented more obliquely from her point of view. In *Dust* many scenes start with an establishing shot of Magda looking, even though the object presented in close-up in the next shot might in reality be too far away for her to see. This occurs for example in the scenes in which the Baas sets out to seduce the young servant Anna: three times we see Magda looking and each time somewhere on the land we see her father talking and presenting gifts to Anna who keeps running away. It is after these short scenes that Magda's fantasy of the breaking window occurs. In the next scene we first see the Baas and Anna on the land together before the camera cuts to a medium shot of Magda watching them from the porch, commenting in a bitter monologue on their affair. In another cut to her own room Magda continues her monologue in front of the mirror before she walks to the window and sees her father pay Anna more money than the other servants. That night she hears them have sex. The sequence of the father's attention forced upon the black servant shows how *Dust* creates a subjective, Magda's, point of view through a variety of devices such as optical and subjective POV shots, fantasy and verbal commentary.

This reconstruction of Magda's point of view helps me reveal the imprecision of the term, since it refers both to the optical POV shot of a character and to a mental perspective, which can be the character's or the narrator's point of view. Physical perception and mental attitude are two different but not quite distinct processes. This confusion does not help clarify the complex issue of the author/narrator, which I discussed in the previous chapter.

Within the structuralist approach, point of view pertains to two different narrative levels, that of the narrative or story, including the relations between characters, and that of the level of narration or discourse, mediating the relation of address between narrator and spectator. Point of view is central to the structuring of the relationship or difference between those two levels of telling (Branigan 1984). The mental point of view can be either a character's or a narrator's perspective, but in both cases it is a construction produced by the text, which mediates the responses of the spectator and thus plays a coordinating role in the construction of the text (Browne 1976). In his more recent work on cinematic narration, Branigan (1992) maintains the distinction between the character who perceives and the narrator who presents, by introducing the term 'focalization' as distinct from 'narration'. I think that precisely because the concept of point of view relates to so many narrational levels in a film, it is important to disentangle those levels more carefully.

Focalization
Despite its clearly photographic origins and concomitant connotations, focalization is a relatively new term in film studies, imported from literary studies where it was first introduced by Gérard Genette.[3] Branigan restricts his use of the concept to characters, which stands in opposition to the original idea in literary narratology according to which narrators can also focalize events. For narratologist Seymour Chatman (1990) the concept of focalization envisaged by Genette blurs the distinction between discourse and story, making the term less useful for cinema. Although I find myself in agreement with Chatman's observation, I do not wish to follow his suggestion and do away with all these terms

(point of view, perspective, focalization) only to introduce new (and to my mind) unnecessarily vague terms such as 'filter' to denote the perceptual experience of character and 'slant' to designate the mental attitude of narrator (Chatman 1990: 143). For reasons of theoretical continuity and clarity I prefer to retain the narratological concept of focalization. But what exactly does focalization in cinema entail?

We recall from the previous chapter that Branigan (1992) narrows the concept of focalization down to character perception and experience. There I defended Branigan's topology of cinematic narration for enabling a detailed and systematic analysis of the many functions of narrativity in cinema, especially with respect to directorship. I was not so much concerned with point of view as the construction of subjectivity, but rather with an analysis of focalization that allowed me to track down configurations of directorship and inscriptions of authorial desire in film.

I now contend, however, that taken in its own right, Branigan's conception of focalization is too narrow and runs the risk of losing sight of the intricate relation between narrator and character. I maintain that focalization is not so much separated from narration but is rather a specific mode of narration. In Branigan's model focalization would be either a function of the implied director (as in montage) or of the diegetic narrator (camera position and movement), yet he exclusively reserves the term as a function of the character. His model further raises for me the question how perception is related to experience or reflection; categories which seem to involve quite different levels of narrativity. Branigan accounts for the transposition of a literary concept to film studies by simplifying focalization almost beyond recognition. It seems to me that such a concept of focalization still begs the question of the construction of point of view in cinema in visual terms.

François Jost (1989) has systematically examined 'point of view' in his comparative narratology of cinema and literature.[4] Jost quite rightly points to the paradox that narratology works with notions taken from cinematography, such as point of view and focalization, whereas film studies have yet to appropriate these terms theoretically. The realm of literature is differentiated from the medium of cinema in that these notions function as metaphors in the former but form material reality in the latter, always already visualized and actualized by means of the camera. In order to avoid possible confusion between focalization and narration, Jost argues, film narratology has to account for the difference between the semiotic level, which can be understood by the metaphor of the camera as eye, and the narrative level, metaphorized by the camera as pen. In other words, film narratology must theorize the visual level and distinguish seeing from telling. Instead of taking the difference between story and discourse as the point of departure for an analysis of point of view, Jost starts from the difference between on the one hand seeing and hearing, and on the other telling.

To that end, and capitalizing on the metaphor of the eye of the camera, Jost introduces a new term in addition to focalization: *ocularization* (22): this refers to the visual regime of the camera showing us what the character sees. Focalization, in contrast, refers to the more cognitive and psychological level of what a character knows. In analogy to visuality, Jost elaborates the metaphor of the microphone as ear to theorize the acoustic regime of cinema by introducing the term *auricularization* (23). Let us look at each of these in some detail.

Ocularization is to be localized in the eye of either the character or – more implicitly – in the diegetic narrator. When the look of the camera can be directly referred back to a character, as is often the case with Magda in *Dust*, Jost speaks of internal ocularization. When the camera look is not attached to an authority within the diegesis, he uses the expression of 'zero' or neutral ocularization. In this case there is no ocular position; or rather the position of the camera is neutral and does not signify anything other than its function of showing; it is not attached to a look. Ocularization being understood as issuing from the eye of the camera, it follows that 'external ocularization' is by definition a contradiction (112).

Jost proceeds to distinguish between primary and secondary internal ocularization; terms that are in line with Metz' conceptualization of cinematic identification with the camera or the enunciator as primary and with the spectator as secondary identification. In the case of primary internal ocularization the visual image contains a signifier of the materiality of the camera (such as a trembling or hand-held camera), a look which in turn can be linked to a character absent from the image. This is the ocular position of the narrator. Secondary internal ocularization constructs subjectivity through contextualization, by montage, the visual qualities of the image, or verbally, as in Magda's monologues spoken into the camera. This is the ocular position of the character. Finally, if camera work or imagery carry the sign of an implied director, Jost speaks of 'spectatorial ocularization' (28). In such a case the implied director creates a perspective that cannot be referred back to an instance in the diegetic world but is directly addressed to the spectator.

Auricularization knows basically the same aspects as ocularization. Primary and secondary internal forms of auricularization are related respectively to a character or narrator. In the case of primary internal auricularization the sound departs from realism and refers directly to the subjectivity of the ear. In film, this can only be inferred from the context. In *Dust*, the peculiar soundtrack in Magda's fantasies is an example of primary internal auricularization. With secondary internal auricularization, acoustic subjectivity is established by montage or the visual style. It would be possible for the sound to derive from a profilmic instance. Finally, when the sound is not at all anchored in a diegetic instance but coming from a point of origin outside the diegesis, we are dealing with zero auricularization, of which film music is the privileged example (57).

There are, however, some complications in the analysis of sound in cinema. Sound is often an undefined sphere rather than being anchored in a specific source and hence, is less individualized than the look. In narrative cinema the soundtrack is usually mediated by the flow of images and acquires its meaning in relation to the image. In itself it remains ambivalent and its 'point of view' (so to speak) is often difficult to determine. Thus, although it is clear that the soundtrack of Magda's fantasies is connected to her character within the diegesis, it is not so easy to decide whether this sound track is meant to represent the sound inside her head (primary internal auricularization) or to create a certain ambiance by the implied director (zero auricularization).

What of focalization in Jost's narratology? In his view, focalization is a 'polymorphous phenomenon' which cannot be easily defined. It can only acquire its meaning in a careful reading of the context in which it occurs. As mentioned earlier, ocularization and auricularization refer to the semiotic level of seeing and hearing, whereas focalization refers to the narrative level of knowing. Jost claims that in cinema, in contrast to the novel, those different psychological attitudes are represented by different codes: the affective by what the character sees, hears or says (the visual and sound track); the cognitive by a complex 'intersemiotics' that makes up the narrative of a film (71–2). The knowledge that focalization distributes to the spectator is to know the position of the narrator towards the character.

Jost distinguishes three modes of focalization: external, internal and spectatorial. External focalization is a form of narration exterior to the character, where the spectator has no inside information about her or him and hence has access to the same or to less knowledge than the character her/himself. In the mode of internal focalization the story is told by the character. The spectator knows the thoughts and feelings of that character and experiences what s/he experiences. Spectatorial focalization, finally, is operative when the cinematic narration gives the spectator an advantage in knowledge over the character, for example through particular *mise-en-scène*, extreme camera angles, or a form of montage giving information of which the character is not aware (as in parallel montage, an example of which we will see in the analysis of *Broken Mirrors* in the next chapter). When showing merges with telling it is possible for a story not to be focalized at all; in cinema this is called transparency.

In Branigan we have a concept of focalization that is exclusively connected to the position of a character, including both mere perception and more complex forms of experience. With Jost the level of perception is broken down into ocularization (seeing) and auricularization (hearing). The narrative information that Jost theorizes as focalization (knowing), is shifted by Branigan to the many different functions of narrator and director. The two narrative models do not altogether exclude one another, although in comparison their different understandings of the same terms might create some confusion.

The main reason for valuing Jost's model – apart from the continuity in theoretical terms mentioned earlier – is because it enables a more lucid understanding of a specific characteristic of cinema: the distinction between the 'literal', that is visual and non-metaphorical nature of point of view, and the mental point of view. Jost points to an unwelcome slippage in literary narratology where those two levels are equated and ocularization and focalization are blended, leading to theoretical confusion. He makes it perfectly clear that to see something is not necessarily a subjective vision; in the first case we deal with a semiotic sign, in the second case with narrative. For example, the use of a subjective camera is not a case of internal focalization; that would mean a confusion of ocularization with focalization. Here, Jost is most critical of literary narratology and insists that the semiotic and narrative levels should be carefully distinguished. Yet, although the two should not be totally blended, focalization cannot be entirely separated from ocularization either. Rather, insofar as perception contributes to narrative knowledge focalization partly builds up from ocularization.

Jost has created a dynamic theory of point of view in cinema that takes into account the material level of a permanent cinematographic ocularization as distinct from but related to the narrative level of focalization. In the following section I will make a pendular movement between theory and film.

Silent Violence

Let me continue my reading of point of view in *Dust* within the framework proposed by Jost. Internal focalization is given to Magda throughout
the film; she tells the story and the spectator lives through her experiences. None of the other characters in the film ever functions as focalizer.
Of the scenes discussed earlier, in which Magda observes her father's
coercive seduction of the black woman, we can now retrospectively
remark that the camera frequently takes up the position of Magda's
eye. In Jost's terms, Magda is given subjectivity through primary
ocularization (the camera eye is linked to Magda), secondary internal
ocularization (Magda's monologue), and focalization (Magda's voice-
over). As her voice-over gives a mental point of view to what she is
witnessing with her own eyes, we can say that the verbal focalization
anchors the ocularization.

If we take up from where we have left the film: Magda hears her
father, the Baas, have sex with the black maid, Anna. It is thus through
Magda's hearing (secondary internal auricularization) that the spectator understands that the Baas has made Anna his mistress. Magda's
tossing and turning in her bed marks her deep discomfort with these
developments. On one such night she sits up and grabs her head while
the hallucinatory sound softly starts. She suddenly stands up to slam
the door. With the sound of the slamming door, the hallucinatory sound
stops and the camera freezes on the black wood of the door. After a
few seconds of black, the camera moves up from the black wood of
the father's bed, while Magda's voice-over projects her dark thoughts
into the future, the images illustrating her words: Magda serving her
father and her maid in bed, Henrik starting to drink and pinching Magda's
bottom, and the work of generations falling to ruin. The hallucinatory
sound increases, enhanced with Henrik's loud laughter, and the scene
ends with a cut back to Magda on her bed grabbing her head.

The verbal level of this scene, the voice-over, signifies internal
focalization. Again it is the focalization here that mediates the zero
ocularization of the visual level of this fantasy scene. The gesture of
grabbing her head suggests that the soundtrack accompanying Magda's
fantasies or hallucinations can be analyzed as signifying her state of
mind (secondary internal auricularization). At the same time the sound
functions to create an uncanny atmosphere and is a subtle cue for the
spectator that the scene is to be taken psychologically and not realistically. I wrote 'subtle' because *Dust* does not give its narration away
easily; the spectator is often thrown into disorientation.

The narrational status of 'mental images' such as fantasies, halluci-nations or flashbacks are complicated and potentially disorienting; this is why Hollywood cinema has developed semiotic signs to indicate starts and endings of a flashback or a dream (foggy or waving image, dissolve, close-up of closed eyes, etc.) and why modernist art cinema wilfully produces confusion by withholding such signs and abandon-ing narrational levels. Mental images derive from mental vision and are hence in between the eye of the character and the eye of the diegetic narrator. Jost designates the term 'modalized ocularization' to mental images (31). Usually, in contemporary cinema, mental images are not semiotically marked, but understood as interruptions of the story, ei-ther in time (flashback), or in mode (fantasy, hallucination) (33). In *Dust*, Magda's fantasies can be seen as modalized ocularization, mostly (but not always) marked by a specific hallucinatory sound.

In the sequence I am presently concerned with, the next shot shows a reflection of a white figure in the glass of the long-case clock, slowly moving forward. The vague and distorted reflection creates a ghostlike image that looks most unreal. At first sight it appears to be an halluci-natory image, but when in another shot Magda is shown in her white nightgown knocking on the door of her father's bedroom, the specta-tor understands it was not another fantasmatic image. Magda's walk-ing down the corridor is presented to the spectator in the strange imagery of a reflection in glass, an image that is repeated after her father has sent her away. The glass clock frames Magda's reflection, which in turn is framed by door jambs and other vertical lines in the image.

Since the reflections are not Magda's experience, they can be attrib-uted to an implied director who deliberately produces a disorienting image by a special *mise-en-scène*, lighting and framing. The image cannot be referred back to a diegetic instance and can therefore be interpreted as a narrational point of view on the status of Magda's inner state: she is like a ghost caught in a coffin-like case and her emotional state is as distorted as her reflection in the glass of the clock. This is what Jost calls spectatorial ocularization, because the director creates a perspective that is directly addressed at the spectator with a specific *mise-en-scène* and camera angle. Spectatorial ocularization, then, can be understood as an overt intervention in the cinematographic style created by the implied director.

Its effects can be measured in the critical representation of white female subjectivity. The visual representation of Magda as white and ghostly suggests white womanhood to be more dead than alive. In his essay on whiteness in cinema, Richard Dyer (1993) has argued that

Hollywood films, in a colonial context, conventionally oppose the chastity and virginity of white womanhood to the vitality and sexuality of the black woman, usually the white woman's servant. Not only is there no occasion for such racist binarism in *Dust* (Anna is shown to be a victim of the white man's prowess), but Magda's virginity is represented as an imposed lack of sexuality, as a source of frustration and bitterness, rather than as a strength allowing for the desired 'calm, controlled, rational' state of whites (Dyer 1993: 156). As we shall see white womanhood in *Dust* is not represented as the ideal but as an ordeal.

The next scene in this sequence shifts back to zero ocularization. When Magda insists that her father answer her, he opens the door and hits her. She slowly slides down the wall and sits on the floor in the corridor, staring ahead. The mode of narration changes to modalized ocularization when the scene suddenly shifts to the father's bedroom where Magda is watching him sleep. Magda begins a long and emotional monologue in which she begs him to show her a sign of his love, while also professing deep self-hatred. She ends her soliloquy crying out: 'Father, look at me. Show me your heart just once. . . . Father, notice me once. Do you think you can die without saying "yes" to me? I am I'. The scene cuts back to Magda sitting in the same position in the corridor.

Although the scene is not accompanied by an hallucinatory sound, the spectator has to infer from the beginning and end position that this was indeed a fantasy. The fact that the scene is unrealistic (the father does not wake up while Magda is talking to him, weeping and touching him, and Anna does not seem to be present in the room) confirms my suggestion that we are dealing with a form of modalized ocularization. Again the spectator witnesses a visualization (filmed in zero ocularization) of Magda's inner thoughts and emotions (internal focalization); the whole of which is a fantasy (modalized ocularization). The combination of affect and cognition produces a profound effect in this scene, because Magda's sad monologue moves the spectator (me, in fact, to tears) and makes her or him sympathize with the woman's plight. At the same time, the spectator has to work out the shifting narrational status of the scene: is it realistic or fantasmatic? The sequence as a whole shows relatively swift changes from one narrational level to another.

In the next scene, therefore, when we witness Magda grabbing a gun, running out of the house, shooting through a window and running away, vanishing as a small white point into the dark night, we do not immediately know whether she has killed her father or whether this was another fantasy. In analytical terms: the spectator cannot at *prima facie* tell whether s/he has been watching internal focalization or zero ocularization. In other words, *Dust* wilfully plays on collapsing the distinction between fantasy and reality. It is only on the basis of contextual evidence that the spectator will be able to solve the riddle and can retrospectively interpret the scene. The sense of disorientation does not last long because in the next scene Magda tends her father's gaping wound in his stomach. He never speaks before he finally dies. While we are watching the agony of the dying father, accompanied by the sound of buzzing flies, the camera focuses on Magda while her voice-over speaks of her numbness; a combination of zero ocularization and verbal internal focalization.

Magda's monologues in *Dust* are a narrative device that is rare in classical cinema but more common in art cinema. Monologues create a peculiar form of narration, mainly because they directly address the spectator and hence break through illusionalism. Whereas voice-over (which is also extensively used in *Dust*) combines internal focalization (the story is told by the character) with zero ocularization (neutral camera), a monologue combines internal focalization with secondary internal ocularization (the story is not only told by the character, but spoken into the camera). The visual and verbal level are then highly subjectivized which most likely places the spectator in a position of identification with the character. At the same time, because the level of discourse is made explicit, the spectator is distanced from the story. The artificiality of this form of narration lies in the character being simultaneously physically present in the world of the story as well as being the narrator. In the case of voice-over narration these two levels are kept separated: the voice belongs to the cinematic discourse and the body to the diegetic story. The monologues in *Dust* thus stimulate the spectator to simultaneously identify with Magda and reflect on the presented story.

Of Heat and Dust

With the death of the patriarch power relations shift. Magda tries to take his place as the boss of the farm, but she never manages to gain control over the situation. She also attempts to befriend the servants Henrik and Anna, who, because of the breakdown of established power relations are structurally incapable of accepting either her authority or her friendship. In one scene Magda breaks open an old chest and gives Anna beautiful robes that belonged probably to Magda's mother. Anna looks proudly at her image in the mirror with Magda helping her to

dress. In the context of South African race relations the contrast between the black woman in the white gown and the white woman in
her ragged black dress is stunning; the masquerade suggests a poor
white servant waiting upon a rich black lady. This image visualizes
Magda's experience of herself as 'a black fish swimming among the
white fish' (as she says in one of her monologues), suggesting a reversal of skin colour. Having acquired proper white womanhood by
repressing desire, sexuality and ambition, Magda has achieved 'ideal'
female subjectivity in a colonial and masculinist context. With absence
and lack lying at the core of her white female subjectivity, Magda can
now only try to live her desires through the mediation of the black
female servant. Dyer has pointed to the narrative technique of Hollywood colonial movies, where the white, sexually repressed heroine lives
her emotions and vitality through her black servant: 'Pent-up feelings of
frustration, anger, jealousy and fear, feelings for which there is no white
mode of expression . . . can only be lived through blacks' (1993: 156).

One day Magda sends Henrik on a bicycle to the post office to draw
money from her father's account. After days of cycling he comes back
without the money, because the bank would not accept Magda's signature. He furiously demands his money and when Magda desperately
tells him she does not have any, he proceeds to rape her. The rape
scene is very disturbing. Of course, any rape scene is horrifying, but
what makes this scene particularly disturbing is the complicating factor of race and the filmic representation of the scene.

The brutal violence of the rape scene is placed very much in the
spotlight by the implied director. The scene is filmed in a montage of
close-ups, the camera positioned at a low angle, moving along with
the struggling bodies. Henrik crashes Magda's head against the wall,
smashes her on the floor and rapes her. While the man is shown to
bang frantically on top of the woman on the kitchen floor, the camera
moves along their bodies to Magda's anguished face. At this point the
scene is intercut with a short fantasy of Magda making love tenderly
to Henrik. No other sound is heard than an hallucinatory soft ringing
in the background. In one take a black man and white woman are shown
to stand in embrace, lovingly caressing each other. The lovers' gestures and movements are slow and respectful. We see hands stroking
bodies without ever seeing faces. The couple is fully naked and the
close-ups reveal the intimate contact between black and white skin.
The fantasy is set outside time and space and outside language. There
is no clear beginning or end nor is there any spatial orientation. All
we see is hands touching parts of bodies. Lighting and framing create

beautiful imagery. The fantasy cuts abruptly back to the rape, with the harsh sounds of Henrik panting and Magda crying. After Henrik has left her the camera retreats to a respectful distance and in a long take shows how Magda slowly gets up and sits in pain against the blood-splashed wall. Her voice-over wonders whether 'this' has made her into a woman and what will be left of her.

This sequence of rape and love is quite unsettling. The combination of a graphic representation of rape with an aesthetic representation of love produces contradictory effects. First, the juxtaposition of two narrational levels (the by now familiar insertion of modalized ocularization (fantasy) into zero ocularization (the camera attached to the narrator), combined with internal focalization (voice-over)) disorients the spectator who, once again, has somehow to figure out that the lovemaking is fantasmatic and not part of the rape. That a woman fantasizes about love while being raped might cause confusion in the spectator. Yet, I do not believe the film endorses an understanding of this scene as a confirmation of the woman's implication or guilt in the rape. On the contrary: the whole sequence marks the difference between the two experiences and indicates the chasm between the violence of rape and the tenderness of love.

Many cinematographic signs help to reinforce the radical distinctions between rape and love. The camera work during the rape is abrupt, shaky and agitated, imitating the gestures of violence, while it is still, slow and intimate during the lovemaking, repeating the gestures of love and care. The rape is edited to a fairly high pace (relative to a film that knows such a slow rhythm as *Dust*), while there is no cut at all in Magda's fantasy. The light is harsh in the rape scene and soft in the love scene. The rape scene is accompanied by ugly human sounds, and the love scene by the ethereal sound of Magda's fantasies. The dishevelled clothes in the rape scene form an obstacle to the violation; clothes have to be opened up and torn in order for the rape to happen, in contrast to the love scene where the nakedness of the bodies creates a feeling of intimacy and closeness. The *mise-en-scène*, too, adds a maximizing effect to indicate the difference between the two scenes: where the horizontal position during the rape scene suggests subjection and humiliation, the vertical position in Magda's fantasy suggests reciprocity.

The cinematic representation, then, visualizes the enormous difference between reality and fantasy, thus creating a narrational point of view on rape as unwanted violence. In representing such a discrepancy between reality and fantasy the film allows no misunderstanding about

Magda's desires: rape is not what she wants. Yet, tragically enough, it is not entirely unrelated to her desires either. The fact that both are Magda's experiences, real and imagined, cannot simply be ignored.

By introducing a female fantasy during an act of male rape, *Dust* represents the inner experience of the woman. Internal focalization here does not reflect her experience of pain, but projects her desire for the pleasure she does not experience. Thus Magda's fantasy reflects back on the rape: it exposes the pain and violence it inflicts on her. She escapes from the real experience into a fantasy that is not completely elsewhere. Many feminists have pointed out that rape destroys the subjectivity of the woman (see the feminist classics: Brownmiller 1975; Dworkin 1976; Barry 1979; as well as more recent work on cultural representations of rape: Kappeler 1986; Bal 1991; Higgins and Silver 1991). By giving the female character internal focalization in the form of a fantasy and by intercutting the woman's fantasy into the scene of rape, *Dust* gives subjectivity to Magda on the level of discourse, where on the level of the story her subjectivity is taken away from her. Thus, the film does justice to the complexity of female subjectivity and of a woman's fantasy life.

But what kind of subjectivity is destroyed? Her utter disarray after the rape makes Magda wonder whether this form of sexuality has helped her to acquire the womanhood she so much wants to have. Her subjectivity is therefore a deeply divided one. How indeed could the violent act that destroys Magda's subjectivity establish the female subjectivity she so desires? All she manages to save is a leftover of identity in the form of desire for the love she has never received. Magda has no other recourse than to retreat from reality into a life of fantasy even further than she already had.

If, given this ambivalent scene, rape for Magda is a tragic perversion of love, that is because it has everything to do with power. Magda is not only raped as a woman, but also as a white woman by a black man. This may, at first sight, seem a familiar story: the story of the black male rapist. A story, according to bell hooks in her essay 'Reflections on Race and Sex' (1990), 'invented by white men . . . about the overwhelming desperate longing black men have to sexually violate the bodies of white women'. And she continues: 'As the story goes, this desire is not based on longing for sexual pleasure. It is a story of revenge, rape as the weapon by which black men, the dominated, reverse their circumstance, regain power over white men' (hooks 1990: 58). There is no doubt that Henrik rapes Magda out of revenge for the earlier violation of his own wife by the Baas. In other words, the rape is shown for what it is: a power struggle between men and in this case, significantly, between black and white men.

Although the scene could be said to reinforce the stereotype of the black man as a rapist, I think that *Dust* undermines this cliché because it shows gender and race to be intricately bound up with each other. In a Foucauldian analysis of the 'complex socio-political-libidinal relation of race and gender', Abdul JanMohamed calls this formation 'racialized sexuality' (1992: 112). In the discourse of racialized sexuality 'the process of racialization is always already a process of sexualization, and the process of sexualization is also always already . . . a process of racialization' (112). At the core of racialized sexuality lies an 'open secret', that is, the white master's rape of the female slave, and hence, his violation of the racial border (104).

Dust problematizes this 'open secret' as a form of male power which initiates a spiral of violence. The desire of the white patriarch for the black man's wife and his power to take her as he wishes, this 'open secret', is witnessed by the Baas's daughter and the black male servant in powerless fury. The violation is revenged by Magda's murder of her father, as well as by Henrik's rape of the white man's daughter. The rape scene, then, headlines painful racial and sexual issues. This is a story of racialized sexuality. In the words of bell hooks, it is a story of the 'sexual sado-masochism' and 'sexual voyeurism' involved in the white male sexual exploitation of black women (57), a hitherto untold story that *Dust* attempts to tell partly from the perspective of the excluded white woman.

The Mad Woman in the Desert

Henrik and Anna leave the farm, while Magda stays behind alone in the vast space of the arid, barren land. The farm soon degenerates and she descends into utter despair and, finally, madness. In the last (fantasy) scene we watch Magda feeding her father as if he were a child, telling him her childhood memories. The film closes with the same image as in the beginning: father and daughter sitting on the porch staring into the distance. Magda's final words recall Morrison's analysis of the ending of American narratives in metaphors of whiteness after the black character has died or disappeared: 'Whiteness, alone, is mute, meaningless, unfathomable, pointless, frozen, veiled, curtained, dreaded, senseless, implacable' (Morrison 1992: 59). Magda's somewhat enigmatic words in voice-over conclude a life of sterility in a country of which the heart is dead:

I have chosen every moment of my own destiny, which is to die here, in this petrified garden, near my father's bones, in this space echoing hymns I could write, but do not write. It would be too easy.

The preceding narratological account of *Dust* shows how the film's point of view is consistently centred on the character of Magda. All modes of narration, internal ocularization and (in this film especially) auricularization, modalized ocularization (the mental images) and internal focalization, represent Magda's experiences or views. *Dust* constructs Magda's subjectivity, not only by giving her a look and a voice, but also by representing her desires and fantasies, in a film full of smothered emotion, repressed sexuality and haunting hallucinations. It represents female subjectivity as fundamentally split. Magda's very subjectivity is contested by the other characters in the story and in society at large. She cannot acquire social agency nor the power of self-determination. The film's conflict is played out in the tension between its construction of female subjectivity on the discursive level, and the ordeal and eventual destruction of white womanhood on the level of the story. It is in representing the struggle for female subjectivity that the feminist rhetoric of *Dust* is situated.

CRUEL EMBRACE

> *The woman*: But I am the one. . . . I am the one who is being destroyed!
> *Malina*: Yes. That is true. One has to live with that.
> *The woman*: Or not.
>
> From *Malina*[5]

A similar feminist rhetoric is at work in Marion Hänsel's next film *Cruel Embrace* (1987). The slow rhythm and lucid imagery of *Cruel Embrace* resemble the cinematic style of *Dust*. *Cruel Embrace* shows the struggle of a woman and a child to establish their respective subjectivities. As in *Dust* the subjectivity of the main characters is cinematically constructed at the level of discourse while that very subjectivity is denied and eventually destroyed within the story.

The opening shot introduces us to a young man staring out at the sea. In a voice choking with emotion he tells an undefined 'you' that he is still alive and is now living on this offshore cargo ship wreck, inviting the 'you' to visit him, Ludo. In the following shot we see him buying some food at the local pub and sending a letter to a 'Nicole'.

Back on his ship he builds a bonfire. When he sits looking into the flames, images are twice intercut of a big fire in a house, after which the young man grabs his head in agony. He walks up the stairs to the deck but stops halfway; we see a short image of him banging his head against a wall; he shakes his head and climbs on. On deck he climbs to the crow's nest; through a POV shot he is shown staring into the sky. A tilt of the camera brings us to a young boy looking at the sky from a window in an old and dusty attic.

The opening sequence of *Cruel Embrace* introduces some of the same narrative structures used in *Dust*, giving the point of view to the young man Ludo, through internal focalization that establishes him as the narrational centre, using secondary internal ocularization (the subjective camera is attached to his look), and modalized ocularization in the form of memory or fantasy – the spectator cannot yet know whether the images of the fire and of the man crashing his head are memories or fantasies. The last extended shot of the sky connects present and past, introducing a flashback that makes up the story of the film.

It takes some time before the spectator can make sense of the story. The little boy is dirty and dressed in rags and lives alone in a large and bare attic, sometimes visited by a beautiful young woman and an angry older woman. One day he is dressed up and taken down to the parlor where an older man, Micho, declares to a middle-aged couple that he is willing to marry their daughter, Nicole, and take care of her little retarded son, Ludovic. Ludo goes outside to wash himself at the pump, squinting at the broad daylight, and then, suddenly, sees the sea. Slowly a smile breaks all over his face. His great love for the sea is born.

The elliptic narrative procedure of *Cruel Embrace* forces the spectator to make a great many inferences about what s/he sees. There are gaps in the story: we do not know for instance why Ludo is locked away in an attic in total neglect and isolation during the first years of his life, although we suspect that it resulted in his mental retardation. Nor do we understand much about his mother, Nicole. Ludo desperately tries to win the love of his mother whom he adores, but for some unknown reason she cannot bring herself to love him. A long part of the film portrays the mutual attempts and failings at love between the mother and child, sending both of them into bitter rage or fits of weeping.

The overall point of view in *Cruel Embrace* lies with the character of Ludo; his story is told through internal focalization. (As we will see later, in the middle of the film internal focalization shifts occasionally to Nicole.)[6] The camera eye is mostly attached to the narrating instance, that is to say that the story is predominantly filmed in zero ocularization, although there are several moments when internal ocularization occurs through Ludo (especially at the beginning and the end of the film), but not nearly as many as in *Dust*. Because the world is presented through the eyes of a young and feeble-minded boy who hardly speaks at all, life does not only appear cruel and enigmatic to him but also to the spectator. We do not understand his mother's behaviour any better than he does. The film thus creates an information gap in the story, a lack that centres on Nicole.

Gradually, the spectator begins to unravel more of the family history than Ludo himself. From remarks of other characters we understand that nobody knows who Ludo's father is (some think Nicole is his older sister). From the context of bourgeois mores in France (or Belgium; the location is undefined) in the 1950s, the spectator must deduce that Nicole's parents married her out to an older man because she has disgraced the family as a young unmarried mother. When, at a certain point, Nicole asks Ludo how old he is, it is intimated that something terrible has happened in Nicole's past. He answers that he is five years old, but she says that he is eight; staring into her room she muses that 'that hot summer' is already eight years ago. She suddenly looks up with eyes full of tears and shouts at him to get out of her sight.

The film leaps ahead in time to show Ludo as an adolescent.[7] Nicole has started drinking and is generally bitter about her life. Ludo's presence is unbearable to her and she wants him sent away to an asylum. Having decided to tell her son the reason why she wants him away from home, Nicole drives Ludo to another village on the beach, near a military base that was used by the American army after the liberation. She takes him to a bar for a drink. Ludo is beside himself with happiness and babbles on to Nicole who seems hardly to listen.

The focalization now shifts to Nicole who remembers her teens, when she went out to this bar and to the beach with her girlfriends. She grows more and more emotional and suddenly speaks of 'him'. When Ludo asks who 'he' is she replies curtly 'the American'. She takes out a mirror of her handbag and with trembling hands puts on lipstick, smearing it all around her mouth. The mirror reflects the sunlight on her face. Then there is a flashback of an American soldier taking Nicole out in a military jeep, both of them laughing happily. The image fades while a strange creaking sound becomes stronger. With a cut back to Nicole closing her mirror, the sound transforms into the cries of squawking seagulls. Nicole cries. When Ludo strokes her hand, she jumps up, throwing over the table, shouting 'don't touch me, bastard'. The film then cuts to Ludo in his bedroom stroking drawings he has made on the wall. The expressive images represent a female face in bright colours, crossed out by violent black lines that turn the mouth into a gaping hole and sometimes blot out the whole face.

By now the spectator understands that Nicole must have been raped by American soldiers and that Ludo is the product of that rape. One morning Nicole sadly asks Ludo to say 'maman' to her, because he has never in his life said it before. Ludo tries to speak but the word remains stuck in his throat and he wraps himself in silence. Nicole bitterly cries that he has every reason not to call her 'maman', screaming that it is 'those three bastards who are your mother'. Ludo cannot bear to witness his mother's pain and runs out of the room leaving Nicole alone.

Through the modalized ocularization (a mental image) of a flashback we see a fourteen or fifteen year old Nicole being brutally raped by American soldiers. The flashback is short (fifty seconds) and suggests rather than actually shows the violent rape. The rapid montage contains forty-one shots, eighteen of which show a swinging lamp that produces the creaking noise heard already in Nicole's previous flashback. The lamp is shown in POV shots through Nicole's eyes, while she is lying down on a table, being raped. Several shots show her terrified eyes. The POV shots of the lamp are intercut with shots (all very short, about one second) that fragmentarily show the introduction to the rape: a soldier beating up Nicole, forcing a bottle into her mouth that makes her bleed, tearing off her clothes, brushing the flame of a lighter along her naked body, raping her and then calling out 'come on guys, she's ready'; other men laugh. A final shot of the swinging light and the creaking noise fade out, concluding the flashback. A cut takes us back to Nicole, weeping silently in her room.

In the next shot, outside in the courtyard, Ludo crashes his head against the wall of the house, until he falls down with blood all over his face. Although he still does not understand what has happened to his mother (in contrast to the spectator), he completely identifies with her suffering and semi-consciously repeats it; not only in this scene, but also by hiding on a beach when he is hurt, the surroundings in which his mother was raped. Ludo is both the sign of the crime and the testimonial witness to his mother's pain. Thus oversignified and without a verbal outlet for his emotions, he becomes self-destructive.

The representation of the rape is highly stylized and concentrates on an image that for Nicole symbolizes the traumatic event: the swinging and squeaking lamp. For the spectator the light gives the scene an eerie atmosphere, in its swing highlighting the actions or keeping them in the dark, thus destroying all linearity, both in terms of vision and of narration. The flickering of the lamp suggests an on-and-off state, of twilight, of almost-non-being, and of horror (it is a typical convention of horror movies). Earlier Nicole has referred to 'that terrible yellow lamp'. For her the lamp has become a metaphor for the horrifying violence done to her; an experience that by its very nature cannot be represented because it happens to and inside the body, and in excess of her own bodily desire. In a metonymical displacement she displaces the violence from her body onto the lamp. The cinematographic representation of Nicole's being raped, focusing on this metonym for the violence, adequately reflects the experience of the violated woman. It indicates the mechanism of 'blocking out' by rape victims; the narrowing down of consciousness during an extreme experience of violence onto a single perception (Dowdeswell 1986: 20). Whereas in *Dust*, as we have seen, Magda retreats into fantasy during the rape, Nicole blocks the experience out by focusing on the lamp. A lamp which, moreover, prevents us from gaining any focus on the scene, signalling the disorder of its raw violence against the light of reason, morality and rationality.

Lynn Higgins and Brenda Silver argue that a disturbing pattern in the representation of rape in dominant culture 'is an obsessive inscription – and an obsessive erasure – of sexual violence against women' (1991: 2). Violence and sexuality are erased from male texts representing rape, turning sexual violence into metaphors or symbols. Therefore, representing rape from a feminist point of view involves more than listening to the voice of the victim; 'it requires restoring rape to the literal, to the body: restoring, that is, the violence – the physical, sexual violation' (4). Both *Dust* and *Cruel Embrace* achieve precisely that restoration: they give a voice to the rape victim, by internal focalization in respectively a fantasy and a flashback, while they also represent the horrific violence of rape in short but poignant visual representations. Moreover, both films extensively narrate the effect of sexual violence upon the female victim.

La mer/la mère

Nicole's flashback of the rape introduces a break in the narrative. Ludo is sent to an asylum where he is very unhappy and sorely misses the sea and his mother. When he is punished for beginning a tentative love affair with a female patient, he (unwittingly?) sets fire to the home and flees. He returns to the sea and builds himself a home on a deserted ship wreck. The wreck can be understood as a metaphor for both Ludo's and Nicole's inner state, their interior devastation. The long flashback of Ludo's story is now finished and the narrative returns to its starting point: Ludo waiting for Nicole's visit. One day Ludo sees his mother walk towards him on the beach. The POV shot almost suggests his vision to be a hallucination – in the mists of the sea Ludo sees a beautiful woman walking down the beach, merging with the waves and the sunlight. Ludo hides in the ship and whines (throughout the film he is shown to hide and whine or groan when he is overwhelmed by emotions). Nicole climbs down into the saloon and looks at the strange paintings of the female faces on the walls of the saloon, now no longer crossed out by black lines, but still images of intense suffering. The son knows his mother's suffering, and he expresses it non-verbally, but he has no means of coping with the implications of that knowledge.

The familiar pattern, showing the failed attempts at love between mother and son, recurs again as soon as they are together. Nicole tries to make peace with Ludo and expresses her wish to become friends with him. But when Ludo replies in a pained voice that she has never loved him, she reproaches him for having ruined her life. Nicole tells him that she is getting a divorce from Micho and is about to marry another man. When Ludo asks her to let him live with them, she answers that he has to go back to the asylum. When she sees how this news upsets Ludo, she soothes him, taking his hand and asking him to say 'maman'. Ludo groans and stutters and finally manages to pronounce the word, almost inaudibly. The moment he can actually say 'maman', however, he gets overwhelmed by an upsurge of repressed emotions and shouts 'maman' louder and louder, banging Nicole against the iron wall of the ship, and crashing her to death. Every time her head hits the wall, the image is intercut with a drawing of the female face.

As in the rape scene, this final confrontation between Nicole and Ludo is highly stylized. In rapid montage medium shots of Ludo bashing Nicole against the wall with a loud metallic bang, are juxtaposed with a close-up of the wall paintings. Nicole's screams can be heard but her face can hardly be seen. Again, her suffering can only be represented outside language; in the graphic depictions of her son's drawings. After a last shot showing a bewildered Ludo looking lost, the scene ends with a close-up of a drawing of that haunting female face with screaming mouth and terrified eyes: an image that has become a sign witnessed by the spectator.[8]

In a dissolve from the drawing to the sea, Ludo is shown floating on a raft with the dead body of his mother, kissing her and putting her arm around him. In her death he has found the maternal embrace he could not find in life. The final image fades away into the waves of the sea. Ludo has brought together the two great loves of his life, *la mer* and *la mère*, the sea and his mother, giving them to one another in a final and desperate gesture of love.

Fatal Destiny

Cruel Embrace explores the horrific consequences of rape down into the next generation. It examines the ever relevant connection between war and rape, be it in a cynical reversal where the liberators become the enemy. There is no way out for the raped woman and her son but to remain forever locked in trauma, hatred and self-destruction. Each time Nicole sees Ludo she is reminded of the barbaric rape she was forced to undergo. By attaching the point of view mainly to Ludo, the child of the rape, who cannot understand why his mother does not love him, the film shows how the mother's pain is transferred to the child born out of violence.

Sexual violence is represented as a traumatic experience that haunts women for the rest of their lives. Both rapes occur in the context of war or colonialism, that is they are micro instances of macro power relations. As such they affect subjectivity at many levels. The rape destroys more than Nicole's virginity and youth; just as we saw happen to Magda in *Dust*, it kills off the very subjectivity of the raped woman at the different levels of agency and desire. Being an unmarried mother at a young age Nicole becomes an outcast in her village. This prevents her from building up a life of her own, being forced by her parents to marry an older man she does not love. Thus, society denies her access to a position of autonomy and self-determination, but also to her own desires. The trauma leads to self-destructive acts such as alcohol abuse; the hatred she has experienced within her own body has destroyed her ability for self-love. As a consequence, she can never love the son born to her after the rape, which is all the more painful because the child itself is innocent. At the point when she is ready to start a new life, the rape overtakes her in a sort of time loop, when she is killed by her son, the very product of the rape. In Nicole's case, rape is a death sentence that is reiterated over and over again; a destiny that cannot be escaped.

The choice of rendering the story in *Cruel Embrace* through internal focalization of Ludo, actually represents the 'lack' of Nicole's subjectivity. By not giving Nicole the main point of view on the level of narration, the film not only signifies the ruination of her very subjectivity but also the great difficulty of telling the story of rape. When, therefore, the film breaks with its sustained focalization through Ludo, shifting it to Nicole for the representation of the experience of rape, this is most revolutionary indeed. The spiral of destruction is stopped at the most crucial point, allowing Nicole to speak of the great unspoken, rather than be spoken about. Through internal focalization *Cruel Embrace* narrates Nicole's pain, rage and despair in her memories of the traumatic experience of that night so long ago. What happened then is shown through Nicole's flashbacks, her mental images shaping the modalized ocularization in which the rape is represented.

Everything directly concerning the actual rape itself, then, is presented from Nicole's point of view. *Cruel Embrace* thus represents the raped woman as subject of narration at the crucial moment that her subjectivity is violated within the story. In doing so the film does not repeat the violent act by which female subjectivity is destroyed, but exposes the very violence of its ruination.[9] In presenting, in contrast, all other events in the story from Ludo's point of view, the half witted boy who can never understand the import of what has happened to his mother, but who speaks the unrepresentable through his bodily pain and his drawings, *Cruel Embrace* traces the ingrievous injustice both woman and child suffer.[10]

COGNITION AND AFFECT

Dust and *Cruel Embrace* hold an emotional grip over me as a viewer; their pathos is one of the main reasons why I wanted to examine them in the first place. It is almost impossible to watch *Dust* or *Cruel Embrace* and remain unmoved. Except for the tragic stories of both films, much of the affective force is connected to the very specificity of the cinematic representation. It seems to me that the above narratological analysis of point of view in feminist cinema brings out an important element in film viewing: the emotional impact on the spectator is closely related to the way in which point of view is negotiated within the film.

The recent turn in film studies to cognitivism, under which the works of Jost can also be counted, has produced an almost exclusive theoretical attention to comprehension of film at the detriment of the affective aspects of film viewing. Contrary to his American colleagues,

however, Jost's theoretical framework shows that a cognitive understanding of point of view in cinema does not necessarily exclude observations of affect. In Jost's analysis, affect is established at the visual
level of ocularization, and cognition at the narrative level of focalization,
both levels working together in complex interaction. This is another
reason for preferring Jost's narratological model to the formalist
cognitivism of Bordwell and Branigan.[11] The approach of American
cognitive narratologists leaves almost no room for the emotional effect
that films can produce. This is surprising in a branch of popular culture that is known for its strong emotional impact on the spectator.
Indeed, such diverse film genres as horror, thrillers or romance and
melodrama exploit the emotive aspect of the movies. I would go as far
as to suggest that more often than not affect precedes comprehension
in film viewing. Images can profoundly move the spectator even before s/he has (yet) completely understood their meaning.

    The key words in the application of cognitive psychology to film
(theory) signal the emphasis on the process of rational understanding,
such as 'knowledge' and 'intelligibility' (see Branigan, 1984, 1993;
Bordwell, 1989). In my view, the absence of the question of affect in
cognitive film theories is problematic for the feminist viewer who wants
to account for the emotional effect certain women's films can have on
her (or him).[12] It is important to realize that a feminist interpretation is
not only (re)produced through cognitive processes, that is, through an
intellectual understanding of the predicament of white woman in the
sexist and racist society of South Africa or of the lifelong trauma of a
raped woman and her child, but also and perhaps even more so through
affect. Female experience is as yet underrepresented within male-
dominated culture and affectivity is a way of expressing the unrepresented and the unrepresentable. Affect can be mobilized by a variety
of cinematic techniques of which point of view is the most important,
because it induces a deep empathy with, for instance, the specific characters of Magda in *Dust* and Nicole and Ludo in *Cruel Embrace*. The
emotional force of these films can therefore not be detached from their
ideological vision.

    American cognitive film narratologists have polemically criticized
semiotic and psychoanalytic film theories for their ideology, jargon
and obscurantism.[13] In concentrating on a cognitive approach that is
unable to account for the emotive effects of film viewing, however,
they themselves go to another extreme. Although Jost does not fall
victim to the trap of unproductive polemics (being French he does not
have to rail against the heritage of so-called 'French' theory), he, too,

underplays the workings of ideology in cinema. In order better to understand the affect of films like *Dust* and *Cruel Embrace* in relation to the ideological effects of point of view, I now turn to a concept in feminist film theory that is closely related to point of view: the male gaze.

The Male Gaze Revisited

In this chapter I have elaborated on a narratological analysis of point of view in relation to female subjectivity, for which I laid the groundwork in the previous chapter. I hope to have shown how such an analysis can cause insight into the cinematic representation of the unrepresentable, such as the traumatic experience of rape. The vicissitudes of desire and fantasy can be traced through the workings of the cinematic point of view, both literal and metaphorical.

As we saw in Chapter 1, the ideological representation of desire in cinema has been analyzed by feminist film theorists as 'the male look' or 'gaze'; terms that directly refer to point of view. My quest for understanding the powerful impact of feminist films like *Dust* and *Cruel Embrace* echoes, I think, Mulvey's attempt, of some twenty years ago, to understand the fascination of Hollywood cinema (1975/1989). Our questions may be similiar (why am I moved or hooked?), but the object of our fascination is quite different indeed (traditional versus feminist cinema). In the following section I want to compare Mulvey's analysis of the male gaze in traditional cinema to my analysis of point of view in women's cinema.

The general claim in psychoanalytic film theory that pleasure in cinema is based on voyeuristic mechanisms, of watching someone without being seen oneself, is predicated on the insight that voyeurism cannot be detached from sexual difference. In other words, there would be nothing wrong with scopophilia, the sexual pleasure in looking, if it were not negotiated through sexual difference and hence through gendered power relations. This is the fundamental significance of the feminist concept of 'the male gaze'. If not mediated through the power of gender, the gaze stops being the gaze and becomes the self-conscious, engaged contemplation of the image, positioned in time and embodied in the spectator. The pleasure of watching the beauty of the imagery in both *Dust* and *Cruel Embrace*, films that in their slow-paced rhythm give the spectators the time to enjoy their looking, makes up what I would call aesthetic scopophilia.

When one considers the technical elements of 'the male gaze' in more detail, it is striking how easily these can be put into film narratological terms. The point of view of the male character gazing at the female body is clearly a case of internal ocularization. This can be filmed in an optical POV shot or in a semi-subjective shot. In classical cinema the male gaze usually consists of two or more shots of the male character looking and of the female character being looked at, the camera look being attached to the eyes of the former.[14]

Internal ocularization can be mediated by internal focalization (the male voice-over in many a film noir), or by the explicitly male narrator in external focalization (most Hitchcock films). Voyeurism, then, is always mediated by internal male ocularization (the semiotics of the camera) and male focalization (narration), either internal (character) or external (narrator). Point of view creates a pleasurable position for the male spectator, who is constructed along gendered lines in enjoying the beauty of the female body and identifying with male power. Mulvey and many other feminist theorists have pointed to the violence of the male gaze; looking more often than not results in raping or killing. The cinematic construction of a male point of view is most disturbing because of this alliance between erotic pleasure and sexual violence.

To my knowledge, voyeurism in classical cinema never occurs in the immediate context of a female focalizer or narrator, let alone through female ocularization.[15] This shows the subversive possibilities of giving a female character the point of view and of attaching the camera look to the eyes of a woman, creating a female gaze. In *Dust* and *Cruel Embrace*, female ocularization obstructs the male gaze: there simply is none in either film. We have seen in these cases how female focalization exposes and criticizes male violence, divorcing it radically from erotic pleasure. In other words, by highlighting female experience the male gaze is almost automatically undermined.

The male gaze can only function at the expense of the representation of the female character being the image, objectified and fetishized. One of the most revolutionary changes that women's cinema has created is the refusal to objectify and fetishize 'woman'. Feminist cinema either avoids fetishization of the female subject, or critically deconstructs it. This is partly prompted by the call for 'realist' images of women, but it mostly follows from making the female character in the film subject of both story and narration. When the female character takes up the position of subject, or struggles to establish her agency and desire, she can no longer be represented as fetishized image.

Needless to say, in both *Dust* and *Cruel Embrace* the female characters are unfetishized. The camera always keeps a respectful distance from the female body and never lingers on any part of either Magda's or

Nicole's body. The lack of fetishization is particularly remarkable in *Dust*, because the character of Magda is played by the actress Jane Birkin whose reputation as a model and actress was based on the image of the sexy, liberated woman. She made her debut as nude model in Antonioni's *Blow Up* (1966) and played in more than forty films that mostly confirmed her objectification and fetishization. As she has said herself in an interview, *Dust* was the first film in her long career that enabled her to play a character role.[16] The film undoes that tradition of fetishization; Magda/Jane Birkin wears no make-up, her hair is dishevelled and she is clothed in a ragged black dress that hides her body. No wonder few spectators recognize Jane Birkin in this image of femininity.

In contrast to the power of the male gaze in classical cinema, these feminist films give the look to the powerless. The change modifies the look itself: *Dust* and *Cruel Embrace* demonstrate that the female look differs sharply from the male gaze. As Kaplan has pointed out. 'For the women does not own desire, even when she watches . . .' (1983: 27). One could say that in different ways both films display and explore how the female subject is deprived of her desire and how her look carries no power. This is shown very clearly in a scene in *Dust*, where Magda watches Henrik and Anna making love. When she is found out by Henrik and challenged by him, she runs away in a flurry. Although her voyeurism springs from curiosity it results in guilt and confusion.

The dispossession of female desire is most extreme in the rape scenes in both films, where the women are at the mercy of the power of their male rapists. I have analyzed how the rape scenes are presented from the woman's point of view and demonstrated how the female look subverts the cinematic stereotype of the male gaze, blocking any pleasure or titillation for the spectator. Instead, the overt presence of the camera and montage makes the spectator aware of her or his voyeurism, playing down any eroticism. The distancing effect breaks through the mechanism of voyeurism, which makes the rape scenes hard to watch. In much the same way, the insistence on the female point of view, both through internal focalization and modalized ocularization, makes the violence of the scenes more explicit and unbearable. Thus, Hänsel's films follow Mulvey's admonition 'to free the look of the camera into its materiality in time and space and the look of the audience into dialectics and passionate detachment' in order to break through the viewing pleasure of male voyeurism (Mulvey 1989: 26).

Dust and *Cruel Embrace* explore the effects of the male gaze for women in a society in which, as Kaplan puts it: 'The man . . . owns the desire and the woman' (27). The question is whether this is the case in *Cruel Embrace*, where the point of view lies mainly with Ludo who, although male, is hardly what one would call a typical masculine subject. For one thing, he is young and 'not all there' and hence has no power. For another, the boy is hurt and wounded. His position outside traditional masculinity is represented by his fear of looking: he often blinks his eyes, turns away from what he does not dare to see or casts his eyes down in embarrassment or fear. In the asylum he is severely punished for any desires that he shows towards a female inmate. Ludo does not master the symbolic at all. It would therefore be too gross a generalization to claim that all men own the gaze. Some men are evidently excluded from the power of the male gaze.

This point may be clarified by recourse to a Lacanian analysis of the gaze, as rigorously performed by Silverman (1992). Silverman argues for a differentiation between the look as the carrier of desire and lack, and the gaze as a carrier of symbolic law. The male gaze as it is usually understood in feminist film theory corresponds more to the look in Lacanian theory (I will come back to this point more extensively in Chapter 5). In the Lacanian scheme, the gaze is understood as an omnipresent space external to the subject. Men do not own the gaze any more than women do, but in Hollywood film the male look 'transfers its own lack to the female subject, and attempts to pass itself off as the gaze' (143–4). When the male look is divorced from the gaze and hence from projection and control, the identity of the male subject can no longer be confirmed nor sustained. In *Cruel Embrace* the desiring look of Ludo is undermined by his being barred from the symbolic.

Gaines (1988) has argued that feminist film criticism should take differences other than sexual difference into account in their theories and analyses. In *Dust* the male gaze is fully negotiated through the category of race. In white patriarchy, the black man does not own the gaze any more than the white woman does. What is more, Henrik is not even subject of his own desire nor of his own wife; the white boss has the power to take the black man's wife Anna as his mistress. That the black woman might have any power over her own body or desire is altogether out of the question. When the white boss has gone, the black man and the white woman enter into a power struggle; a struggle that is temporarily 'won' by the black man's using sexual violence. Although the white woman has committed violence too (Magda has killed her father and oppresses the blacks), she does not acquire the power to act on her erotic desires nor to administer her father's

fortune. The intersection of racial difference with hierarchies of looking in *Dust*, brings to the fore the ideological aspect of power within
cinematic point of view.

In the last few years, feminist accounts of the gaze have tended to
become rather imprecise and vague. In the collection *The Female Gaze*
(Gamman and Marshment 1988), for example, the term 'gaze' seems
to designate very loosely a metaphorical perspective thereby losing
much of its analytic force. When feminist interpretations of the male
gaze become so generalized they run the risk of being severed from
the cinematic discourse in which point of view is anchored. Conversely,
cognitive accounts of filmic narration tend to be oblivious to any ideological meaning in their search for comprehension. Yet, it does not
take much cognitive effort to understand a filmic shot of a man looking at the legs of a woman, whereas the implications in terms of power
and the politics of pleasure of such a point of view are far-reaching.
While a cognitive analysis in itself remains dry and unproductive, since
it fails to draw out important interpretations for feminism, feminist
investigations of the male gaze in cinema can become much more pre
cise and detailed when such analyses take into account narratological
concepts such as ocularization and focalization. It seems to me that
psychoanalytic and cognitive film theories can productively be brought
together and are not necessarily so far apart as to present 'a classic
case of apples and oranges' (Mayne 1993: 7). Rather, as I argued earlier, psychoanalytic and cognitive film theories have much to gain from
mutually informing each other.

CONCLUSION

'I know there is another language. But I cannot imagine how it goes',
remarks Magda in *Dust*. Magda's words signify her desire to escape
from the violence of a symbolic order that reduces women to silent
objects. They simultaneously indicate her impotence in the face of
oppressive social conditions. *Dust* seeks to represent the particular
experience of a woman being caught in gendered and racial power
relations. Cornered from all sides, Magda enters a life and death struggle.
Negated and violated, she lacks a positive experience of female subjectivity, but also basic human assets such as love, friendship and respect, that could ground her sense of self and put her safely into a
world of different meanings.

De Lauretis has defined experience 'as a process by which, for all social beings, subjectivity is constructed' (1984: 158). It is experience, as 'the continuous engagement of a self or subject in social reality', that makes a woman out of the female subject (182). A particular experience of sexuality constitutes the female subject in her specific relation to social reality: sexual experience 'engenders the female subject' (182). The experiential process of subjectivity is a semiotic one, because the subject and social reality are made up of signs. Rereading the semiotician C. S. Peirce, de Lauretis calls this process semiosis. It could thus be said that the films *Dust* and *Cruel Embrace* explore how the experience of sexual violence places the female subject (and her child) at the margins of semiosis. Magda, Nicole and Ludo are barred from semiosis, hence from the process of becoming subjects. They are positioned outside the possibility of access to forms of empowerment that would enable them to make sense of, that is to construct meanings and to gain knowledge from, their experience. They are held hostage within a symbolic system which offers them no grounds for positive self-naming. Thus the possibility of making their own symbolic representation of their experience is precluded.

Magda cannot find words in which to communicate and hence retreats from the world of language altogether. Expelled from the symbolic order she becomes psychotic, wrapped in the silence of her literal and metaphorical desert. Being locked away alone in an attic during his formative years, Ludo in *Cruel Embrace* does not even have normal access to language and as a consequence never reaches adult subjectivity. Nicole drowns her words in tears or alcohol. For her, language in the end appears to be lethal; for when the unspeakable word 'maman' is finally spoken, it kills. Sexual violence, then, is an experience that can in no way constitute subjectivity. On the contrary, it undoes and destroys the speaking subject; the violated subject can only be a 'non-subject'.

The stories that the main characters in *Dust* and *Cruel Embrace* cannot tell themselves, because of the unrepresentability of their experience, are, however, 'told' through the cinematic discourse that Hänsel creates in her films. The construction of a female point of view at the level of discourse, such as I have tried to bring out in this chapter, gives a voice and a look to the characters, securing them well within the process of semiosis from which they are excluded in the fictional world. Hänsel's films thus allow for the unspoken to be spoken, for unrepresentable experience to be communicated. This is where feminist rhetoric can be ground shifting in the Peircian sense: it shifts the ground of representation to another level of signification. It transfers the representation of the female body where experience is silenced and where meaning collapses, to the feminist subject as a producer of meaning. This can be translated as an interstice between the female character in the film, with desires but without agency, and the female subject of feminist consciousness, the implied or the historical director. The hiatus between these two representations of female subjectivity, the spoken subject and the speaking subject, creates the dimension of tragedy that is palpably present in these two films. Experiencing and understanding the injustice of the gap between the female subject who is spoken and the speaking female subject, the spectator can contest the ideology of a symbolic order that commits such violence against female subjectivity.

4 And the Mirror Cracked: On Metaphors Of Violence And Resistance

Feminist film theory has yet to explore and work through anger, which for women continues to be, as it has been historically, the most unacceptable of all emotions.

Tania Modleski[1]

I laugh; therefore, I am implicated. I laugh; therefore, I am responsible and accountable.

Donna Haraway[2]

INTRODUCTION

Feminist film criticism has, from its very beginning, addressed the tradition of misogyny and of violence against women which has become so intricately bound up with dominant cinema. As I pointed out earlier, Mulvey (1989/1975) was the first to unravel Hollywood's investment in voyeuristic structures that couple eroticism to sadism. Many other feminist critics have further elaborated on cinematic violence directed at the female body.[3] It is understood that a critical analysis of violence against women can yield insight into the sources of misogyny in masculinist society.

This quest for knowledge in theory raises not only many poignant questions about cinematic representations of violence, but also runs parallel to developments in feminist film practice. There too, feminists want to come to a critical understanding of violence against women, women's resistance to it, and the vicissitudes of female subjectivity. I am intrigued and concerned by the difficulties which feminist filmmakers face in trying to overcome the long tradition of misogyny in cinema. By what narrative and cinematic devices do they subvert traditions of violence in their films? How do they change representations of sexual violence and construct female subjectivity within such a context of violence? Most feminist films about sexual violence give a lucid analysis of the predicaments and contradictions of women's experiences in a male-dominated culture, without the fetishism, voyeurism and sadism of traditional Hollywood cinema. On the contrary, they evoke a deep sympathy with the plight of the female victims.

As we have seen in the previous chapter, Marion Hänsel's domestic dramas *Dust* (1983) and *Cruel Embrace* (1987) expose violence against women and its destructive effects upon female subjectivity. In this chapter I want to discuss two films made at about the same time, which also tell agonized stories of violence: *De stilte rond Christine M.* (*A Question of Silence*, 1982) and *Gebroken Spiegels* (*Broken Mirrors*, 1984), social dramas made by the Dutch filmmaker Marleen Gorris.[4] Both Hänsel and Gorris portrayed women's violent reactions against male domination in the earlier film and then explored sexual violence against women in the later film: in *Dust* and *A Question of Silence* it is the women who kill and in *Cruel Embrace* and *Broken Mirrors* the men. The portrayal of violence in films is not always centred around women's victimization; women's resistance can become violent too.

These films are not the only ones that explore female violence; feminist filmmakers have made a surprisingly large number of films about violence committed by women, especially in the 1970s and early 1980s. Thus we find female terrorists roaming the screen (in *Die bleierne Zeit*); bank robbers (*Wanda, Das zweite Erwachen der Christa Klages*); freedom fighters (*The Princess Fragrance, Born in Flames*); revolutionaries (*La Negra Angustias*); collective murderesses (*A Question of Silence*); individual killers (*Jeanne Dielman*); mothers and wives who resist the mafia (*Camorra*); daughters (*Dust*), mothers (*Prisonnières*) or wives (*Heller Wahn*) who kill members of their own family; sisters who kill together (*Sister my Sister*); even a little girl that kills (*Celia*) – and in the nineties we see the phenomenon of young female lovers killing (*Heavenly Creatures*).[5] This is far from being an exhaustive list. It looks as if the former goddesses of Hollywood have turned into goddesses of vengeance; has the feminist wave in cinema unleashed the Erinyes onto the silver screen?

The question is why murderous women feature in feminist films. What connects all the murderesses in their differences is the desire to take their lives into their own hands, to liberate themselves from victim roles and to win the struggle for survival. Such a positive reading of female violence may not always be warranted by the films themselves; as we have seen in *Dust*, Magda cannot break loose from gender roles after the murder of her father and she hardly wins her struggle for survival. This points to another characteristic that films on female violence share: violence committed by women is never gratuitous but always a form of resistance against injustice, abuse of power or sexual violence. The films seek to find representations for an experience of anger and frustration, an experience that de Lauretis has described as 'at once social and personal' (1984: 166). Images of female violence, then, are a very specific attempt on the part of feminist filmmakers 'to construct the female subject from that political and intellectual rage', to quote de Lauretis (166).

The theme of female killers may be taken not only as provocation but also as a metaphor, as a cinematic figure representing women's experience. Many feminist filmmakers have used metaphorical representations of violence for their exposure of masculinism. In this chapter I am concerned with the figure of metaphor in feminist cinema as a particular form of rhetoric that symbolizes women's experience. Building on my argument in the previous chapter that the implied director communicates a particular woman's experience to the spectator by cinematic means, such as point of view, I will investigate how this other rhetorical figure, metaphor, is also grounded in experience and how it produces affect and knowledge for the spectator. To that end I will analyze metaphors of violence and their rhetorical effects in the films of Marleen Gorris. I will concentrate mainly on her first two films: *A Question of Silence* which became an international feminist success and won several awards; and *Broken Mirrors* which received much critical acclaim and is well-known within feminist circles, although it did not become such a hit as Gorris' first film (partly due to problems of distributing feminist films, cf Root 1986). Her third film, *The Last Island* (1990), was not so well received and consequently drew less critical attention. In contrast, her fourth film, *Antonia's Line* (1995), became a huge critical and commercial success and among many other prizes won the Oscar for the Best Foreign Film in 1996.

MOVING METAPHORS

A Question of Silence and *Broken Mirrors* always leave me with the distinct impression of having witnessed 'the truth'. This puts me in an almost embarrassing situation, because who believes in 'the truth' in these postmodern times? And yet each time I view her films I experience painfully once again that they are a truthful picture of the world that I inhabit as a woman. This experience is painful because the films are quite ruthless in their views on women's oppression in western society.

My viewing experience of 'truth', then, is connected to the explicit politics of Gorris' films. Her films can be called tendentious in the tradition of left-wing filmmaking, in which, according to Bordwell ' . . . the [story] world stands for a set of abstract propositions whose validity the film at once presupposes and reasserts' (1985: 234). Gorris' political fiction films appeal to a conventional filmic form, that is, to classical narrative and cinematic codes. The films are cast in traditional genres; *Silence* belongs to the genre of the murder mystery,[6] *Broken Mirrors* to the genre of the thriller, *Island* is a mixture of a thriller and of utopian fiction, and *Antonia's Line* is a feminist rewriting of the epic genre. Within these genres the films make use of the narrative code of realism: they produce an illusion of reality.

Although the films are perfectly realist in form I have been impelled to interpret them metaphorically. It is through rhetorical tropes such as metaphors that Gorris conveys her political message: *A Question of Silence* presents the western world as a prison for women; *Broken Mirrors* shows this world as a brothel and in *The Last Island* a potential paradise turns into a worldly hell. Each film is situated in a separate world set apart from normal society; within the microcosm of these enclaves power relations between the sexes explode into violence. In this way the prison, the brothel and the desert island become metaphors for a male-dominated society in which women are subjected to the position of 'the second sex'. *Antonia's Line* breaks away from Gorris' 'violence trilogy' in featuring the geneaology of a matriarchal family within a country village.

Critics have not unanimously viewed these films metaphorically, which raises the question of what makes such an interpretation appropriate and relevant. Rather than opposing realism and metaphoricity, however, I want to suggest that the forceful effect of Gorris' films lies in their simultaneously realist and metaphorical qualities, both equally strong, consistent and emphatic. The metaphorical meaning is never detached from its referent in the fictional reality; it is, as it were, materialized and the spectator cannot separate them. Instead s/he can watch in at once a literal and figurative way. To me this double power of persuasion accounts for the strong truth effect of Gorris' films.

The political impact of Gorris' film, then, must be sought in the interplay between realism and metaphorism. The importance lies in the simultaneity of the two; neglect of either would make the film much less effective. Spectators can choose to deny or ignore one of those levels in the text, thus undermining a potential feminist interpretation. This has often been the case with the films of Marleen Gorris.

Some, mostly male, viewers chose to ignore the metaphorical structure of the films, and to adopt a realist interpretation instead, which resulted in their rejection of the films and accusations of Gorris being a vitriolic man hater.[7] Needless to say I find their reaction short-sighted at best.

Keeping the balance between the realist and the metaphorical is not a problem only for the spectator, but also for the filmmaker. The use of metaphors can be misfired by neglecting the realist level of the film. This, I believe, is the case in *The Last Island*. The extent to which the rhetorical effect of metaphors depends on being grounded in the referent, can be measured in the relative failure of this film. It tells a simple linear story: five men and two women are the only survivors of a plane crash on a desert island. The title of the film refers to an ecological or nuclear disaster, and it is suggested that these people might be the last survivors on earth. They fail in creating a bearable life together. Nick, an elderly military man and fanatic Christian, appropriates the place of 'God'. The desire of macho Jack for Joanna, the younger woman in the group, catalyzes a power struggle between the men, which results in their mutual slaughter. Even the men who in some ways stand apart from traditional masculinity, as homosexual, or as a caring and nurturing husband and father, are drawn into the violent chain reaction of honour and revenge. Joanna and old Mrs Godame remain the sole survivors.

The story of the film can only be understood as a metaphorization of the lethal nature of masculinism at the exclusion of any other possible meaning, which makes the political message of *The Last Island* overbearing. The unambiguous statement about the innate violence of the male species does not allow for any interplay between literal and figural meanings and the specific complexities that cinematic metaphors might achieve. Indeed, many scenes lack credibility because of a lack of realism in a film that otherwise purports to be realist within its genre. More importantly, Gorris has neglected to use specific cinematic strategies so as to effect a differentiation between realism and metaphor, as she did in her former films. The result is a straightforwardly allegorical film that has difficulties convincing the spectator.

A filmmaker and writer who was very much concerned with political interventions in cinema, Sergei Eisenstein made effective use of metaphors in his films of the twenties and thirties. In his writings Eisenstein stressed the importance of 'grounding' the film image in realism.[8] The signifying process of political cinema, such as Eisenstein understands it, depends on a process of metaphorization.[9] This process entails transforming the image from particular picture into global image, or from icon and index into symbol, creating a new vision on the object. It works from the bottom up: the concrete image becomes an abstraction. Eisenstein advises time and again to effectually ground a film image in realism; it is the concrete object that becomes metaphorized. In his essay 'Montage 1937', for example, he expresses his suspicion of too high a degree of abstraction: 'the metaphorical nature of the object' should not 'slide into facile allegory' (1992: 38). The process of metaphorization for Eisenstein lies in cinematic means, such as découpage and montage. As we shall see later, in *A Question of Silence* and *Broken Mirrors* metaphors are created by various techniques such as hand-held camera, framing, camera movement and montage.

Thus, for a cinematic image to be effective there should be a dialectic between its concrete picture (in semiotic terms this can be compared to the iconic and indexical sign) and the 'generalised image' underlying that picture (in semiotic terms this can be compared to the symbolic sign). For Eisenstein it is imperative for a structure to be submitted to metaphorization in order to be received fully by the spectator (1992: 21). In the combination of – or the conflict between – the several cinematic signifiers (the specific picture and the metaphorized image that pervades it) resides 'the implacability and the all-devouring force of artistic composition' in cinema (27).

It follows for Eisenstein that neglect of certain signifiers leads to unsatisfying results. In maintaining those two levels of depiction and generalization that are present in a metaphor the spectator goes through a dialectical process, which enables an experience of pathos (1992: 96). Such a viewing experience does not come about with *The Last Island*, because the film is allegorical throughout. Gorris has not sustained a sense of realism. Moreover, she has neglected the film form. The narrative is reduced to 'facile allegory' because a dialectic between the iconic and the symbolic image is not effectuated. The 'truth' of *The Last Island* hits the spectator hard but fails to ring true.

The careful construction of a cinematic metaphor, then, one that allows for a continuous interplay between literal and figural meanings, is of the utmost importance for the feminist filmmaker who wants both to move and convince her audience. The first two films of Marleen Gorris are excellent examples of this dialectic: *A Question of Silence* and *Broken Mirrors* bring a simultaneously realist and metaphorical film text into effect.

THE PRISON OF GENDER

In *A Question of Silence* a female psychiatrist, Janine van den Bos, has been appointed to investigate on behalf of the prosecution whether three women are sane enough to be accountable for their murder of a male boutique owner. These three women had never met before when together they kill the owner of the boutique where they all happened to be shopping, and one of them was discovered shoplifting. The murder is witnessed by four other women present in the shop.

The film is constructed as a *Bildungsroman* to which the consciousness raising of the psychiatrist Janine is central. In this story, focalized by her, three flashbacks of the murder are embedded. According to Mary Gentile the narrative structure of the film emphasizes the plot of Janine's consciousness raising, allowing the spectator to accept the brutal murder more easily (1985: 155–156). The film connects the psychiatrist's development to the lives of the murderesses by means of parallel editing and identical camerawork and framing. In a closely knit narrative structure *Silence* gradually reveals that the women have no motive in the conventional sense, but that the murder is the indirect outcome of years of humiliation and objectification. The murder being an expression of their unspoken anger, it metaphorically stands for women's outrage at and resistance to masculinist society.

In featuring stereotyped characters from different classes, ages, and race, the film represents the position of women as an oppressed gender in male-dominated culture. The three white murderesses are Andrea, a middle-class executive secretary and single; Christine, a lower middle-class housewife and mother; and An, a lower class waitress in a snackbar and divorced. Janine, the psychiatrist, also white, is upper class and married without children. The silent witnesses of the murder are a white older woman, a black woman and two white punk girls. This typification, rather than individualization, is a characteristic that the feminist films of Gorris share with 'socialist realism'. As such the female characters in *Silence* (and also in *Broken Mirrors*) 'partly operate as types expressive of social groups or classes and historical configurations' (Kuhn 1982: 141). Although in both films the principal roles are given to white women from different class backgrounds, race and age are highlighted in the supporting roles. What Geetha Ramanathan writes of *Silence* also holds true of *Broken Mirrors*: 'By establishing contiguity among a number of women in the text, the film indicates that the story of the murder is a cover-up to the other story: that of bonding in a community of women akin in positionality and politics, different in race and class' (1992: 59).

From the narrative and visual perspective of these individual women it becomes clear that each of them feels she has no right to exist outside her function for men and therefore cannot develop her own identity. Because the female characters consistently are the subject in narrative terms (focalization) and on the visual level (ocularization), they acquire a subjectivity for the spectator which is time and again denied to them within the diegesis of the film. The women, and through identification the female spectator too, find themselves in the situation of 'Woman', that Simone de Beauvoir describes as follows:

> Now, what peculiarly signalizes the situation of woman is that she – a free and autonomous being like all human creatures – nevertheless finds herself living in a world where men compel her to assume the status of the Other.... The drama of woman lies in this conflict between the fundamental aspirations of every subject (ego) – who always regards the self as the essential – and the compulsions of a situation in which she is the inessential.
>
> (de Beauvoir 1972: 29).

Silence exhibits the drama of women who experience themselves as subjects in a society that does not allow for female subjectivity. By creating cinematic parallels between the women's homes and their prison cells, the film shows that in fact very little changes for the women when they are imprisoned. The juxtaposition of similarities between the women's rooms at home and in prison, such as the closed curtains in Christine's room or the cramped space of An's room, creates the metaphor that in their 'normal' lives women are 'imprisoned'. Découpage and montage thus suggest that gender is like a prison.

Silence further represents the oppression of women in metaphors of silence. In various ways the film shows that the female voice has no right of speech and that, not being heard, women are enveloped in silence. Although 'greatly appreciated' by her boss, the secretary Andrea is nevertheless ignored when she makes a proposal at a business conference, whereas the same plan is met with approval when proposed by a man. When Andrea withdraws into herself and absentmindedly stirs her coffee with a spoon, the sound of the spoon draws the attention of the assembly and the man sitting next to her grabs her hand so as to stop the 'noise'. Similarly, nobody listens to the waitress An although she talks and laughs all the time. Her garrulousness seems directed like a weapon against the sexist abuse from her clients in the coffee shop, mainly about her obesity. And as we will see later, the court does not take the psychiatrist's report seriously and meets it, too, with derision.

Whether professional and intelligent like Andrea and Janine, or garrulous like An, women's voices fall on deaf ears. Women are surrounded by an icy silence. Therefore Christine has given up speaking at all; she is literally overcome by silence. (The Dutch title of the film is *The Silence of Christine M.*) Yet it is Christine who 'speaks' most directly about the motive for the murder. When the psychiatrist asks her why they have killed the man, Christine draws simple figures on a white sheet: a man, a woman and a child enclosed in a house, obsessively repeating the drawing of the same figures over and over again. Her drawings indicate her feelings of suffocation in the nuclear family.

In order to understand why the murder, too, can be viewed as a metaphor, I want to explore in more detail how the figure of metaphor appears in cinema and how it is studied in film theory. In classical rhetoric, metaphor is just one of the figures and tropes being studied, but in semiotics and psychoanalysis, metaphor, together with metonymy, has become the most privileged figuration to be theorized. Traditionally, metaphor is a figure 'in which one term stands in for another which it in some way resembles' and metonymy a figure 'in which one term stands in for another to which it is in some way contiguous' (Silverman 1983b: 112–13). The classical characteristics of similarity and contiguity are extended to other sets of terms in structuralism. In *The Imaginary Signifier*, Christian Metz discusses the rhetorical figures of metaphor and metonymy within the framework of both linguistics, 'with its major dichotomy between the syntagmatic and the paradigmatic', and psychoanalysis, 'which introduced the ideas of displacement and condensation' (1982: 153). A metaphor is a figure of condensation which creates paradigmatic relations in a film, and a metonymy is a figure of displacement which creates syntagmatic relations. Metz is, however, quick to point out that these characteristics never occur in a 'pure' binary state, but spill over one into the other.

A metaphor is a figure that refers to the referent by way of similarity. It derives its force and meaning from a continuous movement back and forth between the figural and the literal. Metz recalls how the rhetorical tradition accorded 'the mythical status of primacy' to the literal meaning. In an interesting parenthesis he adds that this can also be turned around 'since the most literal term for invoking certain referents is a figurative one' (156). This throwaway line put me on the track of the intricate way in which metaphors seem to work in cinema. In language, metaphor is a figure of speech, an image evoked by words.

The process of figuration works quite differently in cinema, because a metaphor can be visualized directly and without words into an image. The relation of similarity (or contiguity in case of metonymy) is established through montage to another image, the referent to which it is compared. In other words, a cinematic metaphor, in its being always already visualized, works through literalization. What I experience as the particular force of *Silence* and *Broken Mirrors*, its simultaneous realism and metaphoricity, may very well be Gorris' insightful use of the specificity of cinematic language.

We have already seen the 'direct match of the rhetorical and the iconic' (Metz: 220) in the metaphor of the home as prison. The juxtaposition of images of the women's rooms at home and their cells in prison cannot be analyzed in rhetorical terms, 'once again because there are no words' (Metz: 219), but only in semiotic terms, that is as referential similarity (between the drawn curtains of Christine at home and in prison, or the cramped and messy space of An at home and in prison) and discursive contiguity (established by montage).

In his attempt to read the figure of metaphor through linguistics and psychoanalysis, however, Metz does not put much emphasis on the material aspect of the cinematic metaphor, which he described as 'a pure index of actualisation' in an earlier work (quoted in Wollen 1972: 124).[10] Peter Wollen was among the first film theorists to argue for Peircian semiotics as the foundation of a theory of cinema, which would allow for a less binary and more materialist discussion of the cinematic sign, but 'the topic has not been widely pursued by other film theoreticians', as Silverman observes (1983b: 24). 'In its attentiveness to the referent' (14), C. S. Peirce's semiotic scheme of the sign is more than relevant for the present discussion of the cinematic metaphor as a visualization or actualization within the filmic image.

Peirce categorizes signs according to their relation to the ground (or code) into icons, indices and symbols. An iconic sign resembles the object which it represents; the relationship between sign and denotatum is one of similarity (Wollen 1972: 122). An indexical sign refers to the object that it denotes by virtue of an existential bond (122). A symbolic sign has a conventional, that is non-motivated, relation to its conceptual object (123). These categories are not mutually exclusive but frequently overlap in one particular sign; for example, Peirce describes the photographic image as both iconic and indexical (123–4). For Wollen, this is one of the great advantages of Peirce's classification for a study of cinema. Peircean semiotics can thus be helpful in understanding more complex cinematic figurations like metaphor and

metonymy. If we return once more to the metaphor of the prison in
Silence, we can now see how it is constructed with the help of semiotic signs. The semiotic signs create similarities between home and
prison, which then become each other's metaphor.

Iconicity resides in the photographic image: identical lighting, camera position and framing establish a first layer of similarity between
home and prison. The sound track also functions as an iconic sign:
whether at home or in their prison cells, the women surround themselves with the same silence or noise (the constant radio sound in
Christine's life and the silence in An's private and lonely life con-
trasted to her noisy behaviour in company).

Indexical signs locate the image in time and space, most notably
through camera movement and montage (Silverman 1983b: 23). Indexical similarities establish a common ground for the metaphorical
comparison between home and prison; such as the camera movement
within ·the cramped space of the rooms at home or the prison cells,
and the cross-cutting from home to prison. The juxtaposition of the
images through montage, discursive contiguity in Metz' terms, brings
an element of metonymy into the metaphor. Hence, the metaphor feeds
back into the image: the prison feels as much like home for the women
as home feels like a prison.

Wollen does not refer to this other triad of Peircian semiotics which
according to Silverman explains the process of signification as a complex interaction between the 'sign', the 'interpretant' and the 'object'
(14). Signification, or in Peirce's term, semiosis, is a triadic process in
which the sign mediates between representation and reality: we form
an interpretant (knowledge as in a thought or idea; home is like a
prison for women) of an object (reality; the actual home and prison)
by mediation of a sign (icon, index or symbol). This process is fundamentally dynamic because each interpretant itself becomes a sign that
sparks off a new process of signification. Therefore, semiosis is unlimited and infinite (14–15). The metaphor of the home as prison sets off
a process in which a more abstract idea shapes itself: that gender can
be considered as imprisoning women in a certain role from which they
need to liberate themselves.

For Peirce, the sign stands for the object 'in reference to a sort of
idea, which I have sometimes called the *ground* of the representation'
(quoted in de Lauretis 1984: 172). De Lauretis understands the ground
as the context of the sign and argues that it is fundamentally a social
and ideological formation. Hence by shifting the ground of a given
sign, a signifying practice (such as feminist cinema) can 'effectively

intervene upon the . . . codes of perception as well as ideological codes' (178). In *Silence* the metaphorization of the prison changes the context of imprisonment into its opposite: where usually the prison indicates an order in which a committed offence is punished by deprivation of freedom, in the film the prison becomes a potential safe place which protects women from a masculinist society that is both offensive to women and deprives them of their freedom. Through its cinematic figures *Silence* is literally ground shifting.

Looking and killing

Many critics and spectators have been outraged by the seemingly gratuitous murder of a man by three women (cf Root 1986); one feminist critic did not find it 'so easy to step around the violent act' (Koenig Quart 1988: 158). It seems to me that these critics and spectators fall into the trap of viewing *Silence* only literally, or realistically. The representation of the lives of the three murderesses and the psychiatrist is very realistic indeed in all its banal details, although, as I pointed out earlier, the strong stereotypes of the female characters and the virtual lack of individualization of the male characters directs the film away from realism into social realism. This makes the film into a sustained critique of masculinist society rather than an attack on individual men. In the following analysis of the murder scenes I will try to explain how the representation of the murder in fact metaphorizes female experience of, and reaction to, masculinist violence.

The three flashbacks of the murder are filmed in cinematic techniques that differ significantly from the conventional realist style of the story of the psychiatrist, in which the murder scenes are embedded. In the murder scenes the diegetic sound is lowered and special film music is added for the effect of both estrangement and suspense. The short scenes of about two minutes each are filmed out of a handheld camera which gives the images a wavering quality. Such iconical signs set the murder apart from the rest of the film and indicate that it is to be viewed quite differently.

Many critics have pointed to the complicity of the spectator in the murder scenes (e.g. Kuderna 1992). It is not only silence that makes the spectator complicit, but also – or even more so – the point of view. The construction of point of view in the murder flashbacks is complicated. Usually a flashback in film is personally motivated but here the scenes are not focalized by any specific character. The flashbacks occur in the story of the psychiatrist who is the main focalizer of *Silence*. Not being present at the murder scene she obviously cannot focalize the flashbacks, but the flashbacks of the murder are not focalized by any of the three murderesses either. In the terminology of François Jost the mode of cinematic narration for the flashbacks of the murder is spectatorial focalization, i.e. it functions so as to give the spectator an advantage in knowledge over the psychiatrist Janine. As such it is an intervention of the implied director, whose actual presence is enhanced by the special film music and the particular camera work in these scenes.

The three murder scenes create a specifically female point of view, by extensively privileging ocularization, that is, the women's looks to each other. Indexical signs, grounding the image in time and space, such as camera work, découpage and montage, suggest a deep bond between the women, who look at each other silently, from one to the other, back and forth, without words repeating one another's murderous actions. A special role is given to the hand-held camera, which as soon as it is attached to the eye of Christine, Andrea and An, detaches itself from them and travels along in whirling movements and rapid zooms. Not unlike the diegetic narration in Helke Sander's film *Der subjektive Faktor* (*The Subjective Factor*), the camera in these murder scenes takes on a life of its own, becoming a character in its own right. Together with the camera, the women perform a choreography, attentively, solemnly, and with dedication.

The particular iconical and indexical signifiers in the murder scenes encourage a metaphorical reading; it is a ritual rather than a 'real act'. The absence of a corpse and the persistent focus on the women takes the attention away from the sacrificed man to female resistance against male domination and even more specifically to women's bonding with each other. Hence the many close-ups of the eyes and faces of women looking at each other. The solidarity between the three killing women is extended to the four other women who are present in the shop, the older, the black and the two young women; silent witnesses who in their gravity resemble the chorus in a Greek tragedy. They are a party in the extensive eye contact between the women and watch silently without interfering – just like the audience of the film. The spectator is implicated in the solidarity between the women. S/he is drawn into the scene of the murder in two ways: by identifying with the camera moving around like an independent character; and by identifying with the female characters through the repeated and explicit eye contact between the women in the film. Being part of the scene, and watching silently, the spectator too becomes responsible for the murder. This particular viewing position for the audience and the highly stylized way of filming the scene, make the murder not realistic, but ritualistic. Ritual, as a symbolic act, is by definition (also) metaphorical. Morover, ritual depends for its effect and function on the presence of an audience.

Many feminist film critics have elaborated on the ritualistic aspect of *Silence*. For Linda Williams the 'ritual mutilation and murder of a male scapegoat' (1988: 108) points to the 'wild zone' of women's experience (107). Geetha Ramanathan understands the murder as a speech act and relates it to the motive of silence: 'By placing the conclusive instance of speech – the act of the murder – at the beginning of the narrative as retaliation against the attempt to silence the three women, the film propounds the thesis that women are not heard, not that they do not speak' (1992: 60). For Lucy Fischer the murder is clearly not a real life event, but both a 'silent ceremonial performance' (1989: 293) and a 'highly theatrical modernist drama' (295) that purposefully puts the audience into a position of guilt. Although I agree with the statements about the ceremonial and ritualistic character of the murder scenes, I would, however, not so much use the notion of guilt as that of complicity or, less morally loaded, engagement. Mary Gentile emphasizes the rhetorical engagement that *Silence* encourages in its viewers. Gentile sees a dialectic at work that is reminiscent of the strategies in Eisenstein's films (1985: 156). She points out that the filmmaker's use of standard movie techniques throughout the rest of the film, while rejecting these cinematic conventions for the murder scene, engages the audience both emotionally and critically: 'Gorris is trying to strike an uneasy balance. She wants our attention, our investment in her narrative, but she also wants us conscious, intellectually aware' (162). In other words, by turning the representation of the murder into a metaphor in an otherwise realist narrative, *Silence* encourages the dual perspective of watching at the same time realistically and metaphorically.

Looking and Laughing

Another powerful metaphor is evoked towards the end of the film. To the established order, represented by the judicial system, the violent and seemingly random murder of a man by three women constitutes a violation of the taboo on female violence. For the court the easiest way out is to condemn the women as 'insane', but after her long investigation and growing rapport with the three murderesses, the psychiatrist Janine van den Bos declares them sane. The court now has to actually think about the meaning of the act, which is something it cannot or will not do. Hence, the murder is not acknowledged as 'sexual' violence, in that the legal order denies the importance of sexual difference in the murder case. The masculinist discourse of the judge and the prosecutor proves unable to acknowledge the importance and implications of sexual difference; it denies the significant fact that in this case women have killed a man. In not recognizing the murder as 'sexual' violence, the judicial order cannot understand the motive. The narrative of the film has shown in meaningful details the paramount importance of the paradox that masculinist society is based on and constitutes the differential category of gender, while it at the same time refuses to see that women are different. This refusal rests on the tacit premise of taking the male gender as the norm and the female as the deviation; by giving men subjectivity while women remain non-subjects. Because of its inability to accept sexual difference as a meaningful category the legal discourse becomes violent: the prosecutor breaks off the dialogue, interrupts the speaker, refuses to listen, in short, he does not take women seriously and reduces them to silence. He represents the violence of a culture which strikes half of its members with muteness by its in-difference.

An reacts to this hostile incomprehension with laughter, setting in motion a wave of laughter among the women in the courtroom and gradually among the (mostly female)[11] spectators in the audience. The scene of laughter is one of the final scenes of the film and it repeats the same ritualistic procedure as the scene of the murder. Looking at one another, the women begin to laugh one by one: the three murderesses, the four female witnesses (who are known only to the spectators, not to the psychiatrist or the male characters in the film) and the psychiatrist. The women's laughter is a sign of their understanding of the events in the courtroom; they are aware of their predicament and the total inability of the court to connect cause to effect.

It is a liberating laugh which binds the women together. With their laughter the women shut out those who do not share their insight and understanding. Therefore the laughter is placed outside the order of the dominant discourse; after all, speech is no longer possible. The laughter breaks through the silence that has surrounded the women for so long. It also thwarts all male authority, turning the court case into the farce it has been from the start. Hence the laughter becomes a symbolic sign for women's resistance against the masculinist order.

Ordered to leave the courtroom the murderesses descend the stairs in the middle of the courtroom, still laughing, surrounded by the women who have witnessed the murder. This ritualistic ending evokes the Greek myth of the Erinyes; after their revenge the women are sent back into the underworld, watched by the chorus of laughing witnesses (cf Williams 1988). The final judgement never gets spoken by the male court but the laughter of the female chorus instead says all.

In order to assess the relevance of this metaphorical ending I want to draw out the empowering effects of the women's laughter on the audience. As in the ritualistic scene of the murder, the spectator is inevitably drawn into the scene of the courtroom. The scene is mainly focalized by the psychiatrist Janine van den Bos. Camera and editing give the murderesses and witnesses exclusive ocularization in their exchange of looks. The spectator, in identifying with the female characters, and having understood the pain of their subjection and hence the motive for the murder, is invited to take their position. With the murder they could only watch and silently witness, with great unease presumably; with the impeding judgement in the courtroom they can actually participate, joining in with the laughter of the female characters. As such the laughter has the liberating effect of a catharsis, much needed after having been made silent complices of the ritualistic murder. At the end of *Silence* the audience can participate in a cathartic ritual on the condition of understanding the murder to be a metaphor for the smothered anger and resistance of women. Those spectators who do not accept the murder as metaphor but who see it realistically can only worry about its criminal nature and are thereby excluded from the subversive laughter. They side with the male characters in the film.

Silence has become quite famous for its empowering effect on the women in the audience as they burst out laughing at the end of the film; the laughter in *Silence* is therefore truly 'revolutionary' as Fischer writes (1989: 298).[12] Referring to this last scene, other critics have praised the unique 'politicization of desire' (Dittmar 1986: 80) or 'the reversal of this playful, passionate moment of fantasy erupting all boundaries' (Donnerberg 1984: 72; translation AS). Many female spectators probably remember their own laughter just as Ruby Rich recalls the women's laughter at a public interview with Marleen Gorris in New York after a screening of the film (Rich quoted in Fischer 1989).

It is only because the murder represents a female fantasy of revenge that laughter is possible at the end of the film: nobody would laugh at a real murder. One can laugh a liberating laugh at a metaphor which seeks to represent the violent relations beween men and women. But whereas the murder is metaphorical, the women's resistance and solidarity is as real as can be. The cinematic metaphors in *A Question of Silence*, then, have a forceful effect upon the audience in the subversive

laughter through which the female spectator engages with female re-
bellion. In the end, laughter is the real 'weapon' against masculinist
indifference and a unique way to break through the silence.

PARALLEL PERSPECTIVES

> The mirror almost always serves to reduce us to a pure exteriority –
> of a very particular kind. It functions as a possible way to constitute
> screens between the other and myself. . . . the mirror is a frozen –
> and polemical – weapon to keep us apart.
>
> Luce Irigaray[13]

The stringing together of separate metaphors in *Silence*, like the prison,
the ritualistic murder, the women's silence and the subversive laughter, together produce a contagious vision of feminist resistance. It is a
form of Eisensteinian intellectual montage, described in 'The Fourth
Dimension in Cinema' (1929) as 'the conflicting combination of accompanying intellectual effects with one another' (1987: 193). This
rhetorical strategy is followed with even greater consistency in Gorris'
next film, *Broken Mirrors*. The film recounts two parallel narratives
which on the surface seem unrelated: the story of prostitutes in a brothel,
filmed as a realist drama, and the story of a housewife who falls victim to a serial killer, filmed as a thriller. In both narratives the female
characters are strongly objectified by men: in the brothel women are
humiliated and abused; the serial killer chains his female victims in a
garage, starving them to death.

The parallel presentation of two different stories in *Broken Mirrors*
is another case of spectatorial focalization: its form of narration is
directed at the spectator. In this case the spectator has to work quite
hard at making meaning of the film. Because there is no connection
whatsoever between the two narratives until the very end, the film
encourages throughout a metaphorical comparison between the two.
The spectator has to come to the conclusion that these two separate
narratives really tell the same story; that the two stories each give a
version of the reduction of women to Woman. By embedding the story
of the serial killer within the story of the brothel, the two narratives
become each others metaphor: to objectify women equals prostitution
equals murder.

In his essay 'Montage 1938' Eisenstein stresses the impact of parallel montage on the spectator, as it engages her or him in a creative

process: 'So now we can say that it is precisely the *montage* principle . . . which forces the spectator himself to *create*' (1992: 311). We
find this principle at work in *Broken Mirrors*. In relating separate images or sequences of images to each other through montage, the film
involves the spectator in an active viewing process in order to understand the combination and juxtaposition of the two stories; in the words
of Eisenstein: 'The strength of montage lies in the fact that it involves
the spectator's emotions and reason' (309). Just as in the case of *A
Question of Silence*, the powerful rhetorical impact of the film derives
from the simultaneous realist and metaphorical representation. In the
following analysis I will explore the cinematic strategies that Gorris
uses to make her metaphors both moving and meaningful.

   Broken Mirrors represents women's oppression as the systematic
deprivation of their subjectivity, not through silencing as in *Silence*,
but through violence. The film emphasizes and values the experiences
of women and exposes the symbolic system in all its brutality. Again
the focalization lies emphatically with the female characters, but in
Broken Mirrors the rhetoric is much more complex and radical than in
Silence. The specifically female point of view is filmed very differently in the two stories of the film and has quite a different impact on
the spectator.

   To explore these different strategies I will first analyze a scene from
the brothel story. At the beginning of the film the prostitutes gather
together in the brothel to start their working day. The women represent different stereotypes of prostitutes: Tessa, a black woman finan-
cially supporting her four children in Surinam; (the other prostitutes
are white) Dora, an artist; Linda, a depressed young girl; Francine, an
unfriendly and hard drinking woman; Irma, an uneducated single mother;
Jacky, a snobbish British cocaine addict; and Ellen, the elderly Madame (Diane, the newcomer who needs money for her addicted husband will arrive later). They sit in some sort of parlour, when the
pimp/manager comes in and greets them curtly. Dora makes an obscene gesture as soon as the pimp closes the door of his office. The
women laugh.

   Dora's gesture starts off a short but significant scene. A lovely musical tune is added to the soundtrack whereas the diegetic sound of the
scene is lowered. Then the hand-held camera starts moving around in
the rather cramped parlour, in an almost dancelike choreography. In
an extended take the camera travels freely through the room and casu-
ally films each of the women as they are applying make-up, drinking
coffee, cleaning up or dancing. The camera does not attach itself to

the look of any of the characters but remains independent, filming the female bodies with intimacy but not erotically. The mood is one of harmony: the women take care of each other, exchange jokes or sit quietly by themselves. When the door bell announces the first customer, the music stops, the camera comes to a standstill and the women remain motionless for just a second before getting into action. The scene ends with a cut to the figure of a customer waiting in front of the glass door.

Not unlike the murder flashbacks in *Silence*, this short scene is narrated through spectatorial focalization. There is no character focalization and not even ocularization. The cinematic strategies represent the women three-dimensionally by filming them in time (there is only one cut in the whole take) and in space (the framing of the long shot is quite large in relation to the small and crowded room). This is another way of giving subjectivity to the women both narratively and visually. Like the camera in the murder flashbacks in *Silence*, the rather peculiar camera movements in this short scene of about a minute, draw the spectator into the scene and make her or him become part of the company of women. Identifying with the independent camera the spectator experiences moving around in the room with the women. All these aspects together (the absence of men, the intimacy of the women, the framing, the camera movement and the editing) have the effect of specifically addressing the spectator as female. De Lauretis has argued that a woman's film addresses the female spectator, regardless of the gender of the viewers, when the film 'defines all points of identification (with character, image, camera) as female, feminine, or feminist' (1987: 133). This is certainly the case in this short scene, which is in this sense representative of the whole film.

The privileged position of triple identification – with the independent camera look, with the three-dimensional image and with the female characters – is broken off abruptly by the door bell. Therefore, the customer does not only disturb the intimacy for the prostitutes but also for the spectator. In the next scene the Madame introduces one by one the 'girls' to him (and to the spectator). In an edited series of portraits, each woman is filmed in the same frame and medium shot. The camera look is attached to the male character, fragmenting and eroticizing the female characters. The montage separates the women from each other and from the space they occupy, which makes them into a one-dimensional picture, much like pin-ups, objects exposed for sale to the man's gaze; a position which the women oppose by their ironical looks and remarks.

The spectator shares the literal look of the male customer, but in this context certainly does not share his point of view; in other words, although ocularization lies with the male character he does not focalize the scene. Spectatorial focalization, that is the intervention of the implied director, through the juxtaposition of these two scenes as well as through the camera work, framing and montage, create a contrast between the women as subjects in their own right and the women as objects of the male gaze. The scene thus exposes the effects of the male look upon women. These iconic and indexical signs turn the short sequence into a feminist point of view: the look as sign becomes a metaphor for 'the male gaze'

The effect of this form of rhetoric upon the spectator is far-reaching. The moment a female character makes the transition from a subject to an object position, the spectator makes the transition from the viewing position of empathy and identification to one of critical distance. This procedure returns time and again throughout the film. *Broken Mirrors* engages the viewer emotionally with the women as subjects and then makes the spectator critically aware when the women function as objects for men. Thus, the spectator experiences almost physically the pain of woman's continuous objectification: the pain when she is deprived of her voice, her body, and her freedom. In blocking the way to identification at the moment when the female characters are objectified, the spectator is invited to reflect critically on the objectification of women by men. These alternating positions involve the spectator in a viewing process that is alternately emotional and intellectual.

Lethal Looks

The organization of point of view is quite different in the thriller story. The thriller story in *Broken Mirrors* seems a further elaboration of feminist film theoretical notions, in that it exposes and criticizes the violent, even sadistic, aspects of the male gaze. The thriller story is technically de-coloured, making the world of the murderer and the victim into a grim place. The bleak colour scheme is an iconic sign indicating the metaphorical nature of the 'black-and-white' story. The murderer is introduced with classical means of suspense: when he buries and photographs the dead body of a woman, the camera focuses on his hands, his gloves and his feet, but his face remains outside the frame. Although he is a gruesome sex murderer, he is shown to be a very normal man, working in an office, coming home to a loving wife who has cooked him dinner. This killer is the perfect bourgeois.

The murderer's identity remains unknown because his face is literally kept in the dark. This framing device is maintained throughout
the film until the very end when his identity is revealed. As a consequence of this way of filming the camera can never be presented as
the actual look of the murderer while it exposes at the same time the
violence of his gaze. Technically speaking, there is no occasion for
the murderer's look (ocularization) nor narration (focalization). Within
the thriller story the camera refers directly back to the implied director. Hence the camera work attracts attention to itself and creates a
critical position for the spectator (this is an occasion of what Jost calls
spectatorial focalization).

When the murderer leaves his office to look for a new victim, the
camera follows him from a great distance, constantly on the move
tracking him down from behind all sorts of obstacles, never showing
his face, but just this dark figure going about methodically looking for
another housewife to kill. This is not only high suspense (and the film
music certainly adds to the effect), but the camera movements can also
be understood metaphorically: the indexical sign of the voyeuristic
movements of the camera become a symbolic sign of the voyeuristic
actions of the killer. The spectator watches a male voyeur while identification with his point of view is blocked and can therefore take enough
distance from the voyeuristic male look. Because the camera films the
man without attaching itself to his look, the female character is never
seen through his eyes. The narrator does not present the nameless woman
voyeuristically to the spectator, but instead makes her the focalizer in
some of the scenes in the thriller story. Her perspective is the same as
the spectator's: she does not understand what is happening and asks
aloud the question that the spectator is worrying about all along: 'Why?'

Although the murderer, being faceless, is quite literally deprived of
the gaze, he does avail himself of a voyeuristic gaze in the form of a
polaroid camera that he uses for photographing his victims. After having captured his victim, the murderer does not touch the woman nor
does he batter or rape her. Instead he chains her to a bed in a garage
and photographs her in each stage of her despair, fear, filth and starva-
tion. He pins the pictures methodically on the wall, adding them to the
pictures of his previous three victims whom he photographed from the
beginning of their captivity until their deaths.[14] All the elements from
feminist analyses of the male gaze can be found in this substitute: a
man directs his gaze at a female body; it gives him pleasure to look;
and his gaze objectifies, petrifies even, the woman in his power. As
Kaplan (1983) rightly observes: the problem is not that men look *per*

se, but that they have the power to act on their gaze. *Broken Mirrors* metaphorically shows that looking is not a mere innocent act because it always takes place within a given pattern of dominance and submission.

In this context the act of taking pictures becomes quite threatening; photography metaphorically takes the place of violent sexual abuse. Mulvey has already pointed out the relation between voyeurism and sadism, observing that the 'pleasure lies in ascertaining guilt . . . as serting control and subjugating the guilty person through punishment or forgiveness' (1989: 22–3). The thriller story in *Broken Mirrors* follows Mulvey's description of how sadism fits in with narrative: demanding a story, a battle of will and strength, ending up in victory and defeat. The battle between the serial killer and the housewife ends in the inevitable death of the woman; in *Broken Mirrors* the male look is represented as lethal.

Broken Mirrors never directly shows the murderer's pleasure in watching the submission and powerlessness of his victim; instead it focuses on the suffering of the woman. Because the spectator is blocked from identification with the voyeuristic look, in contrast to classical Hollywood films, s/he does not derive any erotic or sadistic pleasure from looking at the 'guilty' woman. For Mulvey it is fear of castration, the fear that the sight of the 'castrated' woman instills in men, which motivates male sadism. In *Broken Mirrors* this is suggested in the metaphor of the camera as phallus; the murderer is 'castrated' in that he does not perform any sexual act other than the surrogate of photographing the female body. We need little imagination to see taking pictures as an indexical sign of copulation: the film camera always lingers on in close-up when the killer opens his coat – and for one moment the spectator does not know whether to expect a gun, a penis or the camera – and takes out his camera, focuses on the woman and presses. The bulb flashes and the polaroid slides out of the camera. The camera as phallus replaces the sexual act with the physical penis; that is why the woman is not abused or raped. She is metaphorically raped when being photographed. As Susan Sontag writes:

> Still, there is something predatory in the act of taking a picture. To photograph people is to violate them, by seeing them as they never see themselves, by having knowledge of them they can never have; it turns people into objects that can be symbolically possessed. Just as the camera is a sublimation of the gun, to photograph someone is a sublimated murder – a soft murder, appropriate to a sad, frightened time.
> (Sontag 1979: 14–15)

Broken Mirrors explores the utter implications of the voyeuristic gaze. The female victim comes to the conclusion that: 'You hate me so intensely, so terribly; you enjoy to see me beg, to see me beg for mercy'. She refuses to plead with him any longer and remains silent. At this moment the colour comes back into the image; an iconic sign metaphorically marking the insight of the woman. As in *A Question of Silence*, silence is a female form of resistance when all hope is lost. It is only then that the murderer speaks, begging her to speak, calling her a whore. But the woman refuses to react any more; she remains silent, knowing that it is the male gaze and nothing else that sees her as a whore.

The spectator learns this also from the parallel story of the brothel. Men can own the women they look at, because they have the power and the money to act upon their gaze. The murderer possesses the female victim by depriving her of her freedom and eventually of her life; the male customers in the brothel temporarily possess the prostitutes by paying for having sex with them. In the thriller story the objectifying and appropriating gaze leads to violence and murder; in the brothel story it leads to contempt, humiliation and also, violence (Linda commits suicide, and, towards the end of the film Irma gets assaulted and stabbed).

Voyeuristic pleasure is denied to the male spectator, because *Broken Mirrors* carefully avoids any eroticization of the female body. At the same time empathy or identification with any male character is made impossible, because nowhere in the film can they be recognized as individuals. While the film thematizes and problematizes the male gaze, it cleverly avoids voyeuristic pleasure through its employment of cinematic strategies of distantiation. Instead the film shows the pain and suffering caused by the male objectifying gaze. Thus, the cinematic strategy of suspense is turned into a feminist vision. *Broken Mirrors* shows in lucid images the answer to de Lauretis' question 'how did Medusa feel seeing herself in Perseus' mirror just before being slain?' (1984: 109). I would say miserable beyond words.

EMPTY SPACE

As we saw in the first chapter, the feminine is traditionally represented in Hollywood cinema as something unknown, as the enigma creating a place in the narrative structure that remains void (Kuhn 1982: 32–42). This empty space functions as the locus for images, representations and metaphorizations of the feminine. De Lauretis (1984) has extensively analyzed how this process of metaphorization has structured narrativity. The empty narrative space positions the female subject as a structural obstacle or boundary. Narrative is structured around this space: in the beginning of the story the hero makes it his aim to solve the mystery, in the middle he tries to get through to the enigma and in the end he has solved it. As many feminist critics have pointed out, the 'solution' of the mystery lies either in the destruction of the woman (death or prison) or in her incorporation into the symbolic order (marriage); these being the two conventional endings of Hollywood cinema (cf Kaplan 1980).

In the films of Marleen Gorris this narrative structure is reversed: it is not 'Woman' but masculinist society that is metaphorized. In *Silence* explicit violence of women is used as a metaphor for a political approach to sexual difference; in *Broken Mirrors* 'man' himself is metaphorized as an enigma. The male killer does not have a face nor an identity: he is the mystery. Like the male victim in *Silence* he remains an empty space. In both films, Gorris has effected this by keeping the male characters outside the frame and marginalizing them in the narrative. In depicting the male characters as 'other', the films undermine the self-evidence of male power and subjectivity. This reversal of dominant discourse forms a pertinent comment on that discourse: male discourse itself is metaphorized. The reversal enlightens the inadequacy of a form of rhetoric which metaphorizes women. The violent effects of such a discourse is made manifest in its inability to see women as historical and social subjects and in its subsequent power to objectify them.

In contrast, the female characters in both films are shown as subjects in a historical and social context that militates against their subjectivity. De Lauretis has underscored the importance of representing women as social and historical subjects, in order to counteract the metaphorization of the feminine in dominant systems of representation. Earlier in this book I have explored how female subjectivity is related to the notion of experience and how feminist cinema can be a 'political, theoretical, self-analyzing practice by which the relations of the subject in social reality can be rearticulated from the historical experience of women' (de Lauretis 1984: 196). The films by Marleen Gorris prove an example of such a cinematic practice.

De Lauretis argues that women can only become subjects when they live through and represent the contradiction of being both 'Woman' and 'women'; of being both an image of the feminine and a socio-historical subject. This contradiction is what *Silence* and *Broken Mirrors* represent. From the perspective of dominant discourse the female characters in the two films represent 'woman' and 'the feminine' within the binary opposition of sexual difference. Yet within women's own experience (which both films privilege) the category of woman becomes plural; they are women, social and historical subjects. Gorris' films present a great number of women on the screen who differ in age, class and race. These differences break open the dyad of sexual difference, so that women can be represented and signified outside the male order. The dispersion of differences among women creates a context in which personal differences are put to play. Sometimes these differences may lead to conflicts, as in the racist remarks of Francine against Tessa which at one point in the film leads to a verbal fight with Diane and Dora. Mostly the differences among women in *Silence* and *Broken Mirrors* suggest a 'world of difference' in which a political bond and budding friendship between women is at the fore.

In both films one short scene suggests lesbian love within the continuum of female friendship.[15] In *Silence* the secretary Andrea and the psychiatrist Janine silently face one another in Andrea's prison cell. Andrea slowly outlines Janine's body with her hands at several inches away from the body, until they are interrupted by a male guard. In *Broken Mirrors* Diane pays a visit to Dora's private apartment in a typical Amsterdam houseboat. The growing intimacy between the two women suggests mutual desire, although the scene full of lingering looks does not result in explicit lesbianism. These two short scenes emphasize a female continuum of solidarity, friendship and love. Andrea Weiss' observation about *Silence* offering 'the possibility of lesbianism not only as an "alternative lifestyle" but as its own logical conclusion' also holds true of *Broken Mirrors* (1992: 122).

The reversal of dominant discourse (metaphorizing 'man' as the empty space) and representing female subjects as both Woman and women, creates a powerful feminist discourse that specifically addresses the female spectator (whether lesbian or not). Offering a glimmering of utopia the film envisages a shift in consciousness. As I have argued with respect to *A Question of Silence*, the cinematic rhetoric in *Broken Mirrors* is ground shifting. In the next section I want to show how a feminist rhetoric in *Broken Mirrors* is actualized in the metaphorical meaning of the end of the film – when the mirror cracks.

AND THE MIRROR CRACKED

When watching the final dramatic sequence of *Broken Mirrors*, the spectator has already processed quite a lot of suffering and violence: Linda's suicide, continuous humiliation of the prostitutes in the brothel with its 'climax' in the long night of a fraternity's party, the death of the female victim of the murderer and finally the assault on Irma in the brothel. For a full understanding of the impact of the last scene it is important to realize that the spectator is likely to feel emotional tension owing to the suspense, the accumulation of violence, the identification with the female characters and the intellectual understanding of women's position in masculinist society, resulting from the rhetorical strategies discussed earlier.

In the course of the film the main characters Dora and Diane have established a strong friendship with each other. In the final scene they return to the brothel from the hospital where they have taken the badly injured Irma, with the help of a regular and friendly customer (one of the very few men in the film whom the spectator recognizes). While all the women stand or sit dejectedly in the parlour, the man gestures without words that he wants to have sex. The women are outraged and try to reason him into going away, but he stands there shrouded in superior taciturnity, refusing to leave. Through close-ups of all the female characters the spectator experiences their humiliation and powerlessness. Then the alto aria *'fac me vere'* from Haydn's *Stabat Mater* begins to play softly on the soundtrack, getting progressively louder while the diegetic sound is lowered. This music accompanies the images until the very end of the film, channelling the emotions of the spectator into an elegiac mood.

The film then shows a close-up of the hands of the man, removing his gloves, opening his coat and fumbling for something. For just a moment the spectator expects him to reach for a gun but he takes out his wallet pulling out more and more money. This shot is framed in the same way as the shots of the murderer taking his polaroid camera and the man is wearing the same coat. Thus the wallet, the money, is iconically represented as being similar to the camera; both are indexically linked to a gun and all these objects metaphorically represent the phallus. But more importantly, the spectator now understands that this man, the only friendly customer in the brothel, is the same one as the serial killer from the thriller story.

With this one short shot the film addresses the spectator directly. The shot reveals to the audience the murderer's identity. It also brings the two parallel but separate narratives together. This radically alters the viewing position of the spectator who is raised to an altogether different level. She knows more than the female characters in the film, who obviously have no idea of the thriller story and hence do not know this man to be a killer. The intervention by the diegetic narrator on the discursive level does not break off identification with Diane and the other women at the level of the story, but it does put the spectator in a more distant and therefore critical position. Because the narratives assign a metaphorical meaning to each other, s/he interprets the finale of *Broken Mirrors* from a symbolical perspective.

When the customer/murderer flatly refuses to leave and the women get more and more furious and frustrated, Diane picks up a small gun at the same moment as the female voice starts singing the aria on the soundtrack. She points the gun, deliberately diverts it so as to just miss the man when she shoots. He is touched by breaking glass and looks stunned at the few drops of blood on his face. He runs away. For the spectator Diane's act acquires another meaning than just chasing away a man who humiliates the prostitutes; for the audience her gesture is an act of justice, the sentence of 'guilty' that, precisely, *Silence* refused to pronounce on the women. Diane's shooting means a metaphoric trial and execution for the murders the man has committed, and metaphorically at one more remove for sexual violence in general.

The moment the mystery is finally solved – the identity of the murderer – the structure of the film has already convinced the spectator that the identity of the man is completely beside the point; that he is anonymous 'Man'. The way in which the metaphor of the murderer in the thriller story is carefully constructed in *Broken Mirrors*, through framing, lighting, montage and narrative structure, recalls what Paul Ricoeur in his study of metaphor has described as follows: 'The metaphor is not the enigma but the solution of the enigma' (1986: 426). Indeed, when the spectator understands that the murderer is a metaphorical expression of male violence in general, the enigma of his identity is solved. In accepting the reflexive relationship between the two narratives, the spectator understands both of them as a metaphorical expression of the violent power relations between the sexes. The fetters with which the serial killer ties his female victims to a bed is a metaphor of the bondage that keeps women chained to sexual submission. Because the treatment of the prostitutes in the brothel can in the same way be seen as a metaphorization of the sexual objectification and possession of women, the serial killer is clearly not an isolated psychopath but rather one step down on the ladder of sexual violence against women.

When Diane then slowly and solemnly shoots all the mirrors in the parlour, her gestures take on an almost biblical meaning. As the music of the *Stabat Mater* on the soundtrack suggests, this final scene of *Broken Mirrors* represents an indictment against the ancestral suffering of women. The breaking of the mirrors is a ritualistic act of resistance against the male gaze, against cultural representations of femininity, against the objectifying look that make women into whores, against the distorted self-images of women – all of which she shoots to pieces in the symbol of the mirror. Diane's symbolic act empowers her to leave the brothel for good, together with her friend Dora. The film ends with the same scene as it has started with: 'the morning after' a cleaning woman clears up the bloody mess in the brothel, accompanied by the suppliant female voice of the *Stabat Mater*.

THE PASSION OF FEMINISM

'Conflict lies at the basis of every art', writes Eisenstein in his essay 'Beyond the shot' (1987: 145). For feminist filmmakers the basic social conflict is based on gender. One might expect that the thematic conflict in Gorris' films is one between men and women, but although this is not altogether untrue, it unduly simplifies the issues at stake. Rather, the major conflict in both *Silence* and *Broken Mirrors* is expressed in the experience of women who are subjects in a culture that refuses them the status of subject. Gorris has chosen to represent the struggle between the sexes from the exclusive point of view of 'the second sex', which has found its cinematic expression in forms of ocularization and focalization, framing, camera work and montage. As my analyses show, the fundamental collision between women as subjects and women as objects structures the entire form of the two films. This is mainly represented by way of metaphors. Earlier in this chapter we have seen that metaphors are complex signs which mediate our understanding of the object. A string of metaphors creates for the spectator a feminist vision on masculinist society where women are imprisoned in the straitjacket of gender: the world is a prison (*Silence*); or where women are exploited and abused: the world is a brothel (*Broken Mirrors*).

However definite such statements may sound, my interpretation is not the end of semiosis, which, we recall, is fundamentally an unlimited process. De Lauretis (1984, 1987) points to the possible historical, materialist and gendered theory of culture that Peircian semiotics enables. Peirce emphasizes that meanings have effects, in social reality and within the terrain of subjectivity. These effects are the interpretants of signs, which he describes in three general classes. The emotional interpretant is the feeling produced by a sign. The energetic interpretant is a muscular or mental effort in reaction to the sign. And finally a sign may result in a 'habit-change', 'a modification of a person's tendencies toward action', which Peirce calls the logical interpretant (de Lauretis 1984: 174). In this final section of the chapter I will explore some of the effects of Gorris' films.

The prison and brothel are not merely metaphorical figures: in *Silence* women are literally imprisoned and silenced; in *Broken Mirrors* women are literally prostituted and chained to a bed. In fact, one could say she has literalized metaphors. How more graphic can a representation of women's oppression get? This brings me again to the importance of grounding metaphors in realism, for it points to a specific characteristic of the cinematic process of metaphorization: the earlier mentioned material actualization of the figure within the image. It is from the concrete iconic image that the metaphor of women's oppression is transformed into a symbolic image. The metaphor is not an escape, but a liberation, from too literal a meaning, just as the level of realism is a liberation from 'facile allegory'. Thus, the metaphors call for a certain mental effort to understand the object in which they are grounded. In mediating the spectator's understanding of social reality from a female point of view, the metaphors produce their specific energetic interpretants.

Because in cinema a metaphor is depicted in graphic images the transferential process of metaphorization is quite transparent. During the viewing process the spectator traces down the transference between the two meanings of an image, scene or a whole film, and comes to an understanding of both the realist and metaphorical signification of it. The dialectics of this mental effort suggests that the force of cinematic metaphors resides in the simultaneous perception and understanding of both levels of realism and metaphorism. Eisenstein has stressed throughout his written work[16] (as well as realized in his films) that only the construction of those two registers can convince the spectator both intellectually and move her or him emotionally.

Judging from the 'either/or' and 'for or against' reactions by critics, some spectators have opted for only one interpretation at the time. Maybe they are so overwhelmed by feelings that they refuse to make the mental effort to understand, in which case they have stopped the semiotic process at the emotional interpretant. To miss out on one level is missing out on the feminist meaning of the films. To view the films just realistically leads to absurd statements; that feminists are castrating bitches out to kill men (*Silence*) or that all men are whorehoppers and psychopaths out to victimize women (*Broken Mirrors*). To view the films only metaphorically, however, would mean to miss out on the important realization of the forms and issues of women's real oppression and suffering in a male-dominated society.

The highly divisive effects of the films of Gorris on the audience might be explained by the effects of film rhetoric. Above I mentioned the notion of 'conflict'. For Eisenstein conflict is calculated to attract the spectator. However, in his early essay 'the Montage of Attractions', written in 1923, attraction is also meant to subject 'the audience to emotional or psychological influence' and to 'produce specific emotional shocks in the spectator' (1987: 34). As Jacques Aumont points out, there is definitely a certain aggressiveness in Eisenstein's early writings. The efficacy of political cinema results in 'a violence done to the spectator' (Aumont 1987: 47).

It seems to me that this aggressiveness can also be found in feminist cinema of the 1970s and 1980s. As the Dutch scholar Andreas Burnier once wrote: 'Masculinism is a terrible problem, and feminism is an almost equally terrible response to it' (1979: 76; translation AS). In the many women's films about female murderers listed at the beginning of this chapter, there is an edge to the films that may shock the spectator. And there is no doubt that the brutal scenes of violence committed both by women (*Silence*) and by men (*Broken Mirrors*) in the films of Gorris deeply disturb the audience. Judging from her statement in an interview with a Dutch newspaper: 'I want to deal telling blows. That is what the audience will feel at least', Gorris has purposefully subjected her audience to a shock treatment.[17]

Precisely because of the simultaneous realism and metaphorism in the films there is no way out for the spectator (except by blocking out one level of signification). In this respect Gorris' films differ from horror movies (to which they have a resemblance in style). Horror is always an exaggeration which diverts the fantasmatic story from everyday reality. This does not mean that horror does not speak to deep-seated anxieties, but it plays on those fears rather than making them conscious as the films of Gorris do.[18] This is why I think that feminist films about male violence turn out to be quite violent themselves in their effects on the spectator. In the case of the films of Gorris one could say, in the words of de Lauretis (1984), that her rhetoric of violence has resulted in a certain violence of rhetoric, which for many critics and other spectators make them turn away from the signifying process.

But Gorris' films are rich and complex enough to produce more emotional interpretants than just anger and outrage. The films also deeply move the spectator. In his later work Eisenstein was still preoccupied with the efficacy of cinema, but rather than thinking about it in aggressive terms he addresses the issue more in terms of affect. The notions which he uses are 'pathos' and 'ecstasy'. For the exploration of this more positive way of influencing the spectator (there is no doubt as to the manipulative force that Eisenstein ascribes to affect), I rely on Aumont's reading of Eisenstein's texts. Eisenstein refers to the effect of pathos as 'a constant "movement lifting one out of oneself"', which is why he replaces this notion by the idea of ecstasy (Aumont 1987: 59). According to Aumont, affect in film is meant for Eisenstein to result in 'an awakening which puts the spectator's emotional and intellectual activity into operation to the maximum degree' (59). He argues that Eisensteinian pathos or ecstacy is a technique of making the spectator forget himself, yet still with the goal of completing a dialectical process (60).

I find it attractive to think of affect as a double-edged strategy that moves the spectator emotionally as well as activating her or him intellectually. For Peirce the emotional interpretant is a condition for the energetic interpretant. In other words, without emotional response there is no mental effort possible. An example of this technique in Gorris' films is the close-up of the customer's/murderer's gloved hands at the end of *Broken Mirrors*. The shot is part of a scene in which identification with the prostitutes is secured. The spectator shares the women's grief after the frenzied attack on one of them, and their humiliation at the hands of the man who wants to have sex with them in, quite literally, the bloodbath. The emotional interpretant is modified, deepened even, when the spectator discovers this man to be the murderer. Because the particular shot reveals the murderer's identity and brings together the two stories of the film, the spectator is directly addressed by the implied director and invited to make a mental effort in understanding the denouement of the film.

The pathos of the final sequence is most poignantly effected through the plaintive music of the *Stabat Mater*, which on an emotional level moves the spectator/listener deeply, and on an intellectual level compares the suffering of women to the passion of Christ. There are more biblical overtones in *Broken Mirrors* that I have not discussed but which do make much for a general feeling of pathos in the viewing process. Next to Dora's living boat is a strip of waste land where an old man, André, has built a small hut in which he lives. He and Dora are on friendly terms. André is a harmless drop-out who converses rather comically with God and the Virgin Mary. He never comes out of his shack, so the spectator never gets to see him but s/he can hear his funny and sad comments on life interspersed with biblical language. For example, when Diane leaves Dora to go home after their intimate *tête-à-tête*, Dora accompanies her to the street and for a long time follows Diane with her eyes. Meanwhile we hear André expressing his disappointment that Diane is not staying to sleep with Dora. He then rambles on in his Amsterdam dialect about the holy virgin Mary dropping in to sleep in his hut resembling the stable of Bethlehem, her visit being very cosy, and, of course, very chaste.[19]

While comments like these make for comic relief in a film that is generally sad and grim, there is one scene where André's soliloquy takes on the same elegiac significance as the music in the very last scene. The short but significant scene takes place towards the end of *Broken Mirrors*, after the scene in which the nameless victim of the murderer has understood the logic of his violence and has refused to beg any longer. The colour comes back into the image, the woman remains silent and finally she spits at the murderer with utter contempt.

A cut takes us to André's cabin. At the first break of day the camera slowly moves around his hut, while we hear him sadly cite from the *Song of Songs*:

We will not all pass away, but we will all be transformed, in a point of time, in an instant. For, lo, the winter is past, the rain is over and gone. The flowers appear on the earth; the time of the singing of birds is come and the voice of the turtle is heard in our land.

The effect of pathos of this scene is undeniable. The suffering of the individual female characters of the film is elevated to a universal level. André's text refers to a visionary future, a utopian spring, in which 'we' will be transformed. The discrepancy with reality is too pronounced to offer the spectator a sprinkling of hope. Instead, it is a moment of stillness that evokes what should be but is not possible, before the spiral of violence explodes towards the end.

CONCLUSION

The gradual increase of suffering and violence in *Broken Mirrors* is excessive, just as the murder in *Silence*. Together with emotionally pregnant moments, like André's monologue or the music of the *Stabat Mater* in *Broken Mirrors*, and the subversive laughter in *Silence*, the films create an excess of emotion 'which makes the spectator vibrate with the right feelings for the just cause', as Aumont puts it (1987:60). Through metaphorization grounded in realism, Gorris has constructed a feminist rhetoric which cannot fail to leave the spectator unmoved, whether positively or negatively.

What then is the 'logical', final, interpretant of the metaphors – the imprisonment, prostitution and abuse of women in masculinist society? Feelings of sadness, grief, anger and outrage are common reactions to *Silence* and *Broken Mirrors*. Mental effort is required for understanding the complexities of the cinematic metaphors. The logical interpretant involves making sense of those feelings and mental efforts. And the only sense is a feminist one. The final interpretant thus results in a 'habit-change', a modification of consciousness, or in feminist terms: consciousness-raising. The process of semiosis in Gorris' films comes to a rest in the passionate call for the 'just cause', feminist resistance to male supremacy. Thus, the pathos of those two films has everything to do with my initial experience of witnessing the 'truth'. A feminist truth that denounces a hegemonic culture denigrating, denying, and violating female subjectivity. *A Question of Silence* and *Broken Mirrors* have succeeded in representing the passion of feminism and in getting women through the lethal looking glass.

5 Forces of Subversion: On the Excess of the Image

This is the war of the images.
Adrienne Rich[1]

The effort and challenge now are how to effect another vision.
Teresa de Lauretis[2]

INTRODUCTION

The breaking of mirrors – the destruction of traditional patterns of visual and narrative pleasure – has certainly been a necessary phase in feminism, but a similar goal may also be achieved by going through the mirror, in mimetically revisiting and transforming visual and narrative pleasure. Maybe such a process will prove to be equally productive and less painful than smashing mirrors to pieces. This is how I understand the strategy of mimesis as advocated by Irigaray.

Through mimesis Irigaray tries to undo and transform the meanings, images and representations which masculinist culture has made of the signifier 'Woman'. The mimetic process involves revisiting the images, words and definitions of the feminine, in a 'playful repetition' so as to process, transform and appropriate them (1985b: 76). According to Naomi Schor, Irigaray's mimesis is more than a gesture to denaturalize phallogocentrism; it is a positive mimesis which allows the feminine to emerge from the layers of femininity in which it lies buried (1994: 67).[3] Mimesis is, then, the imaginary quest for new self-images.

The metaphor of the mirror as a surface or screen which reflects dominant images of women suggests a possible site of subversive mimesis in cinema: the screen or the image projected on it. The cinematic screen has received little theoretical attention in feminist film theory, with the notable exception of the work of Judith Mayne and Kaja Silverman. Mayne (1990) displaces the privileged concepts in feminist film theory of 'the gaze' and 'the spectacle', by focusing on the screen as the ground for both the image and the gaze (36). As such, the screen has an ambivalent function which has made it a favoured figure for female narration in recent women's films.[4] According to Mayne, the metaphor of the ambiguous screen surface accounts for women's cinema being both complicitous with and resistant to dominant film forms.

Mayne does not, however, feed her stimulating readings of the figure of the screen in women's films back into theory. Silverman (1992) stretches the limits of theory much further. Upon rereading Lacan's fundamental concept of the gaze Silverman comes to the conclusion that the image (or its location, the screen) – rather than the gaze – functions as the site of cultural representation. Hence, she argues, political struggle can most effectively be waged at the level of the image or screen and theoretical attention should be deflected away from the gaze to the image.[5]

In this chapter I explore the notion of the screen or image as that privileged site/sight of cultural change. I will do so by concentrating on a cinematic element that can subvert the very narrative it helps to construct: the image. Thus I will focus on what Barthes has called 'rhetoric of the image' (1977). Following Silverman I will argue that the force of the image as such can displace the voyeuristic look; a 'taming [of] the gaze' as Lacan would have it (1981: 109). In particular, within the context of visual pleasure, I want to examine the relationship between the cinematic image and the representation of female subjectivity. A visual style that privileges the image gives space to psychic configurations deviating from the familiar oedipal trajectory, such as the uncanny and the abject. Visual pleasure is then no longer *per se* dependent on narrative and its collateral structures of voyeurism and fetishism. For my exploration of the subversive force of the visual I discuss two films which, in my view, subvert their narratives at the level of the image: *Bagdad Café* (Percy Adlon, Germany/USA, 1988) and *Sweetie* (Jane Campion, Australia, 1989).

VISUAL EXCESS

In his essay on Eisenstein's films, Barthes (1977) describes how there is a third meaning to a visual image which goes beyond a first (informational) and even a second (symbolic) level. The materiality of the visual image brings about a third meaning which cannot be easily grasped; its meaning is in no way 'obvious' but remains 'obtuse'. This is why the image is fundamentally unspeakable.[6] It is at this third level, which is in fact beyond meaning, which outplays meaning, that the 'filmic' finally emerges: 'The filmic is that in the film which cannot be described, the representation which cannot be represented' (1977: 64).

I reserve the term 'excess' for what Barthes calls 'the third meaning'. By excess I refer to all those qualities of the visual image which construct the narrative but which also always carry a meaning in excess of the film's story.[7] Kristin Thompson (1986) defines excess in opposition to narrative, as that which undermines the unity and homogeneity of the narrative structure. Although Thompson claims to follow Russian Formalism, she approaches cinematic excess exclusively from the Hollywood norm of narrative unity and homogeneity. In many European films (as well as in non-western cinema and certainly within early Russian cinema) visual excess is part and parcel of the cinematic style, meant to purposefully (even paradoxically) create those 'obtuse' meanings beyond the simple story of the film. In my view, visual excess does not necessarily stand in opposition to narrative, but is imbricated in the narrative structure while it at the same time produces a multiplicity of 'obtuse' meanings beyond that narrative. Thus, visual excess is a subversive element creating other meanings, outplaying narrative structures, evoking emotions; it is certainly the 'obtuse' meaning of the visual which carries much of the affect of a film.[8] In this section I will be concerned with these effects of visual excess, in an attempt to speak the unspeakable, that is account for images that break through the mould of 'representation'.

In *Bagdad Café* many images and scenes break with Hollywood film conventions in such a way as to effect an imagery that is best described as 'excessive',[9] Unusual camera angles and framing, colour filters, rapid repetitions or montage, retardation and absurd *mise-en-scène* are characteristic of this film. They have the typical distancing effect that Brecht theorized as *Verfremdung*. The (fifty) shots of the opening sequence of the film until the end of the credits are particularly curious. The sequence depicts the following scene. As tourists in the USA, the Münchgestettners, an obese couple from Rosenheim in Germany, tour the desert on their way to Las Vegas. During a coffee break they begin a quarrel, apparently not the first one. The woman puts on her Bavarian hat with feathers, takes her bag and suitcase and walks out on her husband in the middle of the desert. The images, rather excessive with oblique perspectives, shots from above, yellow colouring, quick montage of jarring frames and the setting in a desolate picnic place in the desert, render the fight between the Münchgestettners somewhat funny, in both senses of the word: the scene is strange and humorous at the same time. There are several reasons why it is humorous to witness this ritualistic marital fight: the man's struggle with objects, the couple's preposterous look as the stereotyped image of Germans, the homely familiarity of their clash. The very strangeness of the filmic images also accounts for the subtle humour of the scene. What does it mean to film such an ordinary thing as a fight between husband and wife in such an extraordinary, even absurd, way?

The images exceed any Hollywood conventions of a realistic visual style at the service of a classical narrative. Referring back to the Peircean terminology of the previous chapter, we can say that the excessive imagery breaks down the Peircean symbolic. The iconic signs depicting the scene are so unconventional as to become indexical: colour, lighting, camera position and movement, and montage direct and coerce the spectator's attention (cf Silverman 1983b): the relationship is as disconnected as the montage is discontinuous, as unstable as the camera angle is slanting and as disharmonious as the images are unsettling. The imagery creates the metaphorical effect of making conventonal relations between men and women (especially when a couple is on holiday) look like grotesque warfare.

With respect to the affect of the excessive imagery, we can also see the strangeness of the cinematic signs in the opening sequence as an expression of the woman's emotional state. Jasmin Münchgestettner finds herself in an all too familiar situation (a fight with her husband), yet far from home (*Heim*). Maybe the fact that she is abroad – 'out of Rosenheim' as the original title was supposed to run – enables her to take the step to walk out on her husband. Now she finds herself, of her own will yet rather lost, alone in a foreign country. The recurring visual play on the word 'Rosenheim' in the film suggests how much Jasmin leaves her home and husband behind. She is not at home – *un-heim-lich* – and surely the sequence renders everything familiar strange: it all becomes quite *unheimlich* (uncanny) for Jasmin who feels nervous and ill at ease in the vast space of the foreign desert with its strange formations of light in the sky. For the spectator, however, the eerie aspect of *Unheimlichkeit* is underplayed by the humour of the images.

The visual excess in the opening sequence in *Bagdad Café* produces a number of effects in the spectator. The first and easiest one may be laughter, but then the excessive imagery draws attention to itself and makes the viewer reflect upon what s/he is watching. S/he has to make a story out of the weird scene. One could say that the excessive imagery indeed constructs the narrative, in much the same way as I viewed the scene metaphorically above, by setting up the scene as a metaphor for marriage as absurd warfare. The opening scene of *Bagdad Café* works quite strongly both with and against narrative. It seems to me that here the image in its excess subverts the very narrative structures it helps to construct: the strangeness of the imagery constructs a meaning but simultaneously undermines a neat narrative. If this is the case, then it appears that the visual can in itself be a subversive force.

As mentioned before, the affective force of the visual resides in the excess or obtuse meaning of the image. The end of the opening sequence is a good example of the emotional effects upon the viewer. The scene ends with the last credits superimposed on images of Jasmin walking down the road alone in the vast desert. The long shots in wide angle present her as a lonely figure. The images are slowed down during the credits. When they take up their normal speed again, the image suddenly explodes in a yellow dazzling light. After a few shots of the sky and of Jasmin looking at it, there is a close-up of a rather anxious looking Jasmin, hot, wiping her face, looking at us. On both sides of her head, she is surrounded by a formation of light in the sky (a recurring image in the film to which I will return later). After the last mention of credits, the image becomes dazzlingly white in a strange way. Jasmin takes a deep breath.

Speed, angle and lighting constitute an excess of the visual, aligning our sympathies with Jasmin. No more giggles at her extraordinary figure, but rather a feeling of compassion with her loneliness in those strange and almost threatening surroundings. The music, too, plays an important role in evoking feelings of forlornness. The play of light remains strange. There is no way to understand this yet (it takes on a specific meaning later in the film). Here, it merely alerts the spectator that things happen around Jasmin; even the skies shift.

The visual excess of the short opening sequence as a whole, then, produces the effect of ridiculing conventional relations between husband and wife, while favouring the woman. As such, the rhetoric of the image can take on a feminist meaning. Before exploring the potential of visual style for a feminist rhetoric, however, I will briefly discuss a more ambivalent way in which excessive imagery is put to use in *Bagdad Café*.

After Jasmin has walked out on her husband, she arrives sweating and puffing at the Bagdad Café, a decrepit gas and oil station and motel, where the owner Brenda has just thrown out her husband. The two women eye each other suspiciously: Brenda, black, lean and scruffy, wiping the tears from her face; Jasmin, white, fat and smug, wiping the sweat from her face. Here, in the middle of nowhere, Jasmin Münchgestettner takes a room. Not used to customers in this deserted place, Brenda feels exasperated by this plain woman who silently moves about in weird clothes (Jasmin had accidentally taken her husband's suitcase with her). Brenda's suspicion of Jasmin echoes Jasmin's fear of Brenda, which we witness in a short fantasy Jasmin has. Jasmin's fantasies are interspersed throughout the film, representing her fears and desires. The fantasies can be analyzed in the same terms as Magda's hallucinations in *Dust*; as modalized ocularization (see Chapter 3). The film thus privileges Jasmin's point of view and constructs her subjectivity. When Jasmin first meets Brenda in the office she get lost and drowned in Brenda's dark eyes. The close-up of Brenda's eye gives way to Jasmin's fantasy in which she is cooked naked in a cauldron while black people chant and dance around the fire. Brenda's voice brings her back to reality.

I first understood this racist stereotype to be a comment on Jasmin's bigotry and fear of black people; a prejudice and fear that she gradually overcomes by befriending Brenda. The excess of the image, in its grotesque representation of a hackneyed image of Africa in the western white imaginary, functions to undermine the very stereotype it produces. Together with the highly stereotyped image of Jasmin herself as the prim and proper German housewife, obsessed with cleanliness and hence forever cleaning even the most absurd things like the gas tank on the roof, I read this fantasy as a comment on white racism, especially on German racism.

However, a classroom experience forced me to reflect upon the fundamental ambivalence of the image and hence a possible different reading of the fantasy. In teaching a mixed class of mostly African, Asian and Latin American, as well as some European students at the Institute of Social Studies in the Hague, it became clear to me that the stereotype of Germanness may be lost on spectators from outside Europe, in which case the stark racism of the image becomes offensive. The difference in reception of this particular scene was indeed completely binarized: the black[10] students were outraged and offended at the blatantly racist representation of blacks as primitive cannibals while the white students invariably laughed at the scene and understood it to be a vitriolic commentary on German racism.

The dissymetrical interpretations of the fantasy point to a fundamental ambivalence of the image; without context or experience it is impossible to settle upon a particular interpretation. Awareness of cultural context and 'situated knowledge' (the term is Donna Haraway's, 1991) are therefore necessary elements in the production of meaning. Rather than resolving ambivalence and privileging a certain reading, it may be more productive to maintain certain tensions. What I have learned from the black students is to acknowledge my own 'partial perspective' (Haraway 1991) in the process of giving meaning to this fantasy scene in *Bagdad Café*. In the following section I will explore the excess of the image in its context and from my own partial perspective.

The body beautiful

In the opening scene discussed earlier we have seen how visual representation can be deployed for a feminist rhetoric. With that potential in mind, I will now turn to a series of scenes which is concentrated around a conventional conjunction of woman and visuality, in order to assess how visual excess works there.

How can the image of a woman posing naked for a male painter, and for the camera, dispel the stereotype that the female nude has become in art and film? I will argue that this is the case in *Bagdad Café*, where Jasmin poses for a male painter. In the following section I will analyze how this traditional scene is subverted and structures of looking are altered. The posing scenes take place in the second half of *Bagdad Café*. They form part of a long sequence in which Jasmin gets accepted by the small community inhabiting the Café. Rudi Cox, a rather eccentric but kind elderly man 'from Hollywood', becomes fascinated by Jasmin's face. In several shots there is an extensive play of light on her face. First a golden light from a lamp gives her an aureole of light around her head, then rays of sun illuminate her as if she radiates from within. Captivated, Rudi asks permission to paint Jasmin. The excess of the image is effectuated here in the lighting and its effect sets the fascination up as the key scene of western painting.

The sequence of Jasmin's success in Bagdad Café is a montage of two parallel narratives: scenes in which Jasmin poses for the paintings in increasing degrees of nudity; and scenes in the Café at night where Jasmin performs tricks learned from a magician's kit she has found in her husband's suitcase. The sequence begins with a painting scene and culminates in a huge success for Jasmin and Brenda's show. Then, however, the sheriff pays a visit to the Café, informing the audience that Jasmin's tourist visa has expired and that she consequently has to return to Germany. In between these two narratives, shots are inserted of the landscape in the red and purple light of the setting sun and of a hiker throwing a boomerang through the air; the boomerang becomes a metaphor for friendship and reciprocity throughout the film.

The posing scenes, seven in all, are thus edited parallel to scenes in and around the Café. The whole sequence lasts about twelve minutes, of which the painting scenes make up approximately three minutes. The scenes in which Jasmin poses for Rudi entertain a relationship of tension with, and to some extent obviously take part of a conventional tradition of the female nude in western art. The question becomes pertinent how the film succeeds in countering the conventions of voyeurism, how it changes the story of vision. In order to understand how this works in the film I will first analyze the scenes according to the ways in which they deconstruct the look, before I come back to the status of the image.

Except for the last posing scene, Jasmin always takes up the same position: she sits straight upon a sofa, each time holding a different fruit in one hand, with a painting of fruits in the background. What changes are her clothes and her hairdo. In the first shot Jasmin poses primly in her Bavarian suit, with ridiculous bag and hat, uncomfortably holding up an egg in one hand. This image represents her as totally other, as the weird tourist from a faraway country. Within the narrative sequence it is after the first painting that Brenda apologises to Jasmin for her bad temper. That same night in the Café Jasmin starts her magic show, conjuring up a flower which she gives to Brenda: the friendship between Jasmin and Brenda begins similarly to flower.

In the subsequent posing scenes with Rudi, Jasmin gradually shows more of her body and lets her hair down. She wears a very decent white petticoat or a corset showing under the Bavarian suit. The fruits become bigger and more colourful. The first four posing scenes are short: between ten and twenty seconds. The formal arrangement remains more or less the same throughout the scenes. Each scene starts with a shot of the back of a painting on which Rudi is working, with a number on it (I to VIII), after which there is a cut to Jasmin. The scenes consist of two types of shots: a middle long shot of Rudi painting and a middle long shot of Jasmin posing. The number of shots is equally distributed between them, but the fewer clothes Jasmin wears the shorter the shots of her become. They have not talked, yet it is clear there is a growing rapport between them. He looks beatifically happy painting away, she slowly relaxes and finally even smiles.

The fifth posing scene is lengthier (seventy-five seconds). The scene starts again with Rudi painting. In a short shot we see Jasmin in her corset holding up an erotic looking orange fruit. The camera does not linger on her body, but cuts back to Rudi who shows her (and the spectator) the previous painting of Jasmin also in her corset, in her hand an orange fruit split open. She is painted with a halo of light around her head. Jasmin sees a little detail in Rudi's signature which visibly moves her.

What she sees is a symbol of the formation of light in the sky that surrounded her after she had left her husband in the desert; the strange light in the beginning of the film. She saw it again when she entered her room at the motel of Bagdad Café and went straight for (Rudi's) painting of that particular sky. She then had a short vision in which the sky in the painting moved and lighted up. When Jasmin recognizes this particular play of light in Rudi's painting of her, she emotionally whispers 'my vision'. She then closes her eyes and very, very slowly pulls down a strap of the corset, baring one big breast. Rudi continues to paint in silence until he says: 'I like that word - vision'.

The scene takes place in an atmosphere that I would describe as reverential. The respect and care with which Jasmin is painted as well as filmed precludes the potential voyeurism of the spectacle. Jasmin is not the passive object of a male gaze, first of all on the narrative level because with her tentative gesture of denuding herself she takes the initiative. On the level of the image this works similarly: because of the silence and the resonating images of her vision, she seems to bestow honour on the spectator by offering the vision of her body through her own vision. The viewer receives the sight of her body as a gift. The scene is by no means desexualized; the corset, the vulva-like shaped fruits and the slow baring of her breast charge the scene with eroticism. Jasmin has changed from a fat conventional German housewife into a beautiful erotic woman.

Witnessing Jasmin's feelings, from discomfort in the beginning to deep emotion when she recognizes her vision in the paintings, the spectator tends to identify with her. An empathy that is strengthened in the parallel scenes of the success and mastery of her 'magic' performance in the Café. Touching on different aspects of 'vision', the scene transforms conventional relations of looking. Watching has become a 'visionary' act instead of a voyeuristic one. To me this particular scene demonstrates that it is possible to change the hackneyed image of a man painting and a half-naked woman posing, playing on voyeuristic ways of seeing and fetishistic representation. In the posing scenes in *Bagdad Café* the spectator is aware of watching and thus also of the erotic pleasure of looking, to which Jasmin consents and in which she participates with pleasure. We as spectators become 'visionaries'.

I have mentioned that Rudi as well as the camera treat Jasmin with respect and care. The character of Rudi is an unorthodox male subject.

His behaviour is puzzling but seductive; he is funny and humorous. Instead of covering up his insecurity with aggression he translates his careful behaviour in playful politeness, retreating as soon as he feels weak or unwanted. In *Bagdad Café* Rudi is repeatedly presented as being vulnerable to Jasmin's rejection. This happens also in the posing scenes. It is unusual in the cinematic play of male look and display of female body to represent the male subject as vulnerable. I want to suggest that in changing the spectacle of the female body, by implication, the male look is modified as well. I recall how in *Cruel Embrace* the half-witted boy Ludo was excluded from the power of the gaze and punished for his desires.

In my analysis there I referred to Silverman's differentiation between the gaze and the look; the former as the carrier of symbolic law and the latter as the carrier of desire and lack. In *Bagdad Café* Rudi is shown to feel desire for Jasmin, but the camera does not attach itself to his desiring look nor does Rudi respond to his desired object with any gesture of appropriation. Rudi's desire is fully negotiated through lack. Thus he remains vulnerable in his desire for Jasmin. In other words, in *Bagdad Café* the male look cannot pass itself off as the gaze and hence remains outside power and control. Therefore, the identity of the male subject can no longer be confirmed but is fully dependent upon the female subject's consent. In very different ways, those two films demonstrate male desire to be fragile when unaccompanied by the violence of the appropriating gaze. They both denaturalize the deceptive identification of gaze and look.

The male look is further disarmed on yet another level: the film makes a spectacle, not of the woman, but of the conventional scene of a nude-woman-posing-for-a-male-painter. The act of painting becomes a scene in itself. Representation is shown to be an act which requires hard work and dedication. By starting each posing scene with a shot of Rudi painting, the film emphasizes the labour of representation, affirmed by the array of paintings strewn around the room. The lack of transparency in this film makes the spectator aware of her or his own act of looking. And this, according to Bal, 'entails the awareness that what one sees is a representation, not an objective reality, not the "real thing"' (1991: 142). Verisimilitude being so inextricably bound up with the medium of cinema, it is of paramount importance to make the spectator aware of the cinematic work of representation involved in imaging the female body, as is the case in these posing scenes in *Bagdad Café*.

The posing scenes, then, discourage the viewing attitude of the voyeuristic look and invite the viewing mode of an engaged look. This mode offers an alternative to 'the male gaze' modifying but not cancelling out visual pleasure. However much the voyeuristic look may be deconstructed, the self-conscious, involved look is fully within desire. But the desire it arouses and sustains is different, because Jasmin's 'directing' the look makes the spectator aware of it, blocking the urge to appropriate.

Let me return to the film now and see how the posing scenes progress. Jasmin next poses with naked breasts holding both her hands in front of them. While painting, Rudi speaks passionately in a strange language. Jasmin withdraws her hands and conjures up a rose, saying 'magic' with a smile. Again in this scene, the film concentrates more on Rudi's act of painting than on Jasmin's body (respectively thirty-two and eleven seconds). Finally, in the last posing scene Jasmin's position is changed. After the initial shot of Rudi working on painting number VIII, the camera moves from one of Jasmin's feet lying on the bed to the other dangling in the air with feminine pink slippers on. The spectator can infer she is apparently lying naked on the bed. Then there is a cut to the finished painting of Jasmin in this posture, lying on her stomach, eating a strawberry, again with an aureole around her head. The camera follows her naked body on the painting in a conventional glide. Our view of the painting is twice obstructed by a curtain blowing in front of it.

The film gives the spectator full view of Jasmin's naked body only in the painting, that is, as a representation. The representation of the female nude here takes on a different meaning from the conventional voyeuristic one, because by this point in the film the naked woman in question is no longer an object, a woman on display. She has instead acquired subjectivity in the eyes of the people within the diegesis of the film and (presumably) in the eyes of the spectator. The gradual change and transformation of Jasmin throughout the film is echoed in the series of painting scenes. By the time that Jasmin is represented as an image, she has become one of the family with the people living in Bagdad Café, her magic show has proved a tremendous success, and she and Brenda have established a friendship. The look of the spectator will therefore be engaged with the character of Jasmin.

The posing scenes obviously relate to the traditional structure of a striptease, from being fully dressed as a Bavarian housewife to being virtually naked lying on a sofa. Yet the film does not build quick erotic tension connected to the surface of the female body culminating in the familiar erotic spectacle, because the imagery is bound up with narrative. By integrating the painting scenes in a narrative of change and transformation, *Bagdad Café* has succeeded in presenting a fat woman as beautiful and erotic, while breaking through the conventional representation of woman-as-spectacle. Jasmin does not 'tease' the spectator but herself. The 'striptease' signifies an inner transformation. With each layer she loses more stiffness and uptightness, changing gradually into a pretty woman full of warmth and humour. In taking off her clothes Jasmin lays off cultural meanings that codify her as ugly and unattractive. She reveals her fat body as desirable. When the woman has come into her own, when she has become a subject, a representation of her body can no longer work to deprive her of subjectivity. As an object of beauty Jasmin may inspire desire, but she will also compel respect and love.

The final painted image of Jasmin, in all her splendid nudity, has very much the effect that Lacan ascribes optimistically to painting in general: 'Something is given not so much to the gaze as to the eye, something that involves the abandonment, the *laying down*, of the gaze' (Lacan 1981: 101). The deconstruction of the gaze is effected by drawing attention to the process of image-making itself. In this respect *Bagdad Café* resembles women's films of the 1980s which, as Mayne (1990) has argued, form a feminist tradition in spotlighting the relationship between women and (cinematic) representation.[11] In presenting the image of Jasmin fully naked on the screen as a painting, her image functions simultaneously as surface and as frame, cancelling out the illusive transparency of the image. According to Mayne recent women's cinema explores this ambivalence of the screen. In *Bagdad Café* the ambivalent functions of the image/screen are put to play in such a way as to subvert conventional representations of women. Jasmin is very much 'the female subject [who] is both complicit with the fictions of patriarchy and resistant to them' (Mayne 1990: 85).

The notion of ambivalence, however, falls short of fully apprehending what is at stake in the imaginary field of representation. In his writings on the gaze in psychoanalysis, Lacan asserts that the scopic field is always already shot through with ambivalence: 'We find here once again the ambiguity that affects anything that is inscribed in the register of the scopic drive' (1981: 83). For an understanding of the fundamental ambivalence of the gaze, I think it is helpful briefly to take a closer look at the Lacanian understanding of the gaze.

Situated at the 'underside of consciousness' (83), the gaze is shot through with illusion and *méconnaissance*, the ill-fated misrecognition of the ego in the mirror, or here, in the gaze of the Other. Lacan uses the metaphor of the scotoma: the gaze is a blind spot in the field of vision. We can never see or encounter the gaze, we can only imagine it and we always imagine the gaze in the field of the Other (84). The gaze is thus illusory in its very function of 'seeingness' (82). Lacan actually ascribes an almost divine omniscience to the gaze, a quality of 'all-seeing'. This all-seeing function of the gaze gives us the impression 'that we are beings who are looked at, in the spectacle of the world'.[12] In other words, the gaze is the experience of being seen by the Other.

Inspired by Silverman's reading of Lacan (1992), I want to introduce the notion of agency rather than dwelling on ambivalence. This will also bring me back to the image or screen. The concept of the gaze as 'seeingness' in the field of the Other radically dismisses any notion of a self-present agency. Lacan (1981) situates the only possible agency for the subject in a play with the screen. The subject maps her- or himself within the scopic regime of the symbolic through the mediation of the screen, which for Lacan is like a play with masks. The agency that Lacan grants us is to put our masks, doubles, images, in place. Or, perhaps in a more postmodern mode, to put them into play. Thus, for Lacan, the human subject has the possibility of playing with the gaze by manipulating the screen. But what exactly is this screen?

In Lacan's diagram of the scopic register the screen collapses with the image (Lacan 1981: 106). Because the image is the psychoanalytic (or cinematic, for that matter) location of the screen, Silverman interprets the screen as cultural representation: 'by "screen" [Lacan] in fact means the image or group of images through which identity is constituted' (1992: 149). Human interaction takes place at the level of the screen; it is an interchange of the images that we have of the other and that we present of ourselves. This reading of Lacan suggests that feminist agency in cinema will be more effective in transforming cultural images and representations than in changing the economy of the gaze.

If we understand, with Silverman, the screen as cultural representation, we can begin to appreciate the subversive force of the visual. *Bagdad Café* plays with the gaze by extensively setting up a scene of painting; on the cinematic screen the image of a woman is part of a process of producing a cultural representation of that woman. Jasmin's agency consists in mediating the screen, making a spectacle of the 'woman-as-spectacle', thus giving the lie to the 'male look'. Her agency lies precisely in the play between her complicity and her resistance when posing for Rudi. Interestingly, Lacan has compared the gaze to the woman-as-spectacle:

this all-seeing aspect [of the gaze; AS] is to be found in the satisfaction of a woman who knows that she is being looked at, on condition that one does not show her that one knows that she knows.

The world is all-seeing, but it is not exhibitionistic – it does not provoke our gaze. When it begins to provoke it, the feeling of strangeness begins too.

(Lacan 1981: 75)

For Silverman this passage has 'staggering implications for film theory', in that the subject is generally both spectator (seeing) and spectacle (being seen), both subject and object (1992: 151). The subject is thus split and divided in her- or himself, rather than binarized as either spectator or spectacle. Although I find myself in agreement with Silverman's observation and subscribe to the political importance of overcoming neat binarizations, I want to emphasize some of the gender implications of Lacan's analogy.

First of all, as I have argued in Chapter 3, the male look can only function by virtue of the construction of woman as spectacle. 'Woman-as-spectacle' is nothing but the flipside of 'the male look'. Lacan's analogy of the gaze with woman as spectacle is hardly surprising or innovative, because it describes a current state as fully within the cultural bind of sexual difference, understood as an asymmetrical power relation. Secondly, Lacan sets the female subject up as being the gaze, in very much the same way as she 'is' the phallus. It may be opportune here to recall the Lacanian juggling with the phallus; a play of being, having and seeming (Lacan 1977). Nobody can really be or have the phallus. The male subject is, however, privileged in seeming to have the phallus. The female subject, in lacking the phallus, cannot seem to have the phallus, but she can seem to be the phallus. She masquerades as the phallus. Similarly, nobody owns the gaze, but the male subject can seem to have the gaze in passing off his look as the gaze ('the male look both transfers its own lack to the female subject, and attempts to pass itself off as the gaze'; Silverman 1992: 144). In the passage quoted above, Lacan positions the female subject within a masquerade to be the gaze. The conditions of the masquerade ('one does not show her that one knows that she knows') illuminate the social contract that binds the female subject to her position within the masculinist symbolic: on no condition can she let down her veil and betray her masquerade, thus exposing the phallus – and the gaze – to be 'a fraud' (Mitchell and Rose 1982: 80), and relations between the sexes 'a comedy' (Lacan 1977: 289).

The agency that the female subject can then exert is to refuse to masquerade her knowledge any longer, that is, to unveil the phallus or elicit the gaze. For Lacan this sheer provocation is rather uncanny: 'When it [woman-as-spectacle] begins to provoke it [the gaze] the feeling of strangeness begins too' (1981: 75). Indeed, if the female subject undoes the binds of the social contract, undermining the symbolic law of the phallus and the gaze, the male subject is bound to feel 'strange'. It seems to me that this is the reason why female exhibitionism unsettles.[13]

Returning to *Bagdad Café*, we can now see that the posing and painting sequence cuts through the masquerade, exhibits woman-as-spectacle and provokes the gaze. Jasmin knows. Rudi knows. So does the spectator. And, yes, it does feel a little strange. The feeling of strangeness is, however, sutured over and kept at bay by two closely connected characteristics which engage a different kind of visual pleasure than the conventional voyeuristic one: humour and excess. The humour is subtle and defused, for example, through the preposterous Bavarian costume, the magic flower, and the formal similarity of the images and scenes. The excessive imagery also makes up for some of the humour of this sequence. The excess here lies in repetition (seven times a posing scene), in progression entailing narrative (increasing degrees of nudity), in exaggeration (paintings everywhere), in bright colours and in striking lighting, in salient fruits, and, of course, in the excessive body of Jasmin herself. So far I have not focused on the most obvious way in which the film succeeds in subverting the cliché of the posing nude: by breaking a taboo – the woman is fat.[14]

The fact that the female body here does not comply with western ideals of white female beauty unsettles the spectator in making her or him acutely aware of the scene s/he is watching: a fat woman posing for a painter. This shows us how much voyeurism is based on the stereotyped beauty of the female body. Conventional beauty solicits the look, whereas what is coded as 'ugliness' draws attention to the work of representation. By imaging the female body differently, *Bagdad Café* breaks with traditional representations that deprive women of their own bodies. Where 'the body beautiful' functions as an iconic sign for female sexuality in dominant systems of representation, the female body that is different from the norm does not function as a signifier but attracts attention to itself as body. Thus Jasmin's corporeality is foregrounded.

The actual embodiment of the female body is, in fact, exceptional in conventional cultural representations. In order to be able to deconstruct the repertoire of cultural representations of 'Woman', it is crucial to insist upon the social and historical status of the image. The endlessly repeated reproduction of woman-as-spectacle in our culture deprives social and historical women of their bodies, while that very system of representation paradoxically condemns 'Woman' to her body and nothing but her body. The overwhelming presence of the female body at the level of the image merely signifies its absence within the symbolic order. In order to ensure the empty space of 'Woman', the image of the female body has to abstract from any characteristics that might subjectivize or embody the female subject. The cultural representation of woman-as-spectacle, therefore, will always strive to veil signs of age, class, nationality and race. Hence the highly conventionalized stereo-type of white female beauty. In a certain sense, 'the body beautiful' even abstracts from sexual difference in the Irigarayan sense: in masculinist culture the female body does not signify sexual identity, but only its differential function as femininity vis-à-vis the male sub-ject. In other words, the western stereotype of female beauty bears no relation to female subjectivity but merely signifies male conceptions and representations of white femininity.

Bagdad Café defies this tradition of representing 'Woman' by imaging a female body that is fat. In Jasmin, the film instead gives the woman her body back. Jasmin's body becomes flesh. Her being embodied gives Jasmin subjectivity, and she is hence positioned as having a gender (female), a nationality (German), an age (forties), an ethnicity (white), and belonging to a class (lower middle class). Jasmin's fat female body, in all its excess, is also no longer represented as quintessentially trans-gressive – as Hollywood tradition would have it – but as 'the site of . . . desirous excess' (Russo 1994: 67). In excess of the conven-tional 'body beautiful', Jasmin's body acquires its erotic beauty through, precisely, its excess: her obesity.[15] This is why in *Bagdad Café* the image of what in contemporary cinema is considered 'ugly' creates a specific eroticism beyond the conventional representations of the female body; the erotic image becomes what de Lauretis calls de-aesthetic (1987: 146).

The image-as-excess, then, subverts the very thing it represents; in this case the female nude. The de-aestheticization of the female body has of course been a major issue in feminist cinema engaged as it is in the process of deconstructing the male gaze and the woman as erotic spectacle, more often than not resulting in the destruction of visual pleasure. *Bagdad Café* does not merely deconstruct or destroy but re-deploys pleasure and desire in its subversion of the image through its light touch of humour and its bold excess and thus actualizes Irigarayan mimesis: it consumes a myth of femininity by setting up the woman-as-spectacle. But in the mimetic repetition lies a turn and a twist; the excess which makes all the difference.

THE GOTHIC IMAGE

In *Bagdad Café* the violent disharmony of the beginning yields to harmony, expressed in a cinematic form which in the end becomes calmer and smoother. The excessive image is only retained in colouring, lighting and mise-en-scène. 'Too much harmony'; not only for one of the permanent guests of Bagdad Café, Debbie, who walks out of the motel leaving the community for good, but probably also for some spectators who may find the spectacle of boundless friendship and happiness hard to take. Yet, *Bagdad Café* has a subtle twist in the end. Jasmin has returned from Germany. She and Brenda are shown to be overjoyed with their friendship.

Just as the posing scenes comment on and transform the traditional aesthetic use of women's bodies, so is the final scene an ironic comment upon the romantic happy ending of Hollywood movies. Building on audience expectation, the film carefully constructs a scene in which Jasmin replies with a tentative 'yes' to all the questions Rudi asks her, to and including his offer of marriage. When the spectator expects the final 'yes', Jasmin hesitates a second and then replies with a little smile: 'I'll talk it over with Brenda'. With refined humour the film thus privileges until the very end female friendship over heterosexual romance.[16]

Where in *Bagdad Café* Jasmin's magic changes the life of the community into wholesome harmony, in *Sweetie* (Jane Campion 1989) magical thinking of the main character Kay cannot avert immanent danger and disaster from family life. What connects these otherwise very different films is the excessive visual style. Imagery in *Sweetie* is excessive in its highly artificial construction. Nothing ever looks normal or predictable. The consistent use of wide angle, deep focus and special lighting render every image strange throughout the film. The effect is again a subtle *Verfremdung*: the everyday world of houses, gardens and streets looks unfamiliar, almost hostile to the people who take up awkward positions within the space they occupy. Although the strangeness of the images has a mildly humouristic effect, the (rather black) humour is definitely undercut by a feeling of *Unheimlichkeit*. And indeed, the crisis in *Sweetie* is situated within the family and home (*Heim*). *Sweetie* tells a story about a family: Kay who lives with her boyfriend Louis in a suburban house in some Australian city. Their paradisaical life is disturbed one day by the arrival of Kay's unruly sister Dawn, nicknamed Sweetie, accompanied by her junkie lover who claims to be her manager. Later their father, temporarily abandoned by his wife, joins them. A trip into the wild Australian outback re-unites the parents, but back home Sweetie's maladjusted behaviour leads to her own death.

The film shows us the emotional life and relations of Kay and her family, who are caught in a complex network of false illusions and odd obsessions. The bizarre style converges with the irrational behav-iour of the characters, creating a psychical reality that remains far re-moved from psychological realism. The cinematic form of *Sweetie* flawlessly catches the moods of the characters by deviating from Hol-lywood cinematic conventions of the camera-of-the-middle and seam-less editing. The film's persistent use of long shots and wide angle, unusual framing, strange *mise-en-scène* and unpredictable camera work builds up a quality of the image that in all its artificiality can be de-scribed as the image-as-excess. These images construct a fragmented narrative that moves along in fits and starts. Again, the excessive im-agery subverts the very narrative it constructs. In its singular style, *Sweetie* shows the subversive potential of the visual.

The uncanny effects of the cinematic style are so strong in *Sweetie* that they often become grotesque. Anna Johnson (1991) describes this particular quality of the imagery in *Sweetie* as gothic. She argues that Campion's gothic style forms part of an Australian art tradition of representing suburbia, traversing from critique and kitsch in the 1970s and 1980s to the more ambiguous representations of menace and per-versity more recently. *Sweetie* never comes close to the horror of evil suburbia in American films (e.g. David Lynch's *Blue Velvet*, to which it has frequently been compared; Johnson 1991: 134–5). Instead it fo-cuses on the stifling home life: 'the claustrophobia of Campion's cinema-tography creates an inescapable atmosphere' (136). The move away from the sensationalist imagery of storms, cliffs and ruins in 18th-century Gothic, to a focus on the cramped space of the domestic interior appears to be connected to Kay's narrative perspective. To tell the family story from a female point of view highlights the threat and oppression of domestic life. It also features a familial relationship which is so often neglected in western discourse, be it fictional or psycho-analytic: the relation between sisters.[17]

The film can be seen as a feminist recasting of the genre of the

Gothic, traditionally a female genre in 18th-century literature. Tania Modleski has argued that Gothics are attractive to women writers, even 'avowed feminists', because: 'Gothics probe the deepest layers of the feminine unconscious, providing a way for women to work through profound psychic conflicts, especially ambivalence towards the significant people in their lives – mothers, fathers, lovers' (Modleski 1984: 83). *Sweetie* rewrites the Gothic genre by focusing on the relationship between sisters instead. It is through the figure of the sister that the frightening aspects of oedipal and love relations are examined. Campion has carefully avoided psychological drama; in privileging excessive imagery over closure and realist narrative she has created a psychic realm where the distinction between imagination and reality, between normal and abnormal, is suspended. Within this universe of madness *Sweetie* shows the *Unheimlichkeit* of the nuclear family. The oedipal narrative has become a gothic story of sound and fury, told by a woman.

The film introduces the spectator directly, with a bit of a shock, to Kay's magical if not animistic view of life, when she resolutely seduces Louis (who has just become engaged to another girl), because she recognizes in his face a sign that was predicted by a fortune teller, namely a question mark on his forehead. For thirteen months they live happily together 'somewhere near the top of spiritual planes', as Kay says in voice-over, when Louis plants a little tree as a symbol of their love in their unbelievably ugly concrete backyard. That same night, Kay, who is mortally afraid of trees, tears out the little tree, root and all.

Trees are the most consistent gothic image throughout the film. Kay's morbid fear of trees has already been expressed in the opening image of the film, when Kay is lying on her bed and tells in voice-over:

Dad built a palace in the branches, she was the princess, it was her tree. I'm afraid someone stands behind a tree watching me, wishing me harm. At night the darkness frightens me. I used to imagine the roots of that tree crawling right under the house, right under my bed. Trees have hidden powers.

Kay imagines the underground roots of trees to spread silently and to crawl like snakes; their hidden powers are suggested to be evil. The monologue betrays an intimate connection between 'she', whom we later understand to be Sweetie, and the uncanny qualities of trees. In the next shot Kay walks fearfully through the suburb, the camera focusing on the surface of the street as if any moment roots of trees could break through the pavement. Kay stops at the house of the fortune teller, which is strangely overgrown with foliage. Gothic tree imagery recurs later in the film, when tree branches cast eerie shadows in Kay's bedroom and in her car at night.

In order to prevent Louis' small plant from becoming an omen and out of fear it will unsettle her life, Kay has to uproot it after a nightmarish vision which presents an uncanny effect of plants. In representing her inner mind the dream is a modualized ocularization, strengthening the prominence of Kay's subjectivity at the discursive level of the film. The short vision shot in black and white starts and ends with an image of pure black. A microscopic image shows small seeds growing, uprooting blocks of earth as the sprouts break through. A threatening sound of wind and of cracking noises accompanies the images. Hands plant Louis' little tree. Microscopic and accelerated images show the shoots growing fast into the air. In a shot from above the stiff sprouts look almost obscene as they develop into small plants. A close-up of two men shaking hands blocks our view of two women dimly discernible in the background. In the next shot the two men with hats and a stick in between them are filmed in close-up from below, in such a way that the image mostly shows the sky. In the final shot the camera decentres the men, who now look like gravediggers, to the right side of the image, where they stand with shovels and Louis' small plant in between them, the rest of the image remaining white and empty. The men look at us with silly grins on their faces. After a few seconds of black, Kay appears in the image in extreme close-up, with harsh light giving her face a silvery lining in the dark of the night. The colour has returned to the image, but the threatening sounds continue and grow stronger. Breathing heavily, Kay walks to the plant and with a gasp tears it out. At that moment all sounds stop.

Sweetie represents organic growth in truly gothic imagery, opposing the menace of uncontrolled plant life to the sterile suffocation of suburban living. Kay's dream or fantasy represents her fear of reproduction and of her own sexuality. It also presents life and death as a cycle or a continuum, which she cannot accept. The uprooting effect that Kay ascribes to trees, is reminiscent of Freud's tentative description of the uncanny as something 'that ought to have remained secret and hidden but has come to light' (*SE*, XVII: 225). In her effort to prevent these 'hidden powers' of roots from making an appearance in broad daylight Kay kills the whole plant. It does not seem farfetched to say that with her magical thinking she tries to allay the hidden powers of her unconscious from emerging. Yet, in trying to keep the unconscious 'under' as it were, she stops the process of life. Growth is then no longer possible, as is indicated in her vision which equates the planting of a tree with burying the dead.

Considering the above, it comes as no surprise that the relationship between Kay and Louis soon begins to show signs of wear. They are no longer happy, their sexual life is hampered and they start sleeping separately. The disharmony is represented within the cinematic image. For example, when Kay and Louis make an appointment to make love – and fail – the scene is filmed as follows. The camera is placed in the corridor, filming obliquely through the open door of the bedroom. With three-quarters of the image black (where the view is blocked by wall and door), we see the couple in an odd angle and from a relative distance getting undressed and lying naked next to each other on the bed. In the next shot, the camera is positioned in front of the door opening, still filming through the door, with much of the image receding in blackness, also due to lighting effects. Without having had sex, Kay sits on the bed and says it feels too much like making love to a brother. They get dressed again. The alienating distance, the gloomy darkness, the cold lighting and the unsettling camera angle turn this 'sex scene' into quite a depressing and even uncanny event.

Dead ringer

The displacement of Kay's fear of her sister Sweetie onto trees is demonstrated in another short fantasy. When Kay tries meditation in a class (following Louis who is a stern meditator), she obstinately refuses to believe it will give her calm. Snapping at the teacher that she 'won't feel any quiet anyway', she finally closes her eyes and has a short vision. The first image shows the teacher in negative colouring, followed by five shots of food on a plate. While the voice of the teacher, saying slowly how to relax, fades away, noisy sounds and voices of children get louder and louder. Images of Louis' forehead and a question mark give way to branches in the dark. A girl's feet dance on a carpet with a flower pattern, followed in quick succession by flickering images of a door opening into the room, of feet dancing on a drain, of the girl's feet, her distorted shadow on the wall as she dances. These images are very short and shot from an extremely low camera angle on the floor. The lighting creates threatening shadows. Finally the camera rides quickly over the ground into the foot of a tree, zooming in on the dark hollow between the roots until the image is totally black. Kay opens her eyes; in a lengthy close-up we look into her staring eyes.

Kay may have succeeded in keeping plant life – and with it her own sexuality – suppressed, she cannot prevent her sister from breaking into her consciousness: the little girl who dances in her fantasy. That night Kay witnesses the return of the repressed: her sister Dawn, alias Sweetie, breaks into the house. Sweetie and her boyfriend uproot the painstaking order of Kay's bourgeois existence. Kay fails to get Sweetie out of her house. From her reactions we understand this has happened many times before and Kay is therefore quite desperate. Even more so, because she knows Sweetie to be 'evil' and is afraid of the harm she will do. Her helpnessness concerning this fate together with her fear of Sweetie's secret intention to do harm, are both aspects that Freud discusses in his account of the uncanny. For Freud, the phenomenon of repetition 'recalls the sense of helplessness experienced in some dream-states' (*SE*, XVII: 237). He explains the dread of evil as a projected state of envy: 'What is feared is thus a secret intention of doing harm' (240). Kay believes Sweetie to be envious of her and is afraid Sweetie will act out of jealousy and do her harm.

It is not only Kay who experiences uncanny feelings; so does the spectator. Like most of the camera work inside the house, the camera is placed at a considerable distance from the figures, obstructing our view with walls and doors, blacking out large parts of the image. The part of the frame that remains visible is lighted in stark constrast to the darkness. The unusual camera perspectives, often from a very low angle, show yards of carpet, wallpaper or ceiling before focusing on bodily parts or objects, thus producing an image in which people are at odds with their surroundings. The home which should be a place of safety does not look familiar but strange and even hostile. The way in which cinematic representation generates uncanny imagery in *Sweetie*, is not unlike the way in which 'Gothics can present us with the frighteningly familiar precisely because they make the familiar strange' (Modleski 1984: 20).

Campion's visual style creates the atmosphere of claustrophobia to which I referred earlier. The spectator enters these cramped interior spaces from an unsettling viewpoint. Interior spaces here refer both to domestic and to fantastic realms; as Johnson puts it: 'Dreamspace, housespace and headspace are collapsed into one' (1991: 138). This complete convergence of inside and outside, is an important aspect of *Sweetie*'s singu-lar style, creating a psychic realm that 'gets under people's skin' (Jane Campion quoted in Johnson 1991: 138). The rhetoric of the image here serves a general effect of the uncanny.

For Kay, Sweetie is an evil and dark spirit, something to be feared, like the hidden powers of trees. Kay's paranoia as well as the uncanny signified and evoked by Sweetie, can be traced back to what Freud calls 'the phenomenon of the "double"' (234). Sweetie functions as a doubling and dividing of Kay's self; she embodies the repressed and distorted aspects of Kay's desires. As Kay's total opposite, fat and punk Sweetie is the figure of everything that the former both desires and represses.

Freud puts forward the idea of the double as an aspect of the retro-spective fantasy of primary narcissism, a fantasy in which a distinction between self and other is beginning to emerge. The double here func-tions as a form of protection for the yet hardly formed ego. In repress-ing this early mental material the double takes on less benign forms, taking the shape of the critical super-ego or of a thing of terror when the ego projects outward all which is unwanted and feared. The figure of the double is uncanny for the subject because it is repressed and projected material. Freud stresses the process of repression which accounts for the uncanny effect: '. . . for this uncanny is in reality nothing new or alien, but something which is familiar and old established in the mind and which has become alienated from it only through the process of repres-sion (*SE*, XVII: 240). Sweetie is familiar, family even, for Kay. She has tried to repress Sweetie's disturbing effects on her life by displacing them onto trees, as we have seen reflected in her fantasies. Thus alienated from her, Sweetie can become an uncanny figure as her double. Sweetie's appearance as the incarnation of the violent return of the repressed, of that which deeply disturbs Kay's life, instills feelings of fear and terror in Kay. From a little dancing princess Sweetie has developed into 'a thing of terror'. The sisters are caught in mutual attraction and rejection; a thwarted relation that is aptly articulated in the uncanny visual style of the film.

Modleski has noted the recurrent theme of the doubling of characters in Gothics written by women. Whereas real mothers are 'conspicuously absent' in Gothics, there is no lack of mother substitutes, who most often function as doubles for the heroine (68). Usually the heroine be-comes obsessed with this other woman, who becomes the recipient of feelings of ambivalence that she fosters for her own mother. If we re-place 'mother' with 'sister', the description of the way in which the Gothic heroines feel about their doubles very much fits Kay's reaction to her sister Sweetie: 'the heroine feels suffocated – as well as desperate and panic stricken in her inability to break free of the past' (70). Kay tries at all cost to prevent her double from collapsing with her self. If we look closer at how Sweetie functions as Kay's double, we see that she continuously violates the boundaries between them. Settling down in Kay's house, Sweetie takes possession of Kay's life, using (and often destroying) her things and her clothes, becoming friends with the neighbour's child and above all interfering with the relationship between Kay and Louis. Sweetie's insatiable need for attention makes her the embodiment of greed and lust. Her abundant sexuality stands in stark contrast with the sexless relationship of Kay and Louis. Louis is sexually aroused when they hear Sweetie and her boyfriend noisily make love. After Sweetie has licked Kay's boyfriend Louis all over his body on the beach, that night Louis wants to lick Kay's feet, who is terrified and angrily rejects him.

Next to fear of repetition, Freud gives fear of castration as a source for the sensation of the uncanny. Modleski speculates that the threat of castration may be understood 'as part of a deeper fear – fear of never developing a sense of autonomy and separateness from the mother' (71). She then argues that the 'unexpected' connection between the two main sources of the uncanny (the fear of repetition and of castration) are 'two aspects of the more primal fear of being lost in the mother' (71). In other words, the experience of the uncanny in Gothics 'has its chief source in separation anxieties', and the figure of the double is one of its main ways of expression. With reference to the psychoanalytic argument of Nancy Chodorow, that it is more difficult for daughters to establish ego boundaries and to separate from their mothers than for sons, Modleski argues convincingly that women's 'sense of the uncanny may actually be stronger than men's' (71). Sweetie functions very much as the double for Kay, from whom she finds it difficult to separate, and to whom she harbours ambivalent feelings of both love and jealousy. The sister can be a figure of even greater envy than the mother, because she is a closer rival for affection of both parents.

I have highlighted Modleski's reading of the double in Gothic literature, because fascination and repulsion for the female figure can be found in another psychic configuration that is closely linked with the uncanny, and that is most certainly represented by Sweetie: the abject.

The Image of Abjection

For Kay things are totally out of control. She does not succeed in getting rid of her sister; the return of the repressed is too strong to simply ward off through the kind of magical thinking that usually helps her out (according to Freud, animism, magic and the omnipotence of thoughts are among the factors that contribute to the experience of the uncanny; *SE*, XVII: 243). Her initial denial that Sweetie is her sister does not get her far either. Kay's feelings of threat, despair and insecurity make her react violently. She has to make Sweetie radically other in order to prevent this double from taking over her life and her self. Initially a configuration of fear, Sweetie soon becomes a figure of disgust. Repression does not work anymore now that Sweetie has materialized in the flesh; Kay has to actively repel and reject her sister. Sweetie is defamiliarized, if not demonized, and becomes the total negative other: she figures as the abject.

Sweetie is a counter-example to Jasmin in *Bagdad Café*, whose fat body becomes sexually desirable and beautiful: Sweetie's fat body remains an image of grotesque excess throughout the film. In her essay on female grotesques Russo raises the question whether the representation of the female body as grotesque 'might be used affirmatively to destabilize the idealizations of female beauty or to realign the mechanisms of desire' (221). This affirmative representation of the female grotesque is definitely put to use in *Bagdad Café* in the endearing figure of Jasmin. Sweetie, however, is a much darker and more ambiguous figure of transgression. The female grotesque in *Sweetie* points in a different direction, that of abjection.

Julia Kristeva (1982) explains the abject as not being an object nor having an object. The abject is the place where meaning collapses. That which signifies an unstable boundary can become abject to the subject. Usually things that are connected to the inside and outside of the body are ab-jected: what can be taken into the body (food); or discharged from the body (vomit, faeces); body fluids like sweat, blood, milk, or pus; a corpse (the border between life and death). The abject is loathed because it confuses the boundaries of the self. It has to be made radically other in order to be excluded and even expelled from the self.

The film represents Sweetie as borderline abject, full of bodily fluids that ooze out of her dirty and fat body: sweat, saliva, urine, blood. With her immoral behaviour she takes on monstrous proportions, crossing all boundaries of decency when she pees and farts in front of her family.[18] Sometimes Sweetie seems hardly human, as when she lapses into straight animal behaviour, barking and biting like a dog, or when she eats small porcelain horses to spite Kay. At the end of the film, Sweetie makes herself into the other of culture, or cultural other, by walking around naked in her parent's garden, covered with mud; a possible reference to Australian Aboriginal rites. As the Aboriginals are the antithesis of suburban Australia, this is another piece of repressed imagery.

Perverse, sinister and cunning, Sweetie closely fits Kristeva's description of the abject as 'What disturbs identity, system, order. What does not respect borders, positions, rules' (1982: 4). Like the uncanny, but much more violent and alien, the abject is an archaic structure that goes back to mental images of primal repression. This can be the threatening territory of animals from which humans have to keep themselves separated (a boundary that Sweetie crosses with her canine behaviour), or the hold of the maternal which has to be rejected when the mother fails to acknowledge the symbolic realm.

We recall how, according to Modleski, the uncanny figure of the double allows women to work through their separation anxieties and their deep ambivalence towards the mother. Like the uncanny, the abject is also a psychic configuration that is related to the figure of the mother. Because the abject marks a struggle for identity and selfhood, Kristeva argues, it should be understood as repressed material dating back to the pre-objectal relationship, to the symbiosis between mother and child. It is directly linked to the 'immemorial violence with which a body becomes separated from another body in order to be' (10). The abject can thus be found at the limit of primal repression: the repression, and abjection, of the maternal body. Psychic processes of abjection are, then, to repel, to reject, to separate; in other words to ab-ject. The abject is 'the violence of mourning for an 'object' that has always already been lost', that is, the maternal body (15). According to Kristeva the struggle for autonomy can only be successful through 'the symbolic light' of the third party, the father.

What throws somebody into a state of abjection is, however, not only incestuous desire for and painful separation from the mother. Kristeva claims that it is mainly brought about by a failure of the paternal metaphor. When the paternal function is absent, weak or otherwise lacking, it produces in Kristeva's words 'this strange configuration' of the abject; that state of someone who cannot establish a relation between subject and object (40). When the oedipal triangle somehow fails, the subject is prevented from finding her or his place; nor can s/he find an object for her or his drives. For Kristeva any warped relationship to the law can only lead to psychosis. Thus, the margins within the symbolic, such as configurations of the abject, are not exactly empowering: the subject who is besieged by abjection, is 'no subject, no object' (47) but merely 'an empty castle . . . "powerless" outside, "impossible" inside' (49).

Many feminist critics have highlighted Kristeva's writings on motherhood and the maternal, either in translation (Moi 1986; Suleiman 1986) or in their own work (Stanton 1986; Silverman 1988), as well as in Kristeva's essay on abjection (Creed 1993; Russo 1994). However, I was struck by Kristeva's insistence on the 'bankruptcy of the fathers' (172) as the source of abjection. The maternal may be a privileged metaphor of the abject for male writers, Kristeva time and again stresses that the abject as 'a kind of narcissistic crisis' (14) is more often than not brought about by the failure of the paternal function. Kristeva's repeated formulations like 'the failure of the triangular relationship' (44); 'the instability of the paternal metaphor' (44); 'the absence, or the failure, of paternal function' (49) or 'a collapse of the Oedipal triangulation' (53), may not look so tragic, but quite appealing to feminists who wish for a certain relaxation of the oedipal plot. However, the painful twists and turns of Kay's family life suggest that the failure of fatherhood imprisons all family members in oedipal fixations rather than liberating them.

There is no doubt that the paternal law in Kay's and Sweetie's family is weak and instable, if not altogether absent. The father strikes a poor and pitiful figure, almost childlike. Like everybody else he is terrorized by Sweetie's excesses, but he nevertheless believes in her as a talented princess, denying her failure in show business. The mother is highly critical of the father 'being in a total fix about Sweetie' and temporarily leaves him because of his stubborn idealization of Sweetie, thus refusing to endorse the paternal law. Whereas Kay shares her mother's criticism of the father, she is also jealous of his attention for Sweetie. Her ambivalence appears most clearly when she watches Sweetie washing their father – as if he were a child – in the bathtub, extensively touching his private parts. Kay's pained expression may signify either disgust or envy, or most probably, both. Here, as elsewhere, Sweetie violates taboos, which is one of the major aspects of the configuration of the abject. In the figure of the watching Kay, the film represents the borderline incestuous relationship as the simultaneous fascination and disgust that come with abjection.

Although Sweetie certainly launches an attack on morality and on the law, the subversive powers that Kristeva ascribes to the abject are absent in this film. The violation of taboos may sometimes give Sweetie momentary *jouissance*, it mostly leads to intensely painful emotions for both herself and for others. Since the father is a weak cry baby who cannot let go of 'his little princess', he instigates a power vacuum that Sweetie abuses for terrorizing the family. In his inability to let the daughters come into their own, the father creates in both of them a hopeless struggle for autonomy and identity; a narcissistic crisis indeed. Although Kristeva's writing does not point to such a possible interpretation, I read the film *Sweetie* as a critique of the fact that in masculinist society but too often the mother is held accountable for narcissistic disorders of her children. In this film it is rather the father who is to be blamed for the lack of boundaries between him and his daughters.

Sweetie cannot reach reality anymore. The final spectacle of a naked and wrathful Sweetie entrenched within her high 'palace' in the crown of a tree in her parents' garden, is difficult to assess. Is the greyish-black mud with which she is covered a reference to Aboriginals, the absent other in Australian white suburbia? Is this grotesque sight an acting out of the anger of a young woman at the betrayal and failure of her father? Or the rage that is caused by the dilemmas of femininity within patriarchy? Or is it rather the comedy of abjection; the apocalyptic laughter that Kristeva hears when the unconscious gushes forth?

Whatever its meaning, the final outburst of excess is shortlived. Sweetie does not survive a fall out of her tree castle. Even in her moment of death, Sweetie is abject with her nude body covered with mud, blood and spit dripping out of her mouth. In a highly symbolical ending, Kay tries to apply mouth-to-mouth resuscitation, smearing herself with Sweetie's blood. But her kiss of life comes too late. In a Gothic twist at the end, Sweetie's sober funeral is slightly delayed, when the gravediggers have to saw off a root of a tree forming an obstacle for the coffin to sink in. As Kay says in voice-over: 'Trees never seem to leave us alone'.

Kay has finally made the effort to reach out for Sweetie. Now that she has lived through experiences of uncanniness and has dared to face abjection; now that she has tried to confront what she has magically tried to repress; only now can she live again. She has understood that life goes on through death. Back home, Louis has returned to her after a short break in their relationship. In one of the last images, in an obtuse angle, through the door opening, we see their feet on the bed touching.

CONCLUSION

Sweetie's excessive imagery creates a world beyond the threshold of the conscious. The excessive meaning of the images in this film resides in the subliminal world of the unconscious. These obtuse meanings cannot be grasped easily at a conscious level. The force of the visual style lies in the strong effects of feelings of uncanniness and even abjection it communicates to the spectator; it is a film that 'gets under your skin' rather than appealing to intellectual reflection about neurotic disorders.

Yet in the overall viewing experience *Sweetie* is not exactly a 'heavy' or dismal film. Although I have not foregrounded the issue of visual pleasure in my analysis of *Sweetie*, the gothic style most certainly gives the film its subtle humour and irony. This does not mean that the film makes fun of the horrors that beset the family, but rather that the film creates enough emotional distance to allow for some ironic relief. Its strange imagery strikes a balance between uncanny discomfort and mild humour. The relative distance of the camera and the unusual lopsided angles make the image strange and at the same time produce a rather comical effect.

As in *Bagdad Café*, the image-as-excess in *Sweetie* has the simultaneous effect of uncanniness and humour. But whereas the excessive imagery in *Bagdad Café* gives way to humour and harmony, a sense of the uncanny is retained in *Sweetie* until the very end. *Sweetie's* idiosyncratic style creates a world where the unconscious reigns. The film renders this subliminal world in a visual imagery that is at the same time lucid and mildly humoristic. Refusing to be a psychological drama the film never explains or interprets. It is up to the spectator to discover in this universe of madness the normal within the anomaly, the familiar in the uncanny and the repressed in the abject.

To come back to the question posed at the beginning of this chapter, whether visual and narrative pleasure can be subverted or displaced instead of being destroyed, I hope to have demonstrated that cinematic pleasure in neither *Bagdad Café* nor *Sweetie* is in any way connected to the traditional visual and narrative pleasure of dominant cinema. The image-as-excess, which in these films takes the form of an image rendered strange, displaces the voyeuristic look. In *Bagdad Café* the excessive image transforms voyeurism and thus displaces the male gaze and forecloses on fetishism. The visual style in *Sweetie* privileges psychic structures such as the uncanny and the abject, which bear no relation to the voyeurism or fetishism of classical cinema. The image, then, as rhetorical element, facilitates different narrative structures and hence different configurations of female subjectivity. The excess is the difference that is brought into the mimetic repetition of myths and meanings of femininity.

The artificiality of the visual style subverts the very narrative it helps to construct: in both films the pleasure of the spectator resides more in the visual *per se* than in narrativity. The rhetoric of the image in the films I have discussed in this chapter displaces traditional narrative pleasure, privileging a female point of view and representing female subjectivity differently. As such, *Bagdad Café* and *Sweetie* place the potential subversive force of the image-as-excess firmly in the foreground.

6 The Navel of the Film: On the Abject and the Masquerade

> You only have to look at the Medusa straight on to see her. And she's not deadly. She is beautiful and she's laughing.
>
> Hélène Cixous[1]

> You all know I am the soul of good taste and decorum.
>
> Bette Midler[2]

INTRODUCTION

At the centre of the black and white fiction film *The Virgin Machine* (*Die Jungfrauenmaschine*, Monika Treut 1988)[3] a fantastic sequence unfolds that seems to defy interpretation by conventional standards. To paraphrase Sigmund Freud, it is the navel of a film, 'the spot where it reaches down into the unknown'; a tangle that resists interpretation and 'which cannot be unravelled' (*SE*, V: 525). It is precisely the unknown that Dorothée, the protagonist of *The Virgin Machine*, wants to explore: in the opening monologue of the film she introduces herself in voice-over as 'Dorothée Müller', who has suffered from the 'illness' of romantic love, this 'fantastic illusion' in which she has strongly believed and which she still desperately desires to understand. The film thus introduces the riddle of love, of sexuality, as the narrative's leading question; as the domain to which the 'navel' of the film text gives access. What that navel is, where it is situated, will become clear in the course of my analysis.

Freud's metaphor of the navel as a figure for an 'unplumbable' passage or spot in a dream is first introduced in the analysis of his own dream about one of his women patients, Irma. In a footnote he refers to the unplumbable spot as 'a navel, as it were, that is its point of contact with the unknown' (*SE*, IV: 111, footnote 1). In her incisive analysis of the Irma dream, Shoshana Felman (1985) argues that the dream serves the discovery of psychoanalytic theory, because it is the very first dream

152

which Freud extensively analyzes in *The Interpretation of Dreams*. The Irma dream is also crucial in another respect: the navel of the dream, its unplumbable spot, is in fact a condensation of three female figures (Irma, another female patient, and Freud's pregnant wife), and Felman forcefully argues that the Irma dream therefore reflects the 'crucial psychoanalytic question of femininity' (1985: 57). The same dream from which psychoanalysis proceeds, articulates 'the very question that psychoanalysis leaves answerless', that is, the question 'what does a woman want?' (57). The navel, then, becomes a bodily metaphor for the 'unplumbable' riddle of female sexuality.

In this final chapter I explore the 'riddle' of lesbian desire and sexuality as represented in the film *The Virgin Machine*. In the first part of the chapter I discuss the fantastic sequence at the heart ('the navel') of the film, which shows a subversive visual representation of the 'unrepresentable' female body and of 'perverse' sexualities. In the second part I discuss the vicissitudes of lesbian desire and masquerade.

Because I deal with questions of desire and sexuality, psychoanalysis provides the theoretical framework for my discussion of the film. However, the film, in representing 'deviant' sexuality, stretches the limits of psychoanalytic discourse. Therefore, rather than taking an orthodox or hegemonic view on psychoanalysis, I look for more subversive ways of understanding representations of lesbian sexuality. This will lead me into an exploration, first of abjection, the obscene and the mucous, and then of lesbian fetishism, the masquerade and humour.

AN HALLUCINATORY FANTASY

Dorothée's quest for love in *The Virgin Machine* echoes the Freudian question 'what does a woman want?' We gather as much from the voice-over monologue during the opening shot of the film, in which we see Dorothée rowing on the river with a male friend, spying with binoculars on people who make love on the shore:

> Once in Hamburg I had a fantastic illusion: I believed in the one and only great love . . . I have dreamt so much of romantic love – that illness. My mother suffered from it too, she with her loose hair, and yet she did not achieve anything. I haven't seen my mother for a long time. One day she left for America. That I should then fall in love with Bruno, my brother! Anyway, I wanted to know what love is all about.

The film is thus structured around Dorothée's curiosity to find out the mystery of love. Being a journalist she sets out to write an article on this subject examining it from many different viewpoints. At the turning point of her quest, when Dorothée leaves Germany for California, we see the following hallucinatory fantasy.

Dorothée has packed her suitcase and walks to the sink to wash her hair. She looks intently at the dripping tap and the dirty water in the sink. Then we see an image filmed underwater, of something that looks like a wet grotto full of weeds. As the camera moves underwater through the grotto, it begins to look like the inside of a vagina or, to be more precise, a birth channel.[4] The next image is a distorted view of Dorothée running after her brother and finding him in an embrace with another man. This is followed by a shot of legs of female shopwindow manne-quins flying through the air. Again we see men kissing, now followed by a shot of men's suits dancing on a merry-go-round. Then Dorothée's eye is filmed in an extreme close-up, introducing the next sequence of im-ages. A microscopic image of larvae crawling in water is followed by a distorted shot of Dorothée's fat ex-boyfriend making movements as if in copulation, seen from her perspective lying under his big body. He sits up and extensively blows his nose. The last shot is again distorted; some-thing like a female breast underwater, squirting milk which disperses into the fluid.

The fantasy sequence ends with Dorothée staring at the sink. Then the telephone rings and she picks it up. While the voice of an anonymous male caller fills the room with his sexual fantasies about a powerful woman, Dorothée returns to the bathroom, empties the bath of its dirty water, and washes her hair.

Because Dorothée is clearly not asleep in this scene, I read the se-quence as a daydream, fantasy or hallucination and not as a dream. This sequence of uncanny images plunges the spectator into semiotic confu-sion. How to interpret signs in a sequence without a narrative structure or logical connections, in which all the images are distorted and at least three are virtually impossible to understand, being obscure, magnified and filmed under water? To say that these images look like the female organ, like larvae, like a female breast, is already giving meaning to images that on the face of it are 'unreadable'. Yet, even thus described the sequence hardly makes sense. The description of the formal structure of the sequence resembles Freud's description of a dream, and in its resistance to interpretation, it can be understood as the film's navel, the unplumbable spot where it reaches down into the unknown. I will there-fore make use of the Freudian model of dream interpretation to read the dreamlike scene in *The Virgin Machine*. In order to do this meaningfully I must first explore the context of the sequence within the film.

'Liebe, Liebe'

Since the fantasy is attached to Dorothée's questioning look/eye at the beginning, the middle and the end of the sequence, I take the images to represent 'love' in her mind; as her internal and modalized ocularization. They are thus linked to Dorothée's desiring subjectivity. This is emphasized by a mechanical voice whispering continually throughout the scene: '*Liebe, Liebe*' ('love, love'). For Laplanche and Pontalis fantasy is a scenario, 'the stagesetting of desire' (1986: 28). In this chapter I will refer to fantasy in this more psychoanalytic sense, that is, as a fantasy scenario representing specific material from the unconscious in order to enable an articulation of desire.

The images in the dream or fantasy all refer to certain experiences or discourses that Dorothée has encountered in her journalistic research on love so far; they are the raw material worked over and distorted into the images of the dreamlike fantasy. The three images underwater can be understood in the context of her interview with Dr Carl Mendel, an endocrinologist. This heavily overweight scientist, who eats voraciously throughout his exposé, explains the experience of romantic love as an effect of hormones: endorphine resulting in a feeling of safety and amphetamine in a feeling of ecstasy. He then links both hormonal effects in a highly unscientific way, not to say in an exulted manner, to the desire of each human individual to go back to the mother, representing the uterus as the paradise lost, the *Ur*-image of deepest harmony which we seek to regain in romantic love. He concludes his narrative, however, by saying that love as a sexual and social phenomenon can only be understood by studying chimpanzees. Here, Dr Mendel refers to the exchange of females among male primates so as to strengthen male bonding. Dorothée goes off to the zoo to take pictures of chimps.

The interview ridicules scientific discourse on sexuality through the preposterous figure of the doctor and his oral fixation on food, the nostalgic obsession with the mother, but also and especially in the actor's camp acting. Regular spectators of New German Cinema will recognize the actor, Peter Kern, for his (mostly gay) appearances in films by Fassbinder, Syberberg and Ottinger. His persona thus functions as an intertextual reference to those films.[5]

Intertextuality is also at play in the character of Dorothée, played by Ina Blum. In the same year that *The Virgin Machine* was released Blum made an appearance in the film *Anita* by the gay filmmaker Rosa von Praunheim. Both movies were filmed by Elfi Mikesch and share an expressionist cinematic style. These scenes thus point to a firm embedding of *The Virgin Machine* within the German subculture of gay and lesbian cinema, with its subversion of gender roles and its exploration of constructions of sexuality. Finally, through Mendel's explanation of the phenomenon of love in monkeys, the scene also ironizes feminist discourse in the reference to the well-known analysis of the 'traffic in women' by Gayle Rubin (1975).

After the interview with Dr Mendel, the next shot in the film shows a pornographic photograph juxtaposed with a picture of a human egg growing into a foetus. While Dorothée examines these photographs on the floor in her room, her attention is drawn by a discussion on television between feminist theologians on the virginity of Mary. Later, when Dorothée's ex-boyfriend tells her about a gruesome American slasher film (against the background of a poster of Rambo), Dorothée is distracted by a discussion on television by American women celebrating pornography for women.

The Virgin Machine thus brings together several powerful discourses on the body and sexuality: biology, pornography, theology and the mass media, and also feminist discourse where these issues proved most controversial as will become clear later in this chapter. Precisely through these juxtapositions the film suggests that these various discourses spill over into each other: they share an equally absurd yet powerful preoccupation with the 'mysteries' of the female body. By stringing together such a variety of images – from photographs of monkeys, foetuses and genitals to televised discussions by women talking about representations of women – the film emphasizes the visual aspect of a cultural obsession with sexual difference. It is through representation, specifically visual, that the female body is explored and colonized: this is a possible meaning of the paratactic structure of the fantasy sequence.

The Impossible Image

Psychoanalytic theory underpins the visual aspect of dreams and fantasies, especially the importance of the visual regime for any knowledge and understanding of sexual difference. In *The Interpretation of Dreams* Freud argues that the dreamwork is subject to mechanisms which facilitate the passage from primary to secondary processes: condensation, displacement and considerations of representability. This last consideration refers to the visual quality of a dream. Freud writes: 'A thing that is pictorial is . . . a thing that is capable of being represented' (*SE*, V: 339–40). So the 'pouring of the content of a thought into another mould' depends on 'representability in visual images' (344). Just as Freud emphasizes the visual aspect of dreams, Laplanche stresses the visual aspect of fantasies: 'As in the case of every fantasy, it should be emphasized, we are dealing with an imagined scene, particularly in its visual aspect' (1985: 98). In other words, the visual stands in a privileged relation to the primary process; for the unconscious to express itself in dream or fantasy it needs a visual representation. Maybe this is one of the reasons why cinema lends itself so easily to representations of the fantasmatic.

If fantasy is typically bound up with visuality, so is sexual difference. Throughout his work on female sexuality Freud has always emphasized the visual aspect of the drama of sexual difference – which for a girl reads more like a tragedy. He writes of the 'strikingly *visible* and large proportion' of the penis of a small boy, in which the little girl 'recognizes the superior counterpart of her own small and *inconspicuous* organ' (*SE*, XIX: 252). The girl 'makes her judgement and her decision in a flash. She has *seen* it and knows that she is without it and wants to have it' (252). Elsewhere, Freud writes that 'the little girl discovers her own deficiency from *seeing* a male genital' (SE, XXI: 233) and he concludes with a visual metaphor: 'it follows that femaleness – and with it, of course, her mother – suffers a great depreciation in her *eyes*' (233). A few years later Freud repeats how the castration complex of girls is 'started by the *sight* of the genitals of the other sex. They at once notice the difference and, it must be admitted, its significance too' (*SE*, XXII: 125) (emphases are mine).

Being 'strikingly visible' clearly entails superiority for Freud but also immediacy of interpretation. What you see is what you know and understand, 'at once'. This position stands in marked contrast to Freud's earlier theories on psychological processes as developed in *The Interpretation of Dreams*, where he states unequivocally that there is no such thing as immediate perception. Indeed, perception is highly unreliable because it passes through primary and secondary processes before it enters consciousness. Freud is therefore careful to avoid graphing his psychical model onto an anatomical model (*SE*, V: 536). When he revises this early model in *Beyond the Pleasure Principle*, by putting perception closer to consciousness, there is still a strong mutual interference between the two modalities and perception is no less under the sway of the psyche than before (*SE*, XVIII, paragraph IV: 24–33). However, Freud has forgotten both his promise and his caution when many years later he deals with female sexuality. 'Seeing' then means instant insight for the girl, whereas the boy enters a psychological process of disavowal and delay between seeing and understanding sexual difference. From Freud's own psychological models, however, it follows that the girl's instant insight cannot come about. It is impossible to have instantaneous perception, realization of the superiority of the male organ and envy and desire for the penis all in one moment, in a magical 'at once'. No vision works instantaneously. It seems that Freud here uses an ideological alibi by lapsing into biology and thus naturalizing the superiority that is culturally assigned to the penis.

In the short sketch 'Medusa's Head' Freud links sight of the female genitals to the terror of castration. He describes the genitals, especially those of the mother, as frightening, horrifying and terrifying. It appears, however, that it is not so much the sight of the female organ as such, it is not the vulva, the clitoris or the vagina that make the spectator 'stiff with terror', but rather the absence of the penis which presents the cause of horror (*SE*, XVIII: 273). In other words, the female genitals are represented to the male psyche as a castrated male organ. Freud seems to suggest here that the female genitals are not 'pictorial' or 'visual' enough to be the subject of representation. They can only be imagined and hence imaged as castration, as the horror of nothing to be seen.

In the fantasy sequence at the centre of *The Virgin Machine*, two highly unconventional images of the inside of the female body are offered. In fact, these images try to represent something which is traditionally considered unrepresentable: the inside and the inner working processes of the female body. As Rozsika Parker and Griselda Pollock (1981) point out, in spite of its persistent fixation on the female nude, western art knows no tradition of representing the female genitals. They argue that the image of the naked woman's body signifies male fear of sexual difference.[6] This point has a specific bearing on cinematic discourse. Being both an art form and a commercial enterprise, cinema takes a particular position vis-à-vis representations of women. Cinema has privileged both the visual and the female body even more than was already the case in western culture.

It is plausible to argue that the excessive visualization of contemporary culture has been built on representations of female sexuality. Cinema took an active part in the over-production of textual and visual representations of the female body. This has resulted in a conventional, if not stereotyped, relation between the female body and sexuality. In cinema the mere appearance of a woman signifies sexuality; her body takes on the meaning of sex, whether desirous or dangerous.

Paradoxically, through this continuous reproduction of representations of their bodies, women have been deprived of their very sexuality and of their own bodies in visual culture. As I argued in the previous chapter, such metaphorizations can only take place in a symbolic absence, indeed, signify the empty space that women occupy in the symbolic order. What looks like an overwhelming presence is in fact veiled absence. In other words, hypervisibility is a mirror reflection of invisibility. I want to argue that the two images of the female body in the hallucinatory fantasy in *The Virgin Machine* juxtapose the terms of this opposition.

As we saw in Chapter 1, feminist film theory has analyzed the role of women in Hollywood cinema in terms of voyeurism and fetishism. In the words of Mulvey, women's appearance is 'coded for strong visual and erotic impact so that they can be said to connote to-be-looked-at-ness' (1989: 19). Mulvey does not put male castration fear literally at the site/sight of the female genitalia, but by extension onto the female figure as such: 'ultimately, the meaning of woman is sexual difference' (21). This semiotic use of the female body in western culture points to fetishism. The tradition of the female nude in art; the over-exposure of the female body in contemporary images (advertisements, music videos); the cult of the female star in cinema all offer the male subject ways of escaping castration anxiety by means of fetishism. By turning the represented image into a fetish object, the male psyche can disavow its dangers and be reassured. As we recall from earlier chapters, the other way out of castration anxiety is through processes of voyeurism and sadism within the narrative: investigating the woman, demystifying and devaluing her and finally ending the narrative (and the woman) by punishment or redemption.

Placed within this cultural context it is obviously a formidable task for feminist filmmakers to represent female sexuality positively and affirmatively. We saw in *Bagdad Café* how nudity can be reclaimed in such a way as to subvert male voyeurism and how both Gorris and Hänsel portray violence while avoiding the repetition of a form of representation that humiliates and objectifies women. In this chapter I want to address more directly the issue of sexuality and the representation of desire and pleasure. I will move, in other words, into the eye of the storm of phallogocentrism.

We saw earlier that for Mulvey the only way to counter voyeuristic and fetishistic modes of representation is the radical destruction of the gendered structures of pleasure and satisfaction in classical cinema. Women, she felt sure, would not 'view the decline of the traditional film form with anything much more than sentimental regret' (1989: 26). Both mainstream and experimental feminist cinema indeed initially avoided glamorous representations of women. A sometimes relentless realism in feminist cinema de-eroticised the female body, the images and the films as a whole.[7]

Representing the female genitals and representing them as beautiful and attractive became a major target of the cultural politics of the second feminist wave. In search of a specifically feminine aesthetic, feminist artists of the 1970s created vaginal and clitoral iconography celebrating female sexuality. *The Dinner Party* by Judy Chicago (1979) is one of the best known examples of this kind of art. Richard Dyer (1990) describes how some feminist filmmakers in the USA created female sexual imagery. Lesbian director Barbara Hammer, for example, made short films with titles like *Multiple Orgasm* (1976), a film in which she superimposes an extreme close-up of a vagina with a finger rubbing the clitoris onto images of landscape vaginal and clitoral shapes of cave and rock formations. In creating such sexual imagery women artists and filmmakers defied a western tradition that considers female genitalia as unrepresentable. They also defy Freud's implicit claim that the female genitals are not representable in visual images other than as incomplete or castrated.

If women artists are indeed capable of representing female genitals in visual images, this raises the question of representability. The mere existence of such feminist art suggests that Freud's 'considerations of representability' may also be considerations of respectability. What can be represented must be respectable and the 'inferior' female genitals clearly do not merit such respect in Freud's view. Freud thinks that the highly praised feminine 'virtue' of shame is in fact related – albeit unconsciously – to a sense of genital inferiority: 'Shame, which is considered to be a feminine characteristic par excellence but is far more a matter of convention than might be supposed, has as its purpose, we believe, concealment of genital deficiency' (Freud, *SE*, XXII: 132). The female genitals are unrespectable because they cannot meet the standard set by the male organ. Hence, being born with a 'substandard' body is something to be ashamed of. If the female genitals are in themselves unrespectable, depicting them can be considered the epitomy of bad taste, whereas the representation of the respectable male genitals constitutes a violation of an altogether different sort. It seems therefore, that for women representability and respectability are intimately connected. Both, however, have to do with entitlement, that is to say, with symbolic power and legitimation. For something to be entitled to representation, it does not only have to be pictorial or visually representable, but it must also fit in with standards of good taste and decorum. Not only shame (*pace* Freud), but representation too, is far more a question of convention than might have been supposed.

By extension I would argue that images and representations are no less under the influence of (social) censorship, than a dream is governed by subjective censorship. Thus, if all genital images are tabooed in polite society and somewhat confined to the periphery of social life – to the 'private' or even 'intimate' sphere – the taboo is particularly strong on female genitals. The social censorship exercised on the representation of the 'intimate' parts of female anatomy is so deeply entrenched that it plunges its roots in the archaic fear of the feminine which I analyzed in the previous chapter. Loathing and disgust are the archaic layer on which the socially enforced sense of 'shame' and 'feminine virtue' are constructed. I agree with Freud, therefore, when he points to an extraordinary coincidence between social effects and psychic processes. Where I take my distance from Freud, of course, is in denouncing the power structures that come to play on the female subject as the result of such socio-psychic mechanisms. The result of these power structures is that female genitalia are not merely repressed socially (like all reference to genitals); they are also repressed psychically – to the extent that they cannot even be conjured up in fantasy life, let alone brought into representation. They are also foreclosed, not just censored.

This socio-cultural context highlights the radicality of feminist films that shamelessly show female genitals or represent them in the transposed form of imagery, for example flowers, vegetables, caves and grottoes. They make female sexuality visible and female desire and pleasure representable in alternative ways. This point needs to be made because Hollywood cinema is still subject to censorship connected to notions of respectability, even after the decline of the Hays code, especially in the case of female sexuality. Consider for example the Hollywood feature film *The Color Purple* by Steven Spielberg (1985), based on Alice Walker's novel of 1982. In the novel the friendship and love relationship with the blues singer Shug helps protagonist Celie to find her way out of a personal hell of sexual violence, hatred and self-loathing. At one point Shug helps Celie to get to know and love her own body. She asks Celie to look at herself 'down there' with a mirror. Celie finds her 'wet rose' a great deal prettier than she had expected and excitedly goes on to explore the rest of her naked body in the mirror. The passage ends with Celie's discovery of (auto-)erotic pleasure, which soon opens the way for a lesbian relationship with Shug.

In the corresponding scene in the film there is an interesting displacement from the sexual lips to facial lips, thus making the image perfectly respectable, but also losing most of its subversive power. In the film, Shug tells Celie to look at herself in the mirror fully dressed up in Shug's red sequined gown. Celie appears too shy to look at herself at all, casting her eyes down and covering her mouth. Shug gently takes away Celie's hand and dares her to laugh at her own reflection in the mirror. Tentatively, Celie starts to smile. Looking at themselves and each other in the mirror, both women open their lips to smile and laugh, finally bursting into a loud and liberating laughter 'because they are beautiful'. Timidly they start kissing each other. The scene ends with the camera discreetly turning away to tinkling chimes, suggesting that the erotic encounter between the women continues.

The displacement from one pair of lips to another, from orgasm to laughter, is quite suggestive. For me, it is reminiscent of Irigaray's subversion of female sexuality, expressed in her famous image of lips kissing and speaking together (1985b). Although I find this a sensitive scene in an otherwise often sentimental film about the struggle of black women, it also indicates the limits of cultural representations of female sexuality. Looking, laughing, kissing: yes. But the uninhibited pleasure that black women can take in the beauty of their own and each other's bodies, let alone sex: no. This heterosexist bias is a way of harnessing female desire into images that, however unconventional in their lesbianism, still respect the standards of decorum dominant in Hollywood-style representation.

The Abject, the Obscene, and the Mucus

It is not *grosso modo* until the 1980s that feminist filmmakers, both mainstream and experimental, start exploring female sexuality in feature films. *The Virgin Machine* is an example of the postmodern lesbian film of the late 1980s which takes the question of female desire and female pleasure as its subject. In view of the foregoing discussion of the relation between representability and censorship, one can begin to understand why the puzzling images of the female body in the fantasy sequence are so radical. Though feminist cinema partakes of a subversive tradition in which grottoes, caves and niches function as sexual imagery, the images in *The Virgin Machine* differ significantly from this iconography in that they are neither beautiful nor metaphorical in any simple way. The images here do not celebrate female genitalia through carefully choreographed allusions: no splendid colours but black and white in coarse grain; no beautiful forms and shapes but obscure passages of slime and

weeds; no dream-like hazy distance, but stark and uncomfortable prox-
imity. The film is also different in representing that which is usually not
seen or even impossible to see: instead of showing the clitoris or labia,
the images are of the inside of the vagina and the uterus; and instead of
a perfectly shaped female bosom, the scene shows spurting of milk from
one isolated breast (transforming it into an almost phallic image). Treut
trespasses the taboo by filming as if inside the female body. Being filmed
with a magnifying lens and underwater, these images are moreover distorted almost beyond recognition. The only other image filmed in this
way are the crawling insects, which are thus semioticallly linked to the
female body. If, following Dr Mendel's narrative, Dorothée desires to
regain her mother's body within her fantasy of romantic love, she surely
does not come up with a paradisaical *Ur*-image.

However much the spectator may be repelled by these images, they
also fascinate because of their unintelligibility and their relentless lack
of familiarity. A first significant aspect of their opaque nature for the
film theorist is the epistemological implication. Here seeing does not
mean knowing. Just as Freud reminds us that (dream) images are fundamentally ambiguous, so does Treut. Rather than offering a final interpretation of these cinematic images I want to stress the significance of
ambiguity. Their ambiguity displaces the spectator and thus forces new
questions upon her or him. Moreover, these opaque images cause upon
the viewers a sort of oscillation between fascination and repulsion, as
well as between literal and metaphorical representation. As such, they
resist interpretation and come close to Kristeva's concept of the abject,
as discussed in the previous chapter.

The abject is the place where meaning collapses. It signifies all that
marks the unstable boundaries of the self, usually things flowing in and
out of the body (food, vomit, faeces, sweat, milk, mucus). As we saw in
Sweetie, the abject is closely related to the repression of the maternal
body and is brought about by a failure of the paternal function. To give
Kristeva's argument a feminist twist, I would say that the release of the
oedipal grip enables the subject to reject and reconstruct dominant discourse by letting the abject emerge. I believe that a degree of relaxation
of the paternal metaphor, or oedipal plot, is attractive for feminist filmmakers who, in de Lauretis' words, want to work 'with and against narrative' (1987: 108) and who want to undo the binary opposition between
subject and object.

We see this at work in Dorothée's vision which has no narrative structure other than a stream of images nor does it display a clear subject–
object structure. Such loosening up of the oedipal plot allows for the

abject to come forth. It opens the door for a return of the repressed or a relaxation of the structures of repression. This allows for that all-important figure in one's life, though unacknowledged by the symbolic realm, to appear: the mother. The images of the inside of the female body, of the insects and of the breast spurting milk, are semiotically linked to each other because they are all three filmed underwater. Thus, they signify each other. Since the milk-giving breast refers unambiguously to the maternal body, the other image of the female body is also signified as maternal. Dorothée's quest goes as far – 'deep' may be a more appropriate expression – as she can take it, to 'the desirable and terrifying, nourishing and murderous, fascinating and abject inside of the maternal body' (Kristeva 1982: 31). The link to the shot of the crawling insects makes the images of the female/maternal body even more abject. I understand this as Dorothée's conscious penetration of the deeper, more archaic layers of the psyche. The site we are being taken to is no longer merely the censored (social) or even the repressed (psychic) – we are crawling on the edge of the foreclosed (unconscious).

It is known that for Kristeva the semiotic realm of the pre-oedipal mother becomes the privileged space for change and transformation of the symbolic (cf Moi 1986). Kristeva points to the subversive powers of the sphere of abjection: authors who devote themselves to figurations of the abject challenge moral, political, religious and aesthetic codes. According to Kristeva such literature is therefore well-suited to represent social, political and spiritual crises. The power of such horror stories lies in the 'first great demystification of Power... that mankind has ever witnessed' (1982: 210).

The way in which Kristeva understands the abject as a liberating transgression of taboos, runs parallel to the ideas of filmmaker Monika Treut about the obscene (1986; see also 1995). Whereas Kristeva characteristically confines herself to male authors and does not consider the possibility of women imaging abjection, Treut develops her ideas in the context of a feminist practice that tries to think through and change women's relation to sexuality. In an introductory essay to an Austrian picture book of lesbian sadomasochism, *Obszöne Frauen* (*Obscene Women*, Krista Beinstein 1986), Treut links the obscene to the abject, to that which is filth and defilement. She consequently sees the obscene as a potent form of transgression: it offends and scandalizes. Like the abject it launches an attack on morality and the law and this contributes to the deconstruction of power. The abject and the obscene show similarities, also in their intimate link to pain and pleasure. The violation of moral, aesthetic and religious taboos and the release of powerful new forces can open up to pure *jouissance*, as both Kristeva (1982: 9) and Treut (1986: 9) point out.

Treut makes no secret of her lust for perverse images of women: 'I am almost addicted to images, also pornographic images, of monstrous, commonplace, exciting, cruel and obscene women. I am looking for mirrors and objects so as to experience my sexuality also visually' (1986: 5; translation AS). Treut believes in a feminist vision of the erotic which seeks to transgress and displace the norm/al, the polite and the conventional. Merely pornographic images do not suffice because they are solely aimed at provoking lust and excitation in the male customer and in his heterosexist objects. A search for new representations of female sexuality leads Treut into the realm of the obscene – even if that may appear 'politically incorrect' to certain branches of the Women's Movement which she chastises for their puritanism (13). One of the fundamental aspects of the obscene is its power to elicit feelings of shame. In Treut's view, the obscene is capable of imaging not only the unrepresentable but also the unrespectable; as such it has an important political dimension. The obscene is exciting as well as morally shocking and politically and aesthetically transgressive.

The fantasy scene in *The Virgin Machine* succeeds in a highly daring and 'obscene' visualization of Dorothée's desires. The scene puzzles, shocks and transcends normal (and hence normative) representation. Hardly a narrative, it is more like a vision, almost a hallucination. It is a scene that refuses to conform to the oedipal plot, that borders on the imperceptible and the unrepresentable, and that remains ambiguous.

The notion of the obscene may explain the objects represented in the sequence, but not the underwater quality of their filmic representation. In order better to understand the radicalness of this short vision, I turn to Irigaray's notion of the mucous. In Margaret Whitford's interpretation, the mucous, the abject bodily fluids, is for Irigaray a way of transforming the dominant system of representation so as to provide women with a 'female symbolic' (1991: 163).[8] According to Irigaray, the mucous can evoke the unthought and the unrepresented, and consequently it can help feminists to symbolize the maternal in a non-phallic way. Because it is situated on the threshold of the body, or within the interior of the body, the mucous is not directly accessible to sight nor can it be seen in a flat mirror. It therefore undoes norms of visibility and of classical representation.

Although Irigaray argues that the mucous defies visualization, I think that the cinematic images in Dorothée's fantasy do visually represent mucosity, since they abound in moistness, wetness and sliminess. Especially the image which can be understood as representing the inside of the female body relates to several qualities of the mucous in Irigaray's inception of the term: it is a threshold, partly open, neither inside nor outside; it is not a partial object that can be separated from the body; it is not easily accessible to vision; and it has no fixed morphological form or shape. In the representations of the female body, *The Virgin Machine* presents the spectator with images defying interpretation, for it is precisely the visualization of the mucous, as well as of the abject, that makes the images so ambiguous and obscene. It also makes them fundamentally undecidable. The film thus creates a female imaginary that resists incorporation into dominant forms of representation. This aspect of the scene's impact is emphasized by the way the images are filmed.

What is at stake in these fantasmatic representations of the female body is the status of the image as such. As Jacqueline Rose argues, 'a confusion at the level of sexuality brings with it a disturbance of the visual field' (1986: 226). By shifting away from the scopic regime of phallus and castration, 'strikingly (in)visible', onto the indeterminate images of the female body *The Virgin Machine* takes up the task of representing the unrepresentable. Imaging the female/maternal body engenders a play between visibility and invisibility, between repulsion and fascination. That is why the fantasy sequence is so difficult to read. In challenging traditional constructions of sexual difference, the film inevitably challenges traditional modes of representation. *The Virgin Machine* shows in these few images that changes in the register of sexuality bring about transformations at the level of representation. We have come a far way from Freudian notions of representing the female body as the horror of nothing to see.

A Wound, a Scar: the Navel

In concentrating on the three most puzzling images within the hallucinatory fantasy, I have read the fantasy sequence as the collapse of oedipal narrative and desire and fascination for the maternal body. Kristeva points to an immediate connection between the abject and fantasy: 'The vision of the ab-ject is, by definition, the sign of an impossible ob-ject, a boundary and a limit. A fantasy, if you wish, but one that brings to the well-known Freudian primal fantasies, his *Urfantasien*' (1982: 154). Laplanche and Pontalis postulate three primal fantasies or fantasies of origins: the primal scene (the origin of the individual), castration (the origin of sexual difference), and seduction (the origin of sexuality). They relate the structure of fantasy to these fantasies of origin: 'Whatever appears to the subject as something needing an explanation or theory, is dramatized as a moment of emergence, the beginning of a history' (1986: 19). This is indeed the narrative structure of *The Virgin Machine*: Dorothée looks for romantic love and then stages her desire in the dreamlike fantasy. I want to argue that although elements of the primal fantasies can be detected in Dorothée's vision, they are rewritten critically.

The first primal fantasy or scene (the origin of the individual), is recast as the ambiguous fascination for the maternal body. The abject images represent what Kristeva has described as the 'immemorial violence with which a body becomes separated from another body in order to be' (10) and as 'the violence of mourning for an 'object' that has always already been lost' (15), that is, the maternal body. In the fantasmatic reconnection to lost objects – the womb, the breast and the milk – Dorothée does not represent the maternal body as lacking and castrated. Yet, the fantasy does not regress into a dream of symbiosis and plenitude either. Instead, refusing to seal over the pain and anxiety of loss, the scene dwells on ambiguity and ambivalence in its images of abjection.

There are references to the lost mother throughout the film, starting with the very first words in the film quoted earlier. Dorothée's initial motivation to visit the USA is to find her mother who supposedly works there as a stripper. It is not until Susie Sexpert tells her that she is 'too old to be worried about your mum' that Dorothée stops looking for her mother. In contrast to Dorothée's quest for the mother there is never any mention whatsoever of a father. The paternal function in this film is conspicuously lacking.

The second primal fantasy (the origin of sexual difference), is related to Dorothée's gay half-brother, with whom she earlier said she was in love. The shots of him in an embrace with another man are alternated with shots of flying legs of mannequins and of dancing men's suits. The last two images may be taken as the empty, 'castrated', signs of sexual difference. Dorothée's fantasy mixes these playful images of sexual difference with the perversions of incestuous and homosexual desire, thus refusing to follow the 'normal' oedipal trajectory.

The third primal fantasy (the origin of sexuality), can be recognized in the sexual act between Dorothée and her ex-boyfriend. Because of his big body and shaven head the man comes across as threatening. The way he is filmed during copulation, in close-up from Dorothée's perspective lying under him, and his blowing his nose after having had sex, make him into a repulsive figure.[9] Heterosexuality is thus presented quite negatively in the fantasy scene. The fantasy sequence as a whole redirects the *Urfantasien* away from their oedipal structure.

Thus *The Virgin Machine* puts Dorothée's fantasy literally at the centre of the narrative and as such as well as in its unreadability, the hallucinatory fantasy figures as the 'navel' of the film. As I argued earlier, in feminist criticism the navel has been related to the maternal body and to the theme of pregnancy. Felman's remark about the 'horrifying confrontation with the unknown of an opened female cavity' vividly brings to mind the abject images of the maternal body in *The Virgin Machine* (1985: 65). The theme of pregnancy is evoked in the image of the breast spurting milk. The navel, Felman emphasizes, is the scar of a wound; it is 'a knot that is cut' and it hence brings us back to the maternal body which is lost, forgotten and 'unplumbable'. In other words, the navel figures as a nodal point of something beyond our immediate knowledge, but also as the metaphor for resistance discovered by Freud to be 'a positively pregnant concept' (66), which allows us 'some textual access into the unknown' (67). In a similar vein, Mieke Bal (1991) has used the navel as a metaphor for deconstructive criticism, opposing it to Derrida's figure of the hymen. The attraction of the figure of the navel lies not only in its gender specificity, as 'the scar of dependence on the mother', but also in its democratic distribution 'in that both men and women have it' (Bal 1991: 23).

Centring a fantasy around a metaphoric navel, the scar that marks the wound of primary loss and separation, *The Virgin Machine* writes the maternal body back into the scenario of Dorothée's desire. I think that out of the nodal point of the hallucinatory fantasy emerges the subversive potential of the bodily metaphor of the navel, in so far as Dorothée's dreamwork transforms the oedipal plot, undermines the superiority of the phallus and rediscovers the daughter's desire for the mother. In so doing, it plunges obliquely but firmly into that foreclosed archaic material that is traditionally kept out not only of polite society for the sake of good taste and decorum, but also out of conventional standards of representation.

THE BOULEVARD OF BROKEN DREAMS

What a blessing is immaculate seduction.

Marlon Riggs[10]

It could be argued that *The Virgin Machine* consists of two films in one: the first is set in Hamburg, Germany and the second in San Francisco, California. Dorothée's quest for romantic love and sexual liberation takes very different forms in these two parts of the world. In Germany, Dorothée is led into some sort of underworld of dream and fantasy, a realm of squalor and ambiguity, where the dark side of sexuality is imprisoned in familial structures: the absent father, the lost mother, the gay half-brother and the ex-boyfriend. The alienating atmosphere culminates in the fantasy sequence discussed above. The distinctly uncanny ambience of the first part of the film recalls the original meaning of the German word *unheimlich*: the familiar, that what belongs to the home, is what becomes most strange.[11]

Significantly, Dorothée does not encounter feminism in Germany. Treut (1986) has written scathingly about the moralism of the German women's movement which she accuses of clinging to a dated and binarized idea of male power and female powerlessness. She sneers at the peaceful ideal of female love based on equality and sisterly solidarity which has subjected women to new forms of oppression. For Treut the political and cultural avantgarde of liberating sexual practices is to be found in the lesbian subcultures on the West Coast of the USA. Here she refers to the California-based Samois group and its spokeswoman Pat Califa, who made the case for consensual lesbian sadomasochistic practices, and to journals like *On Our Backs* (*Entertainment for the Adventurous Lesbian*) and *Outrageous Women* (*A Journal of Women to Women SM*). I find it surprising, however, that she does not acknowledge the background of sexual politics in US feminism, and the 'sex wars' which raged in the 1980s.

Treut singles out the German feminist movement for its puritanism, but paradoxically ignores the puritanical streaks in US feminism. Women's struggle against pornography led to the formation of groups like Women Against Violence in Pornography and Media (San Francisco, 1976) and Women Against Pornography (New York, 1979). For these militant organizations, sexuality was a relatively simple game of power politics excercised by men at the expense of women: pornography was 'sexual fascism' (Eisenstein 1983: 117). Writers representative of this trend, like Andrea Dworkin (1981), Robin Morgan (1980), and Susan Griffin (1981), firmly believed that pornography was the theory and rape the practice. Pornography was defined as an exclusively male prerogative, aimed to fuse sexuality and violence and to ignore the authentic sexuality of women. Visual representations of this kind of sexuality could only be humilitating for women. Within this view, female sexuality became an innocent and pure realm immune from power, fantasy and violence. Groups like Samois were formed in reaction to the campaigns against pornography, which were perceived as censoring sexual practices and fantasies that did not conform to the correct feminist idea of female sexuality. The polemic also raged in other circles: among feminists who did not fall into the trap of censorship and moralism, lesbian S/M was understood to be 'firmly rooted in patriarchal sexual ideology', and rejected it accordingly (Linden *et al.* 1982: 4). These increasingly heated debates resulted in polarizations, both in political and in theoretical terms (see for academic overviews Chapkis 1997; Eisenstein 1983; Snitow *et al.* 1983; Vance 1984).

Another issue at stake was the theatricality of S/M. Sadomasochistic practices are made up of ritual, scenarios, role-playing, and masquerade. They function by a mimetic repetition of stereotyped images, which are often rooted in fascist iconography (see note 11 to this chapter). The aim of the whole consensual practice is pleasure and subversion. For Monika Treut the practice as well as the cinematic representation of S/M signify a subversive mimesis of dominant heterosexuality.

It seems to me that these discussions were not (as yet) taking place in Europe, or at least not in such polarized positions, and consequently that Treut idealizes the sexual eldorado of San Francisco, where Dorothée continues her search for romantic love. Whereas Dorothée's life (though not her fantasy life) in Germany is dominated by relations with men (her boyfriend and her brother), in California she mostly relates to women. There is a marked shift in atmosphere: the story in Germany is rendered in sombre and uncanny imagery and events, while the story in California strikes a much more humorous tone of hedonism.

Dorothée soon falls for the charms of the mysterious and beautiful Ramona, a sex therapist who offers her services in an ad on television: 'You could be addicted to romantic love. My therapy could help you to find a way out'. When Dorothée tells her new friend Dominique, a German woman from Uruguay, that she follows a journalistic quest about romantic love, and that she has now fallen in love, Dominique mockingly asks her 'you don't suffer from it, do you?' But of course Dorothée does. And passionately so.

She watches Ramona perform a male impersonation in a bar for women only. Crossdressed and donning a moustache, Ramona dances for the female audience, partly undressing and using a beer bottle by way of a penis. Her performance culminates in a masturbation act, the beer foam shooting from the bottle in a parodic travesty of male orgasm, much to the thrill of the female audience. Immediately after her performance, Ramona walks over to an excited Dorothée and makes an appointment with her for the next day.

Dorothée has found her Great Love: Ramona treats her to a limousine with chauffeur, champagne and a night on the town, and finally, of course, sex. In contrast to the whirlpool of fun and excess that *The Virgin Machine* has displayed so far in the Californian story, the sex scene strikes a more serious and modest tone. The women make love gracefully rather than passionately, the camera remaining at a respectful distance while the scene unfolds in total silence. This emphatic aesthetization makes the spectator uncomfortably aware that s/he is watching lesbian sex; in other words, it turns her or him into a voyeur who is aware of that voyeuristic position.

The ironic tone of the film is picked up again in an unexpected turn. When Dorothée wakes up in absolute bliss the next morning, Ramona is already dressed and in a hurry to leave. Like a professional call-girl, Ramona makes up the bill of her date with Dorothée, adding up all the consumed items plus her own working hours, leading to a total amount of five hundred dollars. Left alone in stunned bewilderment, Dorothée has only one reaction to her shattered illusions: she is beyond herself with laughter. The film ends with Dorothée happily performing a striptease in the same bar where she had met Ramona, making money to pay the bill. When her friend Dominique asks her what has happened to her dream, she replies with relief: 'that dream has gone'. The closure of *The Virgin Machine* thus playfully ridicules the dream of romantic love, while celebrating the dawn of joyful lesbian lust.

The Parody of Gender

Ramona's transvestite performance deserves closer attention.[12] The scene reverses the classical viewing positions of male gaze and female spectacle. Ramona's performance directs our attention to 'her' phallus. This is where s/he differs from male strippers for a female audience. In a heterosexual setting, the male performer strips but usually does not reveal his penis, keeping on a minimal piece of cloth.[13]

This is at least assumed and made fun of in the British short animation film *Girls Night Out* (Joanna Quinn 1986). One night, Beryl, a lower class, elderly housewife, leaves her husband snoring in front of the television to go out with some friends who have promised her a hot night on the town. In a club called 'The Bull' they watch a bodybuilt man perform a striptease for a noisy crowd of women. Beryl's eyes pop at the man's absurdly bulging biceps and crotch; he looks exactly

like the Tarzan of her dreams. The women drink, crack jokes and become increasingly excited. In their comments they poke fun at bourgeois marriage, especially the unattractiveness of their boring husbands,
but they also make fun of the male performer. When the man struts
the stage in front of Beryl, she reaches out and, gathering as much
from his facial expression of pleasure, fondles his penis. The man suddenly screams out and desperately tries to hide his private parts – Beryl
has undone his pantherprint G-string and triumphantly swings the piece
of underwear in front of the helpless man. The women shriek with
laughter at the sight of his very small penis. Back home a giggling
Beryl hangs the G-string in the bathroom.

Girls Night Out derives much of its humour from the transgressive
behaviour of traditional housewives who go completely wild at the
sight of an attractive young he-man, especially at the final *démasqué*
of his 'small and inconspicuous organ'. By having him exposed fully
nude, the animation film shows the vulnerability of the man-as-spectacle.
In the previous chapter I have discussed the phenomenon of the woman-
as-spectacle and its subversion in *Bagdad Café*. I have also argued
that woman-as-spectacle is one of the key concepts in feminist film
theory. More recently, within cultural studies on masculinity, the phenomenon of the man-as-spectacle has drawn theoretical attention too
(Easthope 1986, Chapman and Rutherford 1988; Kirkham and Thumin
1993; Tasker 1993; Jeffords 1994).

Like the masquerade, the notion of spectacle has such strong feminine connotations that for a male performer to be put on display or to
don a mask threatens his very masculinity or at least plunges it into
paradoxical over-exposure. Lacan notices this effect in his essay on
the meaning of the phallus. He described it as '. . . the curious consequence of making virile display in the human being itself seem feminine' (1977: 291). Male spectacle, the display of naked male bodies
for the scopic consumption by an audience, results in placing the man
in a feminine position. Within existing asymmetrical power relations
between the sexes, to be feminized means to be degraded. As many
critics have observed, this feminization brings about two possible dangers for the performing man: he can easily become the object of ridi-
cule, and he runs the risk of being perceived as a homosexual (Dyer
1982; Neale 1983; Tasker 1993). As Mulvey writes: 'the male figure
cannot bear the burden of sexual objectification' (1989: 20).[14] Of course,
gay critics have taken great relish in this deconstruction of 'masculinity's claim to authenticity, to naturalness, to coherence – to dominate', as Mark Simpson put it (1994: 7). After all, it is only from a

heterosexual standpoint that appearing as a homosexual can be described as a risk.

Being put into a feminine position the male stripper is vulnerable to exposure. But what exactly can be exposed? Why does a male stripper need to hang on to his G-string? From a masculinist point of view, he has, after all, something 'strikingly visible' to reveal. From the previous chapter we recall the play of having and seeming which surrounds the phallus. The male performer may be content to present to the audience that which may correspond to the phallus, but 'what he has is worth no more than what he does not have' as Lacan astutely remarks (1977: 289). According to Lacan, the phallus can only play its role on condition that it be veiled. The male subject may thus pretend to 'have' the phallus. Because the phallus is the ultimate signifier, no man can fully symbolize the symbolic order or the Law. 'Having' is in fact replaced by 'seeming' in order to protect the phallus. In the spectacle of exaggerated masculinity, the male stripper appears to possess the signifier of the phallus – but only as long as his penis is veiled. This points to the constant slippage but also to a systematic misplacement between the organ and the signifier within the dominant heterosexual order. In the act of unveiling the slippage shows and with it the illusion of totality which the phallus represents: the man will be exposed as an imposter for not having the phallus.

In *Speculum* Irigaray (1985a) has put forward that in order for the male subject to 'have' the phallus, he needs an Other who by 'being' the phallus reflects its power. This specular game is crucial to the phallic regime. To withdraw that power would pull the rug from under the feet of the male subject. This is precisely what Beryl in *Girls Night Out* does. As long as his penis is veiled, the male stripper can put on a show of virility, pretending to have the phallus. The moment that together with the G-string his illusion is taken off him, he collapses into a whimpering male trying to protect and veil what has been revealed. The women laugh because they have brought about the loss of phallic power. In disclosing the illusion publicly, they collectively witness that '[t]he status of the phallus is a fraud' (Mitchell and Rose 1982: 80).

The striptease as ultimate spectacle, whether by a woman or by a man, dramatically visualizes the heterosexual play around 'being' or 'having' the phallus. A striptease is precariously situated between desire and anxiety. The final act of revelation is always a disillusion because illusions are being shattered: the illusion of the phallic woman in the case of the female stripper and the illusion of phallic power in the case of the male stripper. *Girls Night Out* can be said to underline the continuous collapse between the organ, the penis, and the symbolic signifier, the phallus, but in the final revelation it points precisely to the impossibility of that collapse. Judith Butler has argued that because the phallus is the privileged signifier of desire, and hence an idealization, the male genitals function simultaneously as 'the (symbolic) ideal' and 'the (imaginary) anatomy', a piece of flesh which is marked by the failure to approximate the ideal (1993: 61). Because of this double function of the male genitals the distinction between penis and phallus cannot be collapsed so easily.

The fact that feminist filmmakers choose to make a comical spectacle out of the phallus seems a subtle subversion of Lacan's wryly humorous observation that the issue of 'to have' or 'to be' the phallus throws relations between the sexes into sheer comedy (1977: 289). The humorous effect of the bar scene in *The Virgin Machine* derives from the satirical appropriation of the phallus, by a woman, in fact by a lesbian, in the location of a bar 'for women only' and for an audience of lesbians. What we see here is a lesbian phallus. Butler has argued that a lesbian phallus is an actual possibility because the phallus is displaceable; the phallus is defined by 'plasticity, transferability, and expropriability' (1993: 61). Since the phallus is a transferable property it can be appropriated by other than the heterosexual male subject who is symbolically entitled to have it. By explicitly referring to those plastic, transferable and expropriable properties, the lesbian phallus destabilizes the distinction between being and having.

In her parody of phallic power and pleasure, Ramona's performative act with the beer bottle explicitly unveils the properties of plasticity, transferability and expropriability inherent in the phallus. She throws into confusion the fixed positions of phallic distribution by appropriating the phallus/beer bottle, and thus challenges any notions of naturalness about sexuality or sexual difference. Ramona's performance reveals that anatomy never 'is', but, in Jacqueline Rose's words, 'only figures' (Mitchell and Rose 1982: 44). By showing the penis to be a sham, her act suggests that every piece of anatomy is a performance that more often than not fails.

If having the phallus is an imposture and if anatomy is a sham, then what exactly does Ramona mime? Butler's notion of gender parody suggests that Ramona mimes what is already a performance: 'Indeed, the parody is *of* the very notion of an original' (1990: 138). Her performance denaturalizes the 'normal' and discloses the 'original' to be a copy; in other words, the 'original' gender identity of masculinity after which Ramona fashions herself is itself an imitation without original. To me these observations beg the question of femininity. If Ramona's drag deconstructs masculinity, the question rises whether her drag reconfirms or deconstructs her femininity. The end of the performance seems to constitute femininity as Ramona's original gender identity. She sinks down on the floor dropping the beer bottle, and rests one hand on her open fly. While the camera lingers on the dark hole in her pants – which is suggestive of the vulva – Ramona looks at us with an ironic smile. The shot functions to ascertain the crossdressing: this show(-off) of masculine sexuality was indeed performed by a woman.

However, when Ramona appears the next day for the appointment with Dorothée dressed up as a sexy and feminine woman, her excessive femininity now appears as a masquerade and a gender parody.[15] Ramona's crossdressing thus has the effect of making her feminine attire look as constructed and unnatural as her drag attire. This supports Butler's point that gender parody displaces the very norms of sexual difference (1990. 148). Once the terms of sexual difference have been shifted there is no innocent return to dominant norms. Interestingly enough Ramona comes closest to figuring as a woman during that short moment at the end of the performance when her female body is suggested to lie behind the masculine masquerade.

What is important here is the subversive effect of the campy parody in *The Virgin Machine*. In this respect, parody resembles Irigaray's idea of mimesis as a repetition with a difference. Whereas mimesis can be read as an affirmation of a copy in order to create a new original, parody can be seen as a deconstruction of the original in order to create a new copy. Both are strategies to bring new representations of femininity into being, and to strike blows at inflexible ideas of identity and sexual difference.

Mis-Fits and Dis-connections

The phallic parody does not account so far for the specificity of the lesbian phallus. In order to be able to answer that question, we need to contextualize the issues at stake. The fierce polemics between 'against pornography' and 'lesbian sadomasochism' political positions, which I mentioned briefly earlier, reopened theoretical debates about fantasy, desire and politics. On the one hand, the anti-pornography feminists were criticized for their denial of the importance of fantasy life and of the ambivalence of desire, as well as for their relentless moralism, while on the other, lesbian sadomasochists were attacked for their neglect of social relations and politics, as well as for their libertarian 'anything goes' attitude.

The heated debates of the 'sex wars' raised the issue of lesbian sexuality, more precisely of its specificity as a libidinal economy and its potential for subverting power relations, and thus for liberating sexuality. Some lesbian feminists rejected the 'lesbian continuum' of Adrienne Rich (1986) and instead affirmed the specificity of lesbian desire, paving the way for queer theory (see *Differences*, vol. 3 (2), 1991; vol. 6 (2–3), 1994). The notion of the lesbian continuum historically forms part of the gynocentric or woman-identified 1970s. By positing the continuity of different degrees of female intimacy, encompassing the sexual encounter, Rich politicized the category 'lesbian'. Her critics argued, however, that she trivialized the lesbian subject by situating it in a wide range of female experiences. Monique Wittig (1992), for instance, rejected the diffuse lesbian subjectivity proposed by Rich and opposed to it a sharper and more exclusive definition: 'a lesbian is not a woman', became Wittig's motto – and many radical lesbians followed her. In her 'lesbian materialism', she aimed to disengage the lesbian from the banality of many other forms of female social intercourse. Wittig grants to the lesbian both an emotional and a political significance, which make this subject capable of advancing specific knowledge claims. The debate on a specific lesbian subjectivity split the lesbian communities and produced increasingly complex discussions on desire and sexuality.[16]

Writing from a continental European perspective, I want to point out some crucial differences in the history of this debate in European and American feminism (see Braidotti 1994b). In Europe, especially in France, feminists on the whole stayed with the idea of a lesbian continuum, reelaborated through theories of sexual difference and *écriture féminine* into an argument of feminine specificity.[17] Generally, it is feminism (and not lesbian culture or theory) that claims the issue of sexuality and itemizes the specificity of female desire and the subversion of female pleasure. We see this most clearly in the philosophy of Irigaray (Chanter 1995), but also find it in the fictional texts of *écriture féminine*. For a writer like Hélène Cixous, female sexuality, including female love for the other woman, can be traced back to the mother as the matrix of all sexuality (this idea emerges in most of Cixous' prolific writing; see e.g. Cixous 1980, 1983, 1986; Cixous and Clément, 1986; see also Stanton 1986). The effect of Cixous' highly aestheticized erotics is that the lesbian does not emerge as a subject position; it is the feminine homosexual woman who occupies that position. Thus, in

European feminism the focus is more on the specificity of female sexuality, including the range of homo-erotic experiences, rather than on the specificity of lesbian sexuality *per se*.[18]

Due to the 'sex wars' in US feminism (and probably also because of more oppressive obscenity laws), the issue of sexuality had different connotations and agendas. This resulted in a peculiar division of labour, where gender, power and identity became topics for the feminist agenda, while sexuality, desire and pleasure became itemized as themes for the agenda of radical lesbian groups (see Braidotti 1994b). This explains how it could happen that Rubin's general call for a theory of sexuality (1984) was taken as the foundational gesture for queer studies (see Rubin 1994). The whole issue of sexuality was thus monopolized by gay and lesbian studies, while feminist theory remained stuck with questions of gender equality and gender identity. This division of labour re-establishes an unfortunate hiatus between gender and sexual identity, which only in its interrelation can illuminate the workings of desire and fantasy. But it also had positive results in the form of studies which are (as yet) unthinkable in European feminism, such as the specific theory of lesbian desire from a psychoanalytic point of view (de Lauretis 1994), or the political investment of subversive power of queer desire from a deconstructive perspective (Butler 1990, 1993).

This transatlantic 'dis-connection' (Stanton 1985) resurfaces in *The Virgin Machine*, when Dorothée enters the wonder world of lesbianism in California. This hiatus between two political cultures of sexuality ends up structuring the film which falls into two irreconcilable halves reflecting Dorothée's subjectivity: a former German romantic and a later Californian hedonistic self.

De Lauretis' catch phrase in *The Practice of Love* (1994) – that it takes two women, not one, to make a lesbian – is a truism that hits home. It also points to the importance not only of dialectical recognition by a consenting other, but also to the empowering role of a community. Ramona's queer act takes place within the lesbian community. It is possible to identify Ramona's phallus as a lesbian one because she performs for women and interacts with women in the absence of men; women who are moreover coded as lesbian in their looks and behaviour. In other words, it is the address as well as the audience of the performance that mark it as lesbian and that attribute a lesbian meaning to Ramona's act. The role of the audience within the scene is important in that it negotiates lesbian desire for the film spectator. The crossdressing performance derives much of its excitement from watching the enthusiastic reactions of the female audience in the bar, through the eyes of a slightly bewildered Dorothée.

The role of the audience in the representation of lesbian desire brings out the theatrical connotations of 'performance'. It is noteworthy that in stark contrast to Dorothée's internal and subjective fantasy life in the German part of *The Virgin Machine*, there are strong elements of public performance of lesbian sexuality in the Californian story. The acting out of desire takes place in public space or quite literally on stage: Susie Sexpert's demonstrations of her paraphernalia of lesbian sex in the streets of San Francisco, Ramona's crossdressing performance and Dorothée's striptease in the women's bar. I would stress the materiality of representation: the public sphere, scenario, stage setting and audience. A focus on the theatrical connotations of performativity foregrounds postmodernist elements of camp, display, surface and address. This suggests a move towards exteriority in the representation of lesbian desire.

Although there are elements of performance in the German story of *The Virgin Machine* (for example a punk female singer), they remain private and linked to Dorothée's desire for her brother. The singer is encountered in a building that looks much like a church (or a theatre), but since there is no clear narrative structure or an audience and because of the wavering camera, the scene can be read as another instance of Dorothée's private fantasy life rather than as a public performance (the song becomes a recurrent musical theme on the soundtrack). We have seen that Dorothée's encounters with sexuality in California, on the contrary, take place in public spaces. Even when she peeps through doors into hotel rooms, what we see through her eyes – kinky sex scenes – is staged for voyeurism. The representation of sexuality in the second half of the film thus becomes a public stage act, 'out there' to watch and to grab. Lesbian sex has become a performance which only makes sense in the presence of a lesbian audience.

The marked stylistic break between the two parts of *The Virgin Machine* results in relegating sexuality in Germany to the realm of dream and fantasy, and to heterosexuality, and in directing sexuality in California to action and performance, and to lesbianism. In other words lesbian sexuality is more 'real' than heterosexuality, because it is more public – it is part of a liveable social community. This break in tone and style may prove problematic for the shrewd viewer in so far as the film fails to integrate the force of primal fantasies and oedipal configurations, so uncannily represented and rewritten in the first part of the story, into the pleasure of acting out lesbian desires. It is as if Dorothée, in leaving Germany, can simply forget her past, which involves a renewed repression of the maternal body, and start a different libidinal life. At first sight, then, the representation of a lesbian utopia in *The Virgin Machine* appears to result in a hedonistic and care free proclamation of sexual desires and practices, unhindered by the cumbersome workings of the unconscious. The problem is solved by a geographical displacement, a self-imposed exile which has the advantage of freeing one's sexuality at least to all appearances.

Having said that, I wonder, however, whether the Californian part of the film is indeed as superficial as that. De Lauretis' reading of the lesbian film *She Must Be Seeing Things* (Sheila McLaughlin 1987) may help to understand the role of unconscious and structuring fantasies in performances of lesbian sexuality, and hence of the performances in *The Virgin Machine*. De Lauretis understands the elements of performance as the signifiers of a lesbian fantasy; the assumption of gender position and the reversal of sexual roles signal 'the position of desiring subject' (1994: 103). She stresses the explicit and visible gap between gender and performance in the lesbian masquerade, describing it as 'an effect of ghosting'. In Lacanian psychoanalysis the address of the masquerade of femininity is to heterosexual men, thus reproducing the order of sexual difference. But what, de Lauretis wonders, if a woman addresses her masquerade to another woman? In such a case the masquerade is not recuperated within the dominant heterosexual order, because the woman is not identified with her role. On the contrary, the lesbian masquerade points to the mis-fit between subject and performer. The way in which de Lauretis analyzes a scene from *She Must Be Seeing Things*, seamlessly fits the camp and postmodernist representation of lesbian sexuality in *The Virgin Machine*, as performed by characters like Susie Sexpert and Ramona: '[The] role-playing is exciting not because it represents heterosexual desire, but because it doesn't; that is to say, in mimicking it, it shows the uncanny distance, like an effect of ghosting, between desire (heterosexually represented as it is) and the representation . . .' (1994: 109–110). De Lauretis argues that it is precisely the gap between character and role, the space between representation and its deconstruction, that displaces the heterosexual framework of desire and creates space for a specifically lesbian desire. Indeed, one can say that it is in its form of address that the lesbian phallus signifies lesbian desire; displaced and expropriated, Susie Sexpert's dildos and Ramona's beer bottle are mis-fits, and only in that disjuncture can they come to represent lesbian desire. Desire can be suggested in the interstices of the performing body, the intervals of the performing texts. It can only be indicated by default. The satirical or comical mode – culminating in the exhilaration of laughter – is in my eyes a perfect form of expression for the fundamentally mis-fit character of desire in its representations.

Lesbian Fetishism

Ramona's performance is only one instance of a representation of lesbian desire in *The Virgin Machine*, and a parodic one at that. Surely it must be possible to represent lesbian sexuality outside parody and masquerade? It has been notoriously difficult to theorize the specificity of lesbian sexuality, and I believe therefore that cinematic representations of lesbianism are important cultural practices from which lesbian theory can benefit.

In *The Practice of Love* de Lauretis (1994) develops a psychoanalytic theory of lesbian sexuality in terms of 'perverse desire', reclaiming perversity from the pathological. In the passage quoted earlier, de Lauretis points to the lesbian investment in a structural fantasy. This is understood to be the primal castration fantasy, a fantasy of original loss and dispossession. De Lauretis proposes to reread those notions of castration and phallus in terms of the perversion of fetishism, for '... the lesbian subject neither refuses nor accepts castration, but rather disavows it' (204). Fetishism offers mobility of desire. But it does more: the fetish gives a freedom from the phallus and from its collapse with the penis. The fetish is a signifier of desire, that is to say, it functions as a sign that designates an (absent) object of desire. 'The lesbian fetish', writes de Lauretis, 'is any object, any sign whatsoever, that marks the difference and the desire between the lovers...' (228). More specifically, the fetish signifies the perverse desire for an originally lost object. It is an imaginary and fantasmatic item which is cut off from the original object (the unity with the maternal body represented by the breast or the womb) and displaced onto another object. De Lauretis argues that the original loss of the female body in the mother can come to mean a loss of her own body-ego for the female subject. Hence, the lost object of lesbian desire is always the female body itself. Castration therefore does not signify 'the loss of the penis in women but the loss of the female body itself and the prohibition of access to it' (243). The lesbian fetish recuperates that lost object, rendering it available and accessible to the subject. In other words, as a psychic structure, fetishism allows the lesbian to reinvest erotically in the body of another woman.

This brief outline of de Lauretis' argument allows me to speculate that a castration fantasy, understood as a fantasy of loss and dispossession, underlies the narrative of *The Virgin Machine* as a whole, and thus provides coherence to the film. In the first, German part of the film Dorothée's hallucinatory fantasy points to the originally lost object: the womb and the breast of the maternal body. In the second, Californian part of the film, the disavowal of castration is underscored in the many performances and practices of lesbian sexuality: Susie Sexpert's show of dildos, Ramona's masquerade as a man, Dorothée's seduction by Ramona, kinky sex scenes in the hotel.

De Lauretis' theory of lesbian sexuality helps to understand how Ramona's act exceeds a mere performance of gender parody. By recasting the lesbian phallus as a fetish, that is, as a sign which negotiates female desire for another woman, de Lauretis argues that what has sometimes been understood as the wish for a penis is in fact 'the wish for a lost or denied female body' (264). De Lauretis argues that lesbians often choose signs of masculinity because in the heterosexual order those are the most explicit and visible signs signifying desire for women. Thus, Ramona's crossdressing performance with the beer bottle represents a public and highly visible display of same-sex desire. The lost female body can, however, also be signified by the reverse discourse, that of femininity. Ramona's exaggerated display of femininity in her later meeting with Dorothée can equally be read as a fetishized scenario which restages 'the loss and recovery of a fantasmatic female body' (265). Here, the masquerade of the femme takes the signs of femininity as a fetish.

In a turn completely in line with the perversity of lesbian desire, the object is lost as soon as it is refound: Ramona is neither the phallic object nor the Great Love, but a lesbian call-girl. She is exactly what she appears to be; you can make what you want of her, so long as you pay cash. Having experienced the vicissitudes of desire, Dorothée can now embark upon a practice of lesbian sexuality in the 'real' world. Free at last, she bursts into the relief of laughter.

'*Cherchez la femme*'[19]

However sophisticated, the above analysis leaves me dissatisfied. The notion of fetishism makes too much of the parodic performance, while it makes too little of the desire and sexuality of the feminine lesbian. De Lauretis' highly intricate rereading of psychoanalysis cannot be easily dismissed. She valiantly stretches the very limits of psychoanalytic discourses of sexuality, and yet, or maybe therefore, also demonstrates the limitations of psychoanalysis for a theory of lesbian desire.[20] At this point I would want to displace the issue of a specific lesbian desire by pointing to a lesson that psychoanalysis teaches us, one that in my view has received too little attention in psychoanalytic theories of lesbian sexuality, and that is the fundamental irrationality and unstability of desire. Because desire is by its very 'nature' (if I may so speak) discontinuous and inconsistent, it follows that subjectivity is necessarily an imposture (Mitchell and Rose 1982: 57) and that identity is a 'failure' (Rose 1986: 91). This is only too obvious from Dorothée's trajectory of desire through the film: voyeurism, boyfriend, abject fantasy, half-brother, telephone sex, dildo display, voyeurism (again), butch masquerade, sex with a femme, and finally a striptease performed by herself. Rather than insisting, therefore, on a specific lesbian desire, I would want to look for the gaps that desire creates, the interstices that desire allows. This turns my attention, once again, to moments of irony and parody in the representation of desire in *The Virgin Machine*.

Enough has been said about Ramona's parodic performance of macho masculinity, but I have not yet highlighted the other significant scene of lesbian sexuality, which is the sexual encounter between Dorothée and Ramona. Interestingly enough, the sex scene in *The Virgin Machine* takes place with two gorgeous looking feminine women. To my knowledge, this remarkable fact (within the context of butch–femme relations in the other scenes of the Californian lesbian subculture) has not received any critical attention. This silence is indicative of the theoretical resistance to the femme lesbian; a tendency that has worried a critic like Biddy Martin (1994) for its implicit misogyny. Martin quite rightly points to the fallacy of both queer and gender theories in the idea that one should escape from gender in the form of disembodiment and gender crossings. Within this view, the feminine becomes the trope for being trapped within the straitjacket of gender. For Martin, this resistance to the feminine 'played straight', i.e. not parodied or camped up, is linked to problems of visibility: 'Women fade again in the face of visible signifiers of difference from norms' (106). The queer emphasis on display, parody and performance, that is on visibility, has led to 'an evacuation of interiority' in which the psyche is reduced to the mere effect of the social (106).

It seems to me that the earlier mentioned split in American feminist theory between gender and sexuality is particularly detrimental here. The unconscious structure of desire and hence the complicating and sometimes implicating roles of fantasy, should not be denied or neglected in any discussion of sexual politics. Yet, a theory of sexuality which attempts to understand the vicissitudes of fantasy and desire with reference to their inner complexities does not necessarily foreclose a critique of the social construction of gender and its power relations. In the inter-relation of identity and sexuality, of desire and gender, embodied femi-ninity may pose less of a problem and threat to (lesbian) feminists.

The Virgin Machine is a rare example of an exploration of female subjectivity and desire, where a crossdressing parody does not fore-close on femininity 'played straight', and where performance does not evacuate the interior fantasy life. The element of parody is undeniably present in Ramona's masquerades as man and as femme. Yet, Dorothée and Ramona make love as women, and not as a butch–femme couple. Dorothée's femininity is never camped up, and therefore the feminine is not 'excluded, undervalued or obscured' from the film (Martin 1994: 112). The way the sexual encounter between the two women is filmed, re-claims for the spectator an aesthetically pleasing, and narcissistically satisfactory, image of female bodies engaged in the pleasures of sex. However, this positive representation of *jouissance* is shortlived, as the film does not buy into the illusion of an harmonious lesbianism. For Treut, no over-arching theories of lesbian sexuality, only the com-plex and contradictory vicissitudes of desire. The virgin is no more, but Dorothée will swing high on the machine of desire.

CONCLUSION

The ways in which female subjectivity and lesbian sexuality are re-spectively represented in the first and second part of *The Virgin Ma-chine* are indeed very different to the point of dissymetry. Whereas the first part is marked by abjection, the second part abounds in parody and laughter. The film shows the liberating effect of working through the unconscious material of that fantasy for the main character Dorothée. While she knows that the Great Love, the One and Only, does not exist, she persists in believing it does: 'I know, but . . .'. Her dream can only disappear after her acknowledgement of the fetishistic nature of her desire and the pattern of disavowal in which she is caught. The only type of 'reconciliation' lies in the acceptance of her being in-wardly split and in contradiction.

However different abjection and parody may be, they are connected in their subversive effects in so far as they are both forms of rejection, transgression and challenge. In their own specific ways, they question fixed ideas and norms, subtly displacing the boundaries of what seem possible, appropriate and respectable. Whether in an abject representation of the maternal body, in the sequence I have metaphorically called the navel of the film, or the humorous unveiling of Dorothée's navel when she dances on stage for a female audience, *The Virgin Machine* has opened up a new discursive and visual space for female subjectivity and lesbian sexuality. And grateful spectators like me can hardly suppress a giggle of relief. The riddles of the sphynx – the enigma of femininity that so worried Mulvey's generation – has turned into the giggles of the bad girls, those for whom decorum is but yesterday's camp.

Epilogue

And the mirror cracked.

Feminism has undone the mimetic mirror of masculinist culture. Whether by going through the looking glass or by smashing it to pieces, it has made the mirror crack. Feminist cinema has therefore profoundly transformed the traditional field of visual representation which 'reflected the figure of man at twice its natural size' (Virginia Woolf 1977: 35), while the image of 'Woman' remained diminished and distorted. Discarding and dismantling old forms of representation, feminist filmmakers have sought new ways of representing women's lives and experiences, of imaging female subjectivity, and of addressing the female spectator.

In *And the Mirror Cracked* I have worked at the interface of feminist cinema and film theory. I have given priority to the film texts themselves, relying on all kinds of film theories – not only feminist – in order to provide satisfactory readings of the texts. While evaluating film theories in both an historical and theoretical perspective, I have thus always placed the films in the foreground. In so doing I hope to have contributed to a new approach and to have offered new perspectives.

It also means that my place of enunciation shifted throughout the book: from the enthusiastic spectator I recalled at the beginning to the critical and self-reflective reader of today. My position as a member of a younger generation of feminist spectators and film critics allows me to survey the historical development of both film theory and feminist cinema with a certain distance. In my method of approaching feminist cinema, this distance, far from marking a critical hiatus or a generation gap, grants me the advantages of both hindsight and of accumulated experience. Empathy with the symbolic capital that is feminist film theory is as much part of my method of analysis as is the emotional bond I feel towards the films themselves. In no way could I define the feminist film critic on the threshold of the 21st century as detached from what feminism has achieved in the second half of the 20th century. On the contrary: I want to state my disagreement with the hasty dismissals of feminist cinema (or feminism *tout court*) as out-dated and old-fashioned, that one can read in both popular and serious film criticism these days. I do so not only out of loyalty and gratitude for what earlier generations of feminist scholars and filmmakers have achieved, but also out of concern for what I see as the historical paradox of feminist cinema and theory as being both too early and too late. Feminist cinema and theory are too early in that their radicality and interdisciplinary span preempt serious attention from established journalists and academics. They are too late in that their political engagement falls on deaf ears and blind eyes in a postmodern culture which, with the general rejection of ideologies, seems to have relinquished any transformative social and theoretical project.

I would claim that feminist cinema has transformed visual culture for ever by acting as a motor of social and symbolic change. In spite of its influence on contemporary cinema, feminist film has, however, remained largely invisible in the sense that it has not been canonized. The lack of canonization coincides with the crisis of cinema and of cinema studies in the institutions of learning. While the story of feminist cinema has not even been told yet, film studies have shifted attention from film theory to cultural studies. This change of academic focus coincides with a radical change of interest and of financial investment in film practice: from cinema to the new multimedia and information technologies. In such a rapidly shifting context, I have deliberately chosen to maintain a continuity with the immediate past, in the hope of contributing to the canonization of feminist cinema, and of the theoretical perspectives offered by film theories in the last twenty years.

The fact that in this book I have put the films before or alongside theory, implies that I have focused on the complexities of the films as texts and on the experiences of the spectator. In other words, I have attempted to trace the new and different effects of the eros and pathos of feminist cinema upon the changing female subjects. In cracking the mirror of classical representation these films have produced new and different forms of visual pleasure which address women primarily, but not exclusively. I will not deny that the quality of affectivity is of the greatest importance to my reception of both feminist film theory and of feminist cinema. Not to be confused with sentimentality, or the cult of emotions for their own sake, affectivity is for me an ethical framework which combines memory, or remembrance of a historical tradition, with positive passions such as affirmation, joy and desire. Affectivity combines the seriousness of analysis or of understanding with the hopeful quest for change or transformation. Throughout this book, while revisiting some of the classical items of the feminist agenda – such as rape, sexual violence, and the constant struggle for female subjectivity – I have systematically stressed the affirmation and the positivity of the difference that feminism can make. I hope the reader will take this as a graceful gesture on her or his behalf; I do think indeed that only a humorous touch, joyful recognition and a sense of appreciative distance can do justice to the ground breaking achievements and complexities of feminist theory and feminist cinema at the turn of the century.

Notes

1 WHAT MEETS THE EYE: AN OVERVIEW OF FEMINIST FILM THEORY

1. See for short and excellent introductions to psychoanalytic notions in film theory *New Vocabularies in Film Semiotics* (Stam *et al.* 1992) and for psychoanalytic notions in feminist (film) theory, *Feminism and Psychoanalysis. A Critical Dictionary* (Wright 1992).
2. See Stacey (1995) on the popular lesbian romance *Desert Hearts* (Donna Deitch, USA, 1985) which, surprisingly, did not receive much academic attention (nor was it followed by other successful lesbian romances).
3. The work of French philosopher Gilles Deleuze is acquiring more relevance in film theory, although significantly not so much for his cinema books (1986, 1989) as for his theories of embodiment and desire and his critique of representation (Boundas and Olkowski 1994). In her study, Studlar refers to Deleuze's critique of Lacanian psychoanalysis, in which he opposes the notion of desire as lack and alternatively proposes the productivity and positivity of desire (Deleuze 1971).
4. This special issue of *Camera Obscura* (1989, no. 20–21) contains an international survey of research on and theories of the female spectator in film and television studies.
5. Scholars have generally focused their empirical studies more on television than on cinema. Such studies tend to concentrate on a specific problematic, especially the influence of violence. See for example Schlesinger *et al.* (1992) who carried out empirical research in relation to women watching violence on television. They included one film in their study, the American court drama on rape, *The Accused* (Jonathan Kaplan 1988). (See note 9 in Chapter 3).
6. De Lauretis has the tendency to substantialize 'narrative' and 'desire' to such an extent that these concepts become personalized agents. This at times gives an almost mythical and universalized aspect to the very terms that she set out to untangle from mythology (i.e. from Propprian folk mythology).
7. Towards the end of the 1980s two anthologies of feminist film theory testify to this paradigm (Penley 1988; Erens 1990). In the 1990s, however, the dominance of psychoanalysis and semiotics is supplemented if not replaced by new perspectives, most notably by cultural studies, multiculturalism and lesbian studies. This approach is echoed by the title of a 1990s anthology, *Multiple Voices in Feminist Film Criticism* (Carson *et al.* 1994).
8. A new approach to the study of culture and society was developed at the University of Birmingham Centre for Contemporary Cultural Studies in the 1960s and 1970s. Stuart Hall is one of the leading figures here (Hall *et al.* 1980). See for readers on cultural studies During (1992) and Grossberg, Nelson and Treichler (1992).

9. Postmodernism is often understood to be a cultural practice (as witnessed in popular culture) as well as to be a theoretical practice, closely linked to poststructuralist thought. For an example of the latter view on postmodernism, see Docherty 1993.

2 IN PURSUIT OF THE AUTHOR: ON CINEMATIC DIRECTORSHIP

1. Halpern Martineau 1991 (1973): 36.
2. Kobena Mercer 1991: 181.
3. I use gender here as the equivalent of sexual difference, understood as the asymmetrical relation between the men and women.
4. Much of my ideas on *auteurism* in this chapter are shaped by the excellent reader *Theories of Authorship* (1981), edited by John Caughie.
5. The new emphasis on the text and on textual analysis underscore how heavily film theory is indebted to and influenced by literary theory; structuralism itself was of course inspired by linguistics (see Silverman 1983b and Andrew 1984).
6. This lecture was printed by Helke Sander herself as a pamphlet in 1981, Basis-Film-Verleih GmbH, Güntzelstr. 60, 1000 Berlin 31. I thank Annette Förster for the material she has given me about Helke Sander and *Der subjektive Faktor*.
7. Rudi Dutschke was a student leader who figures prominently in the historical film footage in *Der subjektive Faktor*. He was shot by a neo-fascist in 1968 but survived the assassination attempt. He finally died of complications related to his injuries in 1980. In the final scene of the film Helke Sander pays a visit to the graves of Meinhof, Baader and Dutschke on the Berlin cemetery.
8. Dutschke (1968) quoted in Rentschler's article 'Life with Fassbinder', 1983: 75.
9. The Oberhausen Manifesto was written and published during the eighth Oberhausen Short Festival in 1962, in which a group of twenty-six filmmakers, writers and artists condemn West German films and plead for a new cinema and a new film language to replace *Papas Kino*, 'daddy's cinema' (Elsaesser 1989: 20–5; Knight 1992: 29). I am struck here by the oedipal notion of 'killing the father', which might be seen as an inherent feature of auteurism: each new author has to react against his predecessors.
10. More recently, the balance has been somewhat redressed by film scholars such as Elsaesser and McCormick who discuss feminist film as an integral part of German culture, and Knight who addresses the position of women in the New German Cinema.
11. The metaphor of the 'empty field' echoes his earlier figuration of the 'Absent One' theorized in his work on suture (Oudart 1977–8). The important point here is the changing notion of cinematic authorship in psychoanalytic film theory.
12. The subject position within the cinematic scene of desire does not necessarily coincide with the biological gender of the author outside the film. Silverman urges us to read libidinal masculinity or femininity in relation to the biological gender of the author, because these positions have different

social and political implications. Another important point that Silverman puts forward, is that the fantasmatic can absorb new material and is subject to change. It can therefore be relevant to look into the role of history in representations of a particular authorial desire.

13. Hoogland (1994) explicitly links narratology to Silverman's psychoanalytic framework. She discusses Silverman's model of the author 'inside' and 'outside' the text in relation to the concept of the female author in literature, *in casu* the works of Elizabeth Bowen. Although Hoogland does not problematize her use of different discourses such as psychoanalysis and narratology, her analysis convincingly suggests a possible intersection.

14. Surprisingly, Branigan criticizes Browne for revealing a 'rationalistic' approach to narration (169). In accusing 'rationalistic' theories such as psychoanalysis of being abstract and metaphysical, Branigan suggests his own approach to be more 'empirical', i.e. less hypothetical. I find Branigan's use of these terms somewhat obscure: he counts most structuralists, such as Barthes, Heath and Metz, but also the linguist Noam Chomsky, among 'rationalists,' whereas Benveniste and Wittgenstein are ranged as 'empiricists,' (171). It remains unclear where Branigan stands himself vis-à-vis these opposing theoretical systems. His claim to have 'attempted to avoid drawing a hard line between classical and modern' sounds rather vague and unconvincing (175), because it is by no means clear how terms like 'rationalist' and 'empiricist' relate to the adjectives 'classical' and 'modern'. It seems to me that a concealed and unresolved polemic underlies Branigan's *Point of View in the Cinema*: although he appears indebted to structuralist theories throughout his book, Branigan's tone is often deprecatory of structuralism. It therefore comes as no surprise that in his next book on film narratology (1992) Branigan shifts his theoretical position more explicitly in the direction of linguistics and cognitive science.

15. To enable quick reference I will render Branigan's hierarchical topology of narration in a scheme:

1. Historical author/director: biographical person, cultural legend.
2. Implied author/director: selection and arrangement of film narration; frame of reference is the entire text.
3. Extra-fictional narrator: statements or appearances, usually by the director, about or in an embedded fiction.
4. Non-diegetic narrator: extra-fictional film elements in story: film music, titles.
5. Diegetic narrator: pictorial equivalent of subjunctive conditional, that is, spectator as bystander 'if I had been present . . . I would have seen . . . and would have heard . . .'; frame of reference is the fictional story world.
6. Non-focalized narration: depiction of character as agent, defined by actions.
7. External focalization: reflection; character experiencing through seeing or hearing; semi-subjective.
8. Internal focalization: character experiencing, private and subjective.
   a. surface: perception, e.g. POV shots.
   b. depth: dreams, hallucinations, memories.

16. The term 'implied author' was first introduced for literary studies by Wayne Booth (1961).
17. The term 'subjective' here is meant as the opposite of 'objective' rather than as an adjective of 'subjectivity'. Its literal meaning does nonetheless refer to focalization as a narrational process that gives a character a higher degree of subjectivity.

3 SILENT VIOLENCE: ON POINT OF VIEW

1. Emily Dickinson, *The Complete Poems*, 1991: p. 648, nr. 1559.
2. I use 'fantasy' here in the colloquial sense of the word and not in a psychoanalytic meaning. Fantasy refers to the scenes that reflect Magda's daydreams, dreams, thoughts, visions and hallucinations.
3. Literary narratologist Mieke Bal (1985, 1991) has further developed the notion of focalization, especially as a tool for a critique of ideology in both literature and art. I restrict myself here to film theoretical elaborations of focalization in cinema.
4. To my knowledge Jost's work has not been translated into English; therefore I discuss his theory of 'point of view' in more detail. See for a concise introduction the section on film narratology in *New Vocabularies in Film Semiotics* (Stam *et al.* 1992).
5. This dialogue is taken from the film *Malina* (1991) directed by Werner Schröeter. Elfriede Jelinek wrote the script based on the novel *Malina* by Ingeborg Bachmann. See the published script *Malina*, 1991. p. 113 (translation AS).
6. Ludo is present in 47 of the 49 scenes; and Nicole in 19 of the 49 scenes.
7. The child that plays Ludo is at this point replaced by an older actor, but Nicole is played throughout the film by the same actress. This results in the rather peculiar effect that in the second part of the film the mother sometimes looks younger than the son, which brings the oedipal implications of their relationship into even sharper relief.
8. There is definitely a hint of the famous painting *The Scream* by Edvard Munch.
9. This is what goes wrong in the court drama *The Accused*, an American Hollywood movie that tries to put forward a feminist view on rape in exploring a victim's struggle for justice, but that fails at the crucial moment. The rape, which is shown at the very end of the film, is told through internal focalization of a male witness. Thus the film takes away the experience from the raped woman. In denying the rape victim a voice and a look to tell her own story, the film repeats exactly the legal discourse that it criticizes. The narrative embedding of the rape as a flashback of a male witness who looked on, rather than allowing the woman to tell her own experience, makes the (very long) rape scene utterly voyeuristic. Once again, the rape victim is spoken.

    The film evoked considerable controversy. Empirical research on women viewing *The Accused* revealed 'universal identification' of female spectators with the rape victim (Schlesinger *et al.* 1990: 163). The film was found to have a great impact:

Many women who viewed *The Accused* felt that it had educational value
(82% of the group who had experienced violence and 75% of those
who had not). Most respondents (97% of the women with experience
of violence and 81% of women with none) thought the film handled the
chosen issues in a reasonable manner. However, a fair proportion were
unsure about the inclusion of the rape scene. It was this that had the
greatest impact. A quarter of the women with experience, and nearly a
third of those without, felt the scene portraying sexual violence should
not have been included for the following reasons: it should not have
been seen as entertainment nor used for financial gain; it sensationalised
sexual violence; and it served no useful purpose in the film (Schlesinger
et al. 1990: 148).

The voyeurism of the rape scene aroused anxieties about men viewing
a film such as *The Accused*. The women were afraid that male spectators
would derive pleasure and sexual gratification from viewing the rape scene.
They also feared that male viewers would blame the rape victim for 'asking for it', because of her sexy attire, her flirtatious behaviour, and her
drinking and smoking dope. This empirical study, then, shows the representation of the rape in *The Accused* to be highly debatable and contested.

10. Critical representations of the harsh reality of sexual violence, as in femi-
    nist films such as *Dust* and *Cruel Embrace*, are particularly pertinent in
    the context of systematic rape of women in wars. Feminists have dis-
    closed the frequent use of rape as a weapon in war (cf Brownmiller 1975).
    At the time of writing this chapter, news was reported about rape camps
    in Bosnia, about enforced pregnancies and the catholic interdiction on
    abortion even in those extreme circumstances. Most horrifying of all, it is
    purported that some rapes were filmed on video and distributed as por-
    nography for the soldiers.
      In the context of the use of rape in warfare, it is interesting to note that
    Helke Sander has made a four hour documentary, *Befreier und Befreite*
    ('Liberators and Liberated', 1991) about the systematic and repeated rape
    of German women by Russian soldiers after the liberation in 1945. In a
    masculinist world that exercises such total power over women's bodies
    and lives, and that displays utter disregard for the happiness of their chil-
    dren, feminist films like *Befreier und Befreite*, *Dust* and *Cruel Embrace*
    provide an urgent and heartrending protest against sexual violence and
    expose the intersection of gender with race and ethnicity.
11. The earlier work of Bordwell and Branigan has also been labeled 'for-
    malist', with their emphasis on a schematic and structural analysis of the
    specificity of the medium, that is of form and style, while abandoning
    questions of meaning.
12. To be sure, within the cognitive approach some attempts are made to
    theorize what keeps the film spectator glued to the screen. Noël Carroll
    (1988) advances an alternative model for movie narration which he claims
    to be more comprehensive and more precise than the models of contem-
    porary film theory inspired by semiotics and psychoanalysis. His so-called
    erotetic model postulates filmic narration as a relation of questions and
    answers: one scene raises a question that is answered in a later scene.

According to Carroll this question/answer model is not only superior in its simplicity but also explains the power of the movies: 'If it is a general feature of our cognitive makeup that, *all things being equal*, we not only want but expect answers to questions that have assertively been put before us, this explains our intense engagement with movies' (Carroll 1988: 181 (my emphasis)). Although Carroll himself is convinced that a restriction to cognitive faculties of the audience is necessary to be able to understand why movies are 'easily accessible and gripping' (212) to many different people, I find such a contention both solipsistic and universalist. All things are not equal after all. Carroll's approach is almost exclusively based on Hollywood movies and is therefore highly ethnocentric.

For Carroll, affect in film is negotiated solely through music (213–25). In isolating music as the carrier of emotive content, he goes as far as to deny the image any emotional impact: 'the music sutures the absence of affect from the image track' (224). Although there is no doubt as to the emotional power of film music nor its full exploitation in filmmaking, Carroll's model expresses a massive denial of the emotive force of images. In my view, Carroll's models suffer from reductive simplifications of minimal explanatory value. Film viewing is more than a rationalistic game of puzzle solving, or games of question-and-answer.

13. The best known and fiercest polemic has been exchanged between Noël Carroll and Stephen Heath in *October*. Carroll wrote a long and polemical review of *Questions of Cinema* (1981) by Heath in 'Address to the Heathen', *October* 23 (Winter 1982) 89–163. Heath responded to this criticism in 'Le Père Noël', *October* 26 (Fall 1983) 63–115. Carroll reacted to the response in 'A Reply to Heath', *October* 27 (Winter 1983) 81–102.

In *Screen* a debate was published between followers of 'Screen Theory' and 'Formalism'. Barry King wrote an extended polemical review of *The Classical Hollywood Cinema* (1985) by David Bordwell, Janet Staiger and Kristin Thompson, published in two parts: 'The Classical Hollywood Cinema' in *Screen*, **27** (6) 1986: 74–88; and 'The Story Continues . . . Barry King Returns to the Wisconsin Project', in *Screen*, **28** (3) 1987: 56–82, in which King extended his review to David Bordwell's *Narration in the Fiction Film* (1985) and Edward Branigan's *Point of View in the Cinema* (1985). In *Screen*, **29** (1) 1988, Thompson responded to King's reviews in 'Wisconsin Project or King's Projection' (48–53); Staiger in 'Reading King's Reading' (54–70) and Bordwell in 'Adventures in the Highlands of Theory' (72–97). Finally, King in turn replied in 'A Reply to Bordwell, Staiger and Thompson' (99–118).

In their latest book, *Post-theory*, Bordwell and Carroll (1996) continue their crusade against anything which is poststructuralist, postmodern or psychoanalytic. Their aversion against what they see as the dogmatism of 'the' modern film theory makes the book into a rather paranoid project. The book is bound to disappoint, because after such fierce criticisms the proposed alternatives are necessarily superficial and common sensual.

14. Such voyeuristic shots have often become quite famous in film history, for example in *Psycho* (Hitchcock 1960) the murderer's look through the hole in the wall at his prospective female victim undressing. Another stereotyped voyeuristic shot is the introduction of the *femme fatale* to both the

male character and the spectator, as in the camera tilt from the floor up to the legs of Lana Turner in *The Postman Always Rings Twice* (Garnett 1946), the camera following the legs of Barbara Stanwyck walking down the stairs in *Double Indemnity* (Wilder 1944) or the swing of Rita Hayworth's hair in *Gilda* (Vidor 1944).

15. If voyeurism is included in the rare case when we are dealing with a female focalizer, it requires a shift from female narration to male ocularization, as for example happens in *Mildred Pierce* (Curtiz 1945) where flashbacks are embedded in Mildred Pierce's (Joan Crawford) story told by her in voice-over. Within the flashbacks (mostly filmed in zero ocularization), men can gaze at women because Mildred's voice is silent; she is no longer a narrator but a character in the story.

16. Source: *Filmkatalogus Cinemien*. Amsterdam: Cinemien 1989, pp. 31 and 51.

4   AND THE MIRROR CRACKED: ON METAPHORS OF VIOLENCE AND RESISTANCE

1. Modleski 1988: 27.
2. Haraway 1997: 182.
3. This body of theory is developed by Kuhn (1982), Kaplan (1983), de Lauretis (1984) Doane (1987) and Modleski (1988), who have most directly addressed issues of violence.
4. Marleen Gorris (1948) wrote and directed four feature films:
   De Stilte Rond Christine M. (*A Question of Silence*), 1982
   Gebroken Spiegels (*Broken Mirrors*), 1984
   The Last Island, 1990
   Antonia's Line, 1995.
   The scripts of the first three films have been published in: *Het Nederlands Scenario* (3) Amsterdam: International Theatre & Film Books, November 1990. Gorris also wrote and directed a television series in five parts *Verhalen van de straat* (*Tales from a street*, 1993).
5. Margarethe von Trotta, *Die bleierne Zeit* (*Marianne and Juliane or The German Sisters*), Germany, 1981
   Barbara Loden, *Wanda*, USA, 1970
   Margarethe von Trotta, *Das zweite Erwachen der Christa Klages* (*The Second Awakening of Christa Klages*), Germany, 1977
   Ann Hui, *Princess Fragrance*, Hong Kong/China, 1987
   Lizzie Borden, *Born in Flames*, USA, 1982
   Matilde Landeta, *La Negra Angustias*, Mexico, 1949
   Marleen Gorris, *De Stilte Rond Christine M.* (*A Question of Silence*), Netherlands, 1982
   Chantal Akerman, *Jeanne Dielman, 23 Quai du Commerce, 1080 Bruxelles*, Belgium, 1975
   Lina Wertmüller, *Camorra*, Italy, 1986
   Marion Hänsel, *Dust*, Belgium, 1984
   Charlotte Silvera, *Prisonnières* ('Female Prisoners'), France, 1988
   Margarethe von Trotta, *Heller Wahn* (*The Female Friend*), Germany, 1982

Nancy Meckler, *Sister my Sister*, Great Britain, 1995
Ann Turner, *Celia*, Australia, 1988
Peter Jackson, *Heavenly Creatures*, Australia 1994.

6. Some critics have referred to *Silence* as a feminist comedy, see for example Gabriele Donnerberg 1984: 61. For me, however, there is nothing comical about the film in spite of the famous laughter on which the film ends.

7. In my forthcoming study of Marleen Gorris I will dedicate a chapter to a reception study of her work.

8. See for example 'Montage 1937' (Eisenstein 1992) and Nizhny's *Lessons with Eisenstein* (1962).

9. At one point in his essay 'Montage 1937' Eisenstein distinguishes metaphor from what he calls 'the general image' in subordinating the former to the latter: separate metaphors are combined into a dynamic general image. Yet throughout that same essay and elsewhere a slippage often occurs between the terms metaphor and general image.

10. Peter Wollen argues that Metz' early theory of cinema exaggerates the importance of analogies with verbal language and hence underplays the dimension of the iconic sign. According to Wollen, there are two different kinds of heritage that bring Metz to this onesidedness in his early work: the romantic aesthetics of André Bazin, with its preference for the natural and organic 'ontology of the photographic image' (124–41), and Saussurian semiology, with its prejudices 'in favour of the arbitrary and the symbolic' and of 'the spoken and the acoustic' (139).

11. The fact that it was mostly women in the audience who laughed was commented upon in reviews and articles; the laughter was sometimes read as 'immoral' and 'incredible'.

12. I am reminded here of Cixous' provocative image of the laughing Medusa as beautiful (1980: 255). See for a exploration of symbolic violence in relation to women in Greek drama and myth, Geyer-Ryan (1994).

13. Irigaray, 'Divine Women', in *Sex and Genealogies*, 1993.

14. See for a feminist critique of photography and the image of 'Woman', Pollock 1990.

15. Adrienne Rich describes lesbian existence in her famous essay 'Compulsory Heterosexuality and Lesbian Existence' (1986) as a continuum of women's experiences, solidarity against men and political bonding.

16. See for example Eisensteins essays 'Montage 1937 (1992)' and 'Montage 1938' (1992).

17. *NRC Handelsblad*, March 29, 1989.

18. See for an excellent feminist analysis of the horror movie, Carol Clover, 1992.

19. I disagree with the interpretation of Els Maeckelberge (1991) that the references to Mary in *Broken Mirrors* can be read as a liberative theology for feminists. Although Gorris makes use of Christian imagery, the references to Mary by André are too much of a mockery to be able to claim, as Maeckelberge does, the *Broken Mirrors* offers a liberating image of 'the Immaculate and Pure position of women in a violent society' (1991: 166).

196 *Notes*

5 FORCES OF SUBVERSION: ON THE EXCESS OF IMAGE

1. Rich, 'The Images', from *A Wild Patience Has Taken Me This Far*, 1981: pp. 3–5.
2. De Lauretis 1987: 135.
3. See for discussions of Irigaray's notion of mimesis Whitford 1991 and Burke, Schor and Whitford 1994, especially the essays of Braidotti, Schor and Weed.
4. Mayne analyzes *Redupers* (Helke Sander 1977), *Illusions* (Julie Dash 1982), *I've Heard the Mermaids Singing* (Patricia Rozema 1987) and *The Man Who Envied Women* (Yvonne Rainer 1986).
5. Perhaps unnecessarily I reiterate my remark made in Chapter 3 that the Lacanian concept of the gaze exceeds the notion of 'the male gaze' in feminist film theory. Within the Lacanian scheme Silverman maintains a sharp distinction between the gaze and the look. (Here she makes use of the possibility of the English language to distinguish gaze and look, both rendered as 'le regard' in French. 'Look' is Silverman's translation of Lacan's 'l'œil', or the eye.) The Lacanian concept of the look encompasses the feminist notion of the male gaze, that is, scopophilic voyeurism.
6. *Camera Obscura* dedicated a special issue to 'Unspeakable Images' (no. 24, September 1990).
7. There are many elements to one cinematic shot:
   Photography: light, colour, tonality
   Framing: focal length/perspective relations, frame dimensions, camera angle and movement
   Mise-en-scène: setting, make-up, costumes, composition
   Actors: gestures, facial expressions, movement
   Time and space: duration (short or long take); representation of three-dimensional space
   Sound: diegetic or non-diegetic; loudness, pitch, timbre; hi-fi, stereo
   (cf Bordwell and Thompson, *Film Art*, 1986).
8. The idea that the image always expresses something which is in excess of conventional representation comes close to Gilles Deleuze's critique of representation (1968, 1981; also see Patton 1994). For Deleuze, representation should not be related to the Freudian theory of the libido, and hence of lack, but on the contrary to the positive notion of pure expression. The power of the image can then be read as a force, a passion, an affect which is beyond classical representation. I think that it may be very fruitful and productive to rethink contemporary visual culture along the lines of Deleuzian philosophy, but it lies outside the scope of this book.
9. I drew much technical information from the published post-production script with full *découpage* of the film *Bagdad Café* in *L'Avant-Scène Cinéma*, pp. 19–117, November–December 1988.
10. I use 'black' and 'white' here as political terms designating asymmetrical social positions.
11. I am, of course, aware that *Bagdad Café* is directed by a male filmmaker. However, in my viewing experience Percy Adlon's film is an example of feminist filmmaking by a man. Also, several women were active in realizing this film. Adlon's films are co-written with and produced by Eleanore

Adlon. Moreover, in several interviews Marianne Sägebrecht, the actress who plays Jasmin and also has the leading role in two other films by the Adlons (*Zuckerbaby*, 1985 and *Rosalie Goes Shopping*, 1989), has stated her intense involvement with the script and the making of the film.

12. I want to draw attention to the 'phallic proportions' that the Lacanian notion of the gaze acquires here. The structural similarities between phallus and gaze are striking: they both signify (and veil) lack symbolizing the desire of the Other; nobody can own or have either phallus or gaze; and the male subject stands in a privileged relationship to both.

13. Silverman argues that exhibitionism unsettles 'because it threatens to expose the duplicity inherent in every subject, and every object' (1992: 152). I believe that her argument does not clash with mine but I elaborate on different aspects of the same problematic.

14. Of course, fat has become a feminist issue (Orbach 1978) just as anorexia and bulimia have become the dominant pathology for women of today (Orbach 1986; Bordo 1993).

15. The contemporary cult of female beauty is deliciously caricatured in the animation film *Body Beautiful* (Joanna Quinn, UK, 1990) in which obese housewife Beryl wins a fitness contest. (I briefly discuss Quinn's earlier cartoon with Beryl as the main character, *Girls Night Out*, in the next chapter.)

16. The reference here to a possible lesbian love affair between Jasmin and Brenda is no more than implicitly suggested. In his next film, *Salmonberries* in 1991, Percy Adlon explored a lesbian relation between the German librarian Roswitha and the Eskimo foundling Kotz, played by k.d. lang.

17. The relation between sisters is, probably not uncoincidentally, a popular topic in women's films, as for example in *Sisters or the Balance of Happyness* (1979) and *Marianne and Juliane (The German Sisters)* (1981) by Margarethe von Trotta; and more recently *Sister My Sister* (1995) by Nancy Meckler and *Six Days, Six Nights* (1995) by Diane Kurys.

18. See Creed (1993) for an exploration of the monstrous feminine as the abject in the horror film.

6 THE NAVEL OF THE FILM: ON THE ABJECT AND THE MASQUERADE

1. Hélène Cixous, 'The Laugh of the Medusa', 1980: 255.

2. Bette Midler announcing Madonna on the benefit pop concert 'Aid for Africa' in 1985.

3. Monika Treut has made videos since 1976 (e.g. *Bondage*). In 1984 she completed a dissertation in literary studies entitled *Die grausame Frau* ('The Cruel Woman'), a study of sadomasochism (Basel/Frankfurt 1984). Since 1984 she has worked together with Elfi Mikesch in a film production company called 'Hyäne Filmproduktion'. Treut and Mikesch co-directed the film *Seduction. The Cruel Woman* (1984). Then Treut made some films that dealt with transsexuality: *My Father Is Coming* (1990) and *Max* (1992). See for an analysis of the reception of Treut's controversial work, Knight 1995.

4. The image, though in black and white, is remarkably similar to the startling beginning of *The Tin Drum* (Schlöndorff 1978–9), where the camera moves with the baby through the birth channel as it is born.

5. Peter Gern has also directed gay films himself, e.g. *Gossenkind* ('Child of the gutter', 1991). See for the phenomenon of the 'actor as intertext' in New German Cinema, Thomas Elsaesser 1989: 284–9.

6. In my understanding Richard Dyer sligthly misrepresents Parker and Pollock's argument in focusing too much on the 'mysterious, hidden and threatening' female genitals (quoted in Dyer 1990: 182). In western art it is not the actual genitalia but the image of the female body as such that signifies her difference, and hence on an unconscious level provokes male fear (Parker and Pollock 1981: 126–7).

7. A privileged example of feminist realism for film theorists has been *Jeanne Dielman, 23 Quai du Commerce, 1080 Bruxelles* (1976) by Chantal Akerman.

8. For Irigaray one of the most important aspects of a female symbolic is to find images of the divine; see for example 'Divine Women' (1993: 55–72).

9. 'Repulsive' and not abject, because the major elements of abjection are absent in this shot: ambiguity, loss of boundaries, mucosity, etc. In *My Father Is Coming* Treut again focuses on the repulsive male body in a sex scene between the father of the film title, Hans, and porn star Annie Sprinkle. The camera films Hans' fat stomach from below and then takes a position from under his armpit. While the frame is filled with an extreme close-up of quivering flabs of white flesh, hairs, wrinkles, pimples, and drops of sweat, Annie's voice tells us to let pleasure fill each and every cell of the entire body with erotic power.

10. Marlon Riggs in his experimental film on black male homosexuality, *Tongues Untied* (USA, 1989).

11. The general feeling of gloom and immanent threat in the German part of the story, enhanced by the *mise-en-scène* as well as the black and white imagery, creates a theatrical setting that is reminiscent of fascist aesthetics. Treut has written about the theatrical connection between fascism and sadomasochism (1986, 1995). As mentioned in note three, she has made a film about sadomasochism with Elfi Mikesh in 1984, *Seduction. The Cruel Woman*, which explores the theatre of S/M and fascism. Treut believes that women should take up the theatrical gesture and play with the cultural signs of fascism, in order to disentangle the *un*conscious relation between violence and sexuality. In making this connection conscious and turning it into theatre, or rather, into highly aestheticized cinema, Treut claims to deconstruct the fascist tradition as well as open up a space for new representations of sexuality (see Treut 1986: 18). In this respect, she shares with other directors of the New German Cinema the relentless search of pushing the boundaries of representability to the limit so as to deal with a painful history and to effect change and transformation.

12. The phenomenon of crossdressing and gender ambiguity has drawn serious attention from feminist critics. See Epstein and Straub (1991) and Garber (1992).

13. Usually, male strippers performing to a female audience keep on a piece of underwear that veils their penis. However, starting with the immense success of male performing groups such as the Chippendales, some male

strippers have begun actually to strip down to their penis. For example, the London Knights strip completely naked, keeping their organs in erection by penis rings and continuous frantic movements. At the same time, their show has hard core elements including a display of violence in imitating rape and S/M scenes with girls from the audience.

14. Male groups performing for a female audience try to avoid these dangers through different strategies. The Chippendales do this by perfecting their performance in a highly professional if not sleek show, the London Knights by putting on a display of exaggerated and aggressive masculinity. Not that this has saved The Chippendales from 'accusations' of being gay. In any case male performers keep their distance from the female audience in that they are not for sale, in contrast to female strippers who tend to work in brothels or nightclubs where male customers can buy 'a girl' for sex. Hence, for the male performer, there is a bottom line to his degradation.

15. In teaching this film regularly in class, I have noticed that there are always some students who have not understood that the feminine woman Ramona is the same person as the macho man performing in the bar. They are usually quite shocked to be fooled in their perceptions and expectations of gender.

16. See Hoogland 1997 for a lucid critique of the use of lesbianism in feminist theory. As her book came out while mine was going to press, I could not include her work in the body of this chapter.

17. *Écriture féminine* (lit.: 'a feminine writing') is an experimental practice of writing by women which started in France during the 1970s, exploring the feminine in language. Writers Hélène Cixous and Luce Irigaray are seen as its most important exponents, but also writers who have claimed their distance from feminism, such as Julia Kristeva and Marguérite Duras. See for introductions Marks and de Courtivron 1980; see also Andermatt Conley 1984; Braidotti 1991; Shiach 1991; Whitford 1991; see for a lesbian critique Roof 1991.

18. The advanced emancipation of gays and lesbians, especially in such northern countries as Scandinavia and the Netherlands, may be another reason why the lesbian movement is less visible in Europe than in the USA. Gay and lesbian subcultures are so much integrated into the mainstream, that some gays and lesbians complain that they have become 'normal' thereby losing their specificity, and hence their 'queerness'.

19. Lit.: 'look for the woman'. I derived this subtitle from a published discussion on *The Practice of Love* (de Lauretis, 1994) in the Dutch journal *Lover*, vol. 21 (4), 1994: 50–6.

20. This is the major argument of Elizabeth Grosz' 'interrogation' of *The Practice of Love* – that psychoanalysis cannot be the primary paradigm for thinking lesbian sexuality (1994). Grosz even goes as far as to question whether it is possible to postulate a specific lesbian desire. Her criticism sounds slightly disingenuous, however, since she herself has endeavoured into a specific theory of lesbian sexuality in terms of fetishism (1991).

Bibliography

Andermatt Conley, V., *Hélène Cixous: Writing the Feminine*. Lincoln and London: University of Nebraska Press, 1984.

Andrew, D., *Concepts in Film Theory*. Oxford: Oxford University Press, 1984.

Ang, I., *Watching Dallas*. London: Methuen, 1985.

Aumont, J., *Montage Eisenstein*. London: BFI Publishing and Bloomington: Indiana University Press, 1987.

L'Avant-Scène Cinéma, November–December. Script of *Bagdad Café*, 1988: 19–117.

Bal, M., *Narratology: Introduction to the Theory of Narrative*. Toronto: University of Toronto Press, 1985.

Bal, M., *Reading 'Rembrandt'. Beyond the Word–Image Opposition*. Cambridge, New York (etc.): Cambridge University Press, 1991.

Barry, K., *Female Sexual Slavery*. New York: Avon Books, 1979.

Barthes, R., *The Pleasure of the Text*. New York: Hill and Wang, 1975.

Barthes, R., 'The Death of the Author', in *Image/Music/Text*. Glasgow: Fontana/Collins, 1977: 142–148.

Barthes, R., 'The Third Meaning. Research notes on some Eisenstein Stills' in *Image/Music/Text*. Glasgow: Fontana/Collins, 1977: 52–68.

Beauvoir, S. de, *The Second Sex*. Harmondsworth: Penguin, 1972 (1949).

Berger, J., *Ways of Looking*. London: BBC and Penguin Books, 1972.

Bergstrom, J. and Doane, M.A. (eds), *Camera Obscura. A Journal of Feminism and Film Theory*. Special Issue 'The Spectatrix', nos 20–21, 1989.

Bobo, J., 'Reading Through the Text: The Black Woman as Audience', in M. Diawara (ed.), *Black American Cinema*. New York and London: Routledge, 1993: 272–287.

Bobo, J., *Black Women as Cultural Readers*. New York: Columbia University Press, 1995.

Booth, W., *The Rhetoric of Fiction*. Chicago: University of Chicago Press, 1961.

Bordo, S., *Unbearable Weight. Feminism, Western Culture, and the Body*. Berkeley: University of California, 1993.

Bordwell, D., *Narration in the Fiction Film*. London: Methuen, 1985.

Bordwell, D., *Making Meaning. Inference and Rhetoric in the Interpretation of Cinema*. Cambridge, MA and London: Harvard University Press, 1989.

Bordwell, D. and Carroll, N. (eds), *Post-Theory. Reconstructing Film Studies*. Madison/Wisconsin: The University of Wisconsin Press, 1996.

Bordwell, D. and Thompson, K., *Film Art. An Introduction*. New York: Alfred A. Knopf, 1986 (rev. edn).

Boundas, C. V. and Olkowski, D. (eds), *Gilles Deleuze and the Theater of Philosophy*. London and New York: Routledge, 1994.

Braidotti, R., *Patterns of Dissonance. A Study of Women in Contemporary Philosophy*. Cambridge: Polity Press, 1991.

Braidotti, R., *Nomadic Subjects*. New York: Columbia University Press, 1994a.

Braidotti, R., 'Feminism By Any Other Name', in *Differences*, vol. 6 (2–3), Summer–Fall, 1994b: 27–61.

Branigan, E., *Point of View in the Cinema. A Theory of Narration and Subjectivity in Classical Film*. Berlin: Mouton Publishers, 1984.

Branigan, E., *Narrative Comprehension and Film*. New York and London: Routledge, 1992.

Browne, N., *The Rhetoric of Filmic Narration*. Ann Arbor, Michigan: UMI Research Press, 1976.

Brownmiller, S., *Against Our Will. Men, Women and Rape*. Harmondsworth: Penguin Books, 1975.

Bruno, G., *Streetwalking on a Ruined Map. Cultural Theory and the City Films of Elvira Notari*. Princeton: Princeton University Press, 1993.

Burke, C., Schor, N. and Whitford, M. (eds), *Engaging with Irigaray. Feminist Philosophy and Modern European Thought*. New York: Columbia University Press, 1994.

Burnier A., *De zwembadmentaliteit*. Amsterdam: Querido, 1979.

Buscombe, E., 'Ideas of Authorship', in J. Caughie (ed.), 1981: 22–34.

Butler, J., *Gender Trouble*. New York and London: Routledge, 1990.

Butler, J., *Bodies That Matter. On the Discursive Limits of 'Sex'*. New York and London: Routledge, 1993.

Carroll, N., *Mystifying Movies. Fads and Fallacies in Contemporary Film Theory*. New York: Columbia University Press, 1988.

Carson, D., Dittmar, L. and Welsch, J. R. (eds), *Multiple Voices in Feminist Film Criticism*. London and Minneapolis: University of Minnesota Press, 1994.

Casetti, F., *D'un regard l'autre. Le film et son spectateur*. Lyon: Presses Universitaires de Lyon, 1990.

Caughie, J., *Theories of Authorship. A Reader*. London and New York: Routledge and Kegan Paul, 1981.

Chanter, T., *Ethics of Eros. Irigaray's Rewriting of the Philosophers*. New York and London: Routledge, 1995.

Chapkis, W., *Live Sex Acts. Women Performing Erotic Labour*. London: Cassell, 1997.

Chapman, R. and Rutherford, J. (eds), *Male Order. Unwrapping Masculinity*. London: Lawrence and Wishart, 1988.

Chatman, S., *Coming to Terms. The Rhetoric of Narrative in Fiction and Film*. Ithaca and London: Cornell University Press, 1990.

Chicago, J., *The Dinner Party. A Symbol of Our Heritage*. New York: Anchor Press, 1979.

Cixous, H., 'The Laugh of the Medusa', in Marks, E. and de Courtivron, I. (eds), *New French Feminisms*. Amherst: University of Massachusetts Press, 1980: 245–64.

Cixous, H., *Le Livre de Promethea*. Paris: Gallimard, 1983.

Cixous, H., *Entre l'écriture*. Paris: Des Femmes, 1986.

Cixous, H. and Clément, C., *The Newly Born Woman*. Theory and History of Literature Series no. 24. Manchester: Manchester University Press, 1986.

Clover, C. J., *Men, Women, and Chain Saws. Gender in the Modern Horror Film*. London: British Film Institute Publishing, 1992.

Cook, P., 'The Point of Self-Expression in Avant-Garde Film', in J. Caughie (ed.), 1981: 271–81.

Creed, B., *The Monstrous-Feminine. Film, Feminism, Psychoanalysis.* London and New York: Routledge, 1993.

Deleuze, G., *Différence et répétition.* Paris: Presses Universitaires de France, 1968.

Deleuze, G., *Masochism. An Interpretation of Coldness and Cruelty.* New York: G. Braziller, 1971. Reprinted as *Masochism: Coldness and Cruelty.* New York: Zone Books, 1985.

Deleuze, G., *Francis Bacon. Logique de la Sensation I & II.* Paris: Éditions de la Différence, 1981.

Deleuze, G., *Cinema 1. The Movement-Image.* Minneapolis: University of Minnesota Press, 1986.

Deleuze, G., *Cinema 2. The Time-Image.* Minneapolis: University of Minnesota Press, 1989.

Dickinson, E., *The Complete Poems,* edited by T. H. Johnson. London and Boston: Faber and Faber, 1991.

Differences, 'Queer Theory. Lesbian and Gay Sexualities', **3** (2), 1991.

Differences, 'More Gender Trouble: Feminism Meets Queer Theory', **6** (2–3), 1994.

Dittmar, L., 'Beyond Gender and Within It: The Social Construction of Female Desire', *Wide Angle,* **8** (3/4), 1986: 79–88.

Doan, L., *The Lesbian Postmodern.* New York: Columbia University Press, 1994.

Doane, M. A., *The Desire to Desire. The Woman's Film of the 1940s.* Bloomington: Indiana University Press, 1987.

Doane, M. A., 'Film and the Masquerade: Theorising the Female Spectator', (1982). Reprinted in *Femmes Fatales. Feminism, Film Theory, Psychoanalysis.* New York and London: Routledge, 1991: 17–32.

Docherty, T. (ed.), *Postmodernism. A Reader.* New York: Columbia University Press, 1993.

Donnerberg, G., 'Warum *Die Stille um Christine M.* kein "patriarchalisches Erzählkino" ist, obwohl theoretisch alle Bedingungen dazu erfüllt sind', *Frauen und Film,* **36**, 1984: 61–72.

Dowdeswell, J., *Women on Rape.* Guildford, Surrey: Biddles Ltd, 1986.

During, S. (ed.), *The Cultural Studies Reader.* London and New York: Routledge. 1992.

Dworkin, A., *Our Blood. Prophecies and Discourse on Sexual Politics.* London: The Women's Press, 1976.

Dworkin, A., *Pornography: Men Possessing Women.* New York: Perigee/G.P. Putnam's, 1981.

Dyer, R., 'Don't Look Now: The Male Pin-Up', in *Screen,* **23** (3–4), 1982: 61–73.

Dyer, R., *Now You See It. Studies on Lesbian and Gay Film.* London: Routledge, 1990.

Dyer, R., 'White', reprinted in *The Matter of Images. Essays on Representations.* London and New York: Routledge, 1993: 141–63.

Easthope, A., *What A Man's Gotta Do. The Masculine Myth in Popular Culture.* London: Paladin, 1986.

Eisenstein, H., *Contemporary Feminist Thought.* Boston: G. K. Hall & Co., 1983.

Eisenstein, S. M., *Selected Works. Volume I. Writings 1922–34*, edited and translated by R. Taylor. Bloomington: Indiana University Press, 1987.

Eisenstein, S. M., *Selected Works. Volume II. Towards a Theory of Montage*, edited by R. Taylor and M. Glenny. Bloomington: Indiana University Press, 1992.

Elsaesser, T., *New German Cinema. A History*. New Brunswick: Rutgers University Press, 1989.

Epstein, J. and Straub, K. (eds), *Body Guards. The Cultural Politics of Gender Ambiguity*. New York and London: Routledge, 1991.

Erens, P. (ed.), *Issues in Feminist Film Criticism*. Bloomington: Indiana University Press, 1990.

Felman, S., 'Postal Survival, or the Question of the Navel', *Yale French Studies*, **69**, 1985: 49–72.

Fetterley, J., *The Resisting Reader. A Feminist Approach to American Fiction*. Bloomington: Indiana University Press, 1978.

Fischer, L., *Shot/Countershot. Film Tradition and Women's Cinema*. Princeton: Princeton University Press, 1989.

Flitterman-Lewis, S., 'Woman, Desire and the Look: Feminism and the Enunciative Apparatus in Cinema', in J. Caughie (ed.), 1981: 242–50.

Flitterman-Lewis, S., *To Desire Differently. Feminism and the French Cinema*. Urbana and Chicago: University of Illinois Press, 1990.

Förster, A., *Subjektitude. Het Tweede Gezicht 2*. Amsterdam: Cinemien, 1982.

Förster, A., 'Helke Sander', in *Het Nederlandse Jaarboek Film 1985*. Weesp: Wereldvenster, 1985: 82–9.

Foster, H. (ed.), *The Anti-Aesthetic: Essays on Postmodern Culture*. Port Townsend, Washington: The Bay Press, 1983.

Foucault, M., 'What is an Author?', in *Language, Counter-Memory, Practice*. Ithaca: Cornell University, 1977: 113–39.

Freud, S., *Interpretation of Dreams*. In: *Standard Edition*, edited by J. Strachey. London: Hogarth, vols IV and V, 1964 (1900).

Freud, S., 'The Uncanny', *SE*, XVII (1919) 218–56.

Freud, S., 'Beyond the Pleasure Principle', *SE* XVIII (1920) 3–64.

Freud, S., 'Medusa's Head', *SE*, XVIII (1922 (1940)) 273–4.

Freud, S., 'Some Psychical Consequences of the Anatomical Distinction Between The Sexes', *SE*, XIX (1925) 243–58.

Freud, S., 'Female Sexuality', *SE*, XXI (1931) 223–43.

Freud, S., 'Femininity', *SE*, XXII (1933) 112–35.

Gaines, J., 'White Privilege and Looking Relations: Race and Gender in Feminist Film Theory', *Screen*, **29** (4), 1988: 12–27.

Gamman, L. and Marshment, M. (eds), *The Female Gaze. Women as Viewers of Popular Culture*. London: The Women's Press, 1988.

Garber, M., *Vested Interests. Cross-dressing and Cultural Anxiety*. London: Penguin Books, 1992.

Genette, G., *Narrative Discourse*. Ithaca: Cornell University Press, 1980.

Gentile, M. C., *Film Feminisms. Theory and Practice*. Westport and London: Greenwood Press, 1985.

Gever, M., Greyson, J. and Parmar, P. (eds), *Queer Looks. Perspectives on Lesbian and Gay Film and Video*. New York and London: Routledge, 1993.

Geyer-Ryan, H., *Fables of Desire*. Cambridge: Polity Press, 1994.

Gledhill, C. (ed.), *Home Is Where the Heart Is. Studies in Melodrama and the Woman's Film.* London: British Film Institute, 1987.

Griffin, S., *Pornography and Silence: Culture's Revenge Against Nature.* New York: Harper and Row, 1981.

Grossberg, L., Nelson, C. and Treichler, P. (eds), *Cultural Studies.* New York: Routledge, 1992.

Grosz, E., 'Lesbian Fetishism?', *Differences*, **3**, 1991: 39–54.

Grosz, E., 'The Labors of Love. Analyzing Perverse Desire: An Interrogation of Teresa de Lauretis's *The Practice of Love*', *Differences*, **6**, (2–3), 1994: 274–95.

Hall, S. *et al.* (eds), *Culture, Media, Language.* London: Hutchinson, 1980.

Halpern Martineau, B., 'Subjecting Her Objectification *or* Communism Is Not Enough' in C. Johnston, *Notes on Women's Cinema*, (1973) SEFT, Glasgow: Screen Reprint, 1991: 32–40.

Hamer, D. and Budge, B. (eds.), *The Good, the Bad and the Gorgeous. Popular Culture's Romance with Lesbianism.* London: Pandora, 1994.

Haraway, D., 'Situated Knowledges: The Science Question in Feminism and the Privilege of Partical Perspective', in *Simians, Cyborgs, and Women. The Reinvention of Nature.* London: Free Association Books, 1991: 183–201.

Haraway, D., *Modest_Witness @ Second_Millennium. FemaleMan© Meets OncoMouse™.* New York: Routledge, 1997.

Haskell, M., *From Reverence to Rape. The Treatment of Women in the Movies.* Chicago and London: The University of Chicago Press, 1987 (rev. edn).

Heath, S., 'Comment on "The Idea of Authorship"', in J. Caughie (ed.), 1981: 214–20.

Heath, S., *Questions of Cinema.* London: Macmillan, 1981.

Higgins, L. A. and Silver, B. R. (eds), *Rape and Representation.* New York: Columbia University Press, 1991.

Hoogland, R., *Elizabeth Bowen: A Reputation in Writing.* New York: New York University Press, 1994.

Hoogland, R., *Lesbian Configurations.* Oxford: Polity Press, 1997.

hooks, b., *Yearning. Race, Gender, and Cultural Politics.* Boston: South End Press, 1990.

hooks, b., *Black Looks. Race and Representation.* Boston: South End Press, 1992.

hooks, b., *Outlaw Culture. Resisting Representations.* New York and London: Routledge, 1994.

Irigaray, L., *Speculum of the Other Woman.* Ithaca: Cornell University Press, 1985a.

Irigaray, L., *This Sex Which Is Not One.* Ithaca: Cornell University Press, 1985b.

Irigaray, L., *Sex and Genealogies.* New York: Columbia University Press, 1993.

JanMohamed, A. R. 'Sexuality on/of the Racial Border: Foucault, Wright, and the Articulation of "Racialized Sexuality"', in D. C. Stanton (ed.), *Discourses of Sexuality. From Aristotle to Aids.* Ann Arbor: The University of Michigan, 1992: 94–116.

Jardine, A., *Gynesis. Configurations of Woman and Modernity.* Ithaca and

London: Cornell University Press, 1985.

Jeffords, S., *Hard Bodies. Hollywood Masculinity in the Reagan Era*. New Brunswick: Rutgers University Press, 1994.

Jelinek, E., *Malina. Ein Filmbuch*. Frankfurt am Main: Suhrkamp Verlag, 1991.

Johnson, A., 'The Root of Evil. Suburban Imagery in Jane Campion's *Sweetie* and Bill Henson's series *Untitled 1985/1986*', in E. McDonald and J. Engberg (eds), *Binocular. Focusing, Writing, Vision*. Sydney: Moët and Chandon, 1991.

Johnston, C., 'Women's Cinema as Counter-Cinema', in *Notes on Women's Cinema*, (1973) SEFT, Glasgow: Screen Reprint, 1991: 24–31.

Jost, F., *L'Œil-Caméra. Entre Film et Roman*. Lyon: Presses universitaires de Lyon, 1989.

Jost, F., *Un Monde à Notre Image. Énonciation, Cinéma, Télévision*. Paris: Meridiens Klincksieck, 1992.

Jump Cut Special Issue 'Lesbians and Film', 24/25, 1981.

Kaplan, E. A., *Women in Film Noir*. London: British Film Institute Publishing, 1980.

Kaplan, E. A., *Women and Film. Both Sides of the Camera*. New York and London: Methuen, 1983.

Kaplan, E. A., *Rocking Around the Clock. Music Television, Postmodernism, and Consumer Culture*. New York and London: Routledge, 1987.

Kaplan, E. A., *Postmodernism and Its Discontents. Theories, Practices*. London and New York: Verso, 1988.

Kappeler, S., *The Pornography of Representation*. Cambridge: Polity Press, 1986.

Kirkham, P. and Thumin, J. (eds), *You Tarzan. Masculinity, Movies and Men*. London: Lawrence and Wishart, 1993.

Knight, J., *Women and the New German Cinema*. London and New York: Verso, 1992.

Knight, J., 'The Meaning of Treut?' in T. Wilton (ed.), *Immortal Invisible. Lesbians and the Moving Image*. London and New York: Routledge, 1995: 34–51.

Koch, G., 'Warum Frauen ins Männerkino gehen', in G. Nabakowski, H. Sander and P. Gorsen (eds), in *Frauen in der Kunst. Band I*. Frankfurt am Main: Suhrkamp Verlag, 1980: 15–29.

Koenig Quart, B., *Women Directors. The Emergence of a New Cinema*. New York etc.: Praeger, 1988.

Kristeva, J., *Powers of Horror. An Essay on Abjection*. New York: Columbia University Press, 1982.

Kuderna, J. and Kuderna, C., 'Lauter ganz normale Frauen', in Frauenfilminitiative, *Mörderinnen in Film*. Berlin: Elefanten Press, 1992: 135–7.

Kuhn, A., *Women's Pictures. Feminism and Cinema*. London etc.: Routledge and Kegan Paul, 1982.

Lacan, J., *Écrits. A Selection*. New York and London: Norton, 1977.

Lacan, J., *The Four Fundamental Concepts of Psychoanalysis*. New York and London: Norton, 1981.

Laplanche, J., *Life and Death in Psychoanalysis*. Baltimore and London: The Johns Hopkins University Press, 1985.

Laplanche, J. and J.-B. Pontalis, 'Fantasy and the Origins of Sexuality', in

V. Burgin, J. Donald and C. Kaplan (eds), *Formations of Fantasy*. London and New York: Methuen, 1986: 5–34.

Lauretis, T. de, *Alice Doesn't. Feminism. Semiotics. Cinema*. Bloomington: Indiana University Press, 1984.

Lauretis, T. de, 'Oedipus Interruptus', *Wide Angle*, **7** (1/2), 1985: 34–40.

Lauretis, T. de, *Technologies of Gender. Essays on Theory, Film, and Fiction*. Bloomington: Indiana University Press, 1987.

Lauretis, T. de, 'Sexual Indifference and Lesbian Representation', *Theatre Journal*, **40** (2), 1988: 155–77.

Lauretis, T. de, 'Film and the Visible', in Bad Object-Choices (eds), *How Do I Look? Queer Film and Video*. Seattle: Bay Press, 1991: 223–64.

Lauretis, T. de, *The Practice of Love. Lesbian Sexuality and Perverse Desire*. Bloomington: Indiana University Press, 1994.

Linden, R. R., Pagano, D. R., Russell, D. E. H. and Leigh Star, S. (eds), *Against Sadomasochism. A Radical Feminist Analysis*. East Palo Alto: Frog in the Well, 1982.

McCormick, R. W., *Politics of the Self. Feminism and the Postmodern in West German Literature and Film*. Princeton: Princeton University Press, 1991.

Maeckelberge, E., *Desperately Seeking Mary. A Feminist Appropriation of a Traditional Religious Symbol*. Kampen: Kok Pharos, 1991.

Marks, E. and de Courtivron, I. (eds), *New French Feminisms*. Amherst: University of Massachusetts Press, 1980.

Martin, B., 'Sexualities Without Genders and Other Queer Utopias', *Diacritics*, **24** (2–3) 1994: 104–21.

Mayne, J., *The Woman at the Keyhole. Feminism and Women's Cinema*. Bloomington: Indiana University Press, 1990.

Mayne, J., *Cinema and Spectatorship*. London and New York: Routledge, 1993.

Mayne, J., *Directed by Dorothy Arzner*, Bloomington: Indiana University Press, 1994.

Mercer, K., 'Skin Head Sex Thing: Racial Difference and the Homoerotic Imaginary', in Bad Object-Choices (eds), *How Do I Look? Queer Film and Video*. Seattle: Bay Press, 1991: 169–210.

Metz, C., *Psychoanalysis and Cinema. The Imaginary Signifier*. London: Macmillan, 1982.

Miller, N., 'Changing the Subject: Authorship, Writing, and the Reader', in T. de Lauretis (ed.), *Feminist Studies. Critical Studies*. Bloomington: Indiana University Press, 1986: 102–20.

Mitchell, J. and Rose, J., *Feminine Sexuality. Jacques Lacan and the École Freudienne*. New York: W. W. Norton and Company, 1982.

Modleski, T., *Loving with a Vengeance. Mass-produced Fantasies for Women*. New York and London: Methuen, 1984.

Modleski, T., *Studies in Entertainment. Critical Approaches to Mass Culture*. Bloomington: Indiana University Press, 1986.

Modleski, T., *The Women Who Knew Too Much. Hitchcock and Feminist Theory*. New York and London: Methuen,1988.

Modleski, T., *Feminism Without Women. Culture and Criticism in a 'Postfeminist' Age*. New York and London: Routledge, 1991.

Möhrmann, R., 'The Second Awakening of Christa Klages', in S. Frieden,

Bibliography 207

R. W. McCormick, V. R. Petersen and L. M. Vogelsang (eds), *Gender and German Cinema. Feminist Interventions*. vol. I. Providence and Oxford: Berg, 1993: 73–83.

Moi, T. (ed.), *The Kristeva Reader*. New York: Columbia University Press, 1986.

Monaco, J., *How To Read A Film*. New York and Oxford: Oxford University Press, 1981 (rev. edn).

Morgan, R., 'Theory and Practice: Pornography and Rape', in L. Lederer (ed.), *Take Back the Night: Women on Pornography*. New York: Wm. Morrow, 1980.

Morrison, T., *Playing in the Dark. Whiteness and the Literary Imagination*. Cambridge and London: Harvard University Press, 1992.

Mueller, R., 'Introduction', in *Discourse*, **6**, 1983: 4–9.

Mulvey, L., 'Visual Pleasure and Narrative Cinema' (1975), reprinted in *Visual And Other Pleasures*. London: Macmillan, 1989: 14–26.

Mulvey, L., 'Afterthoughts on "Visual Pleasure and Narrative Cinema", inspired by King Vidor's *Duel in the Sun*' (1981), reprinted in *Visual And Other Pleasures*. London: Macmillan, 1989: 29–37.

Neale, S., 'Masculinity As Spectacle', *Screen*, **24** (6), 1983: 2–16.

Nowell-Smith, G., 'A note on "history/discourse"', in J. Caughie (ed.), 1981: 232–41.

Orbach, S., *Fat Is A Feminist Issue*. London: Hamlyn, 1978.

Orbach, S., *Hunger Strike. The Anorectic's Struggle as a Metaphor for our Age*. New York: Avon Books, 1986.

Oudart, J.-P., 'Cinema and Suture', in *Screen*, **18** (4) 1977–8: 35–47.

Oudart, J.-P., 'The Absent Field of the Author', in J. Caughie (ed.), 1981: 261–70.

Parker, R. and Pollock, G., *Old Mistresses: Women, Art and Ideology*. London: Routledge and Kegan Paul, 1981.

Patton, P., 'Anti-Platonism and Art' in C. V. Boundas and D. Olkowski (eds), *Gilles Deleuze and the Theater of Philosophy*. London and New York: Routledge, 1994: 141–56.

Peirce, C. S., 'Logic as Semiotic: The Theory of Signs', in R. E. Innes (ed.), *Semiotics: An Introductory Anthology*. Bloomington: Indiana University Press 1985.

Penley, C. (ed.), *Feminism and Film Theory*. New York: Routledge. London: BFI Publishing, 1988.

Penley, C., Lyon, E., Spigel, L. and Bergstrom, J. (eds), *Close Encounters. Film, Feminism, and Science Fiction*. Minneapolis and Oxford: University of Minnesota Press, 1991.

Pollock, G., 'Missing Women. Rethinking Early Thoughts on Images of Women' in C. Squers, *The Critical image. Essays on Contemporary Photography*. Seattle: Bay Press, 1990: 202–19.

Pribram, E. D. (ed.), *Female Spectators. Looking at Film and Television*. London and New York: Verso, 1988.

Radway, J., *Romancing the Reader: Women, Patriarchy and Popular Literature*. Chapel Hill: University of North Carolina Press, 1984.

Ramanathan, G., 'Murder as Speech: Narrative Subjectivity in Marleen Gorris' *A Question of Silence*', *Genders*, **15**, 1992: 58–71.

Rentschler, E., 'Life with Fassbinder: The Politics of Fear and Pain', *Discourse*, **6**, 1983: 75.

Rich, A., *A Wild Patience Has Taken Me This Far. Poems 1978–1981*. New York and London: W. W. Norton, 1981.

Rich, A., 'Compulsory Heterosexuality and Lesbian Existence', in *Blood, Bread, and Poetry: Selected Prose 1979–1985*. New York: W. W. Norton, 1986: 23–75.

Ricoeur, P., 'The Metaphorical Process as Cognition, Imagination, and Feeling' in H. Adams and L. Searle, *Critical Theory Since 1965*. University Presses of Florida, 1986: 424–34.

Roof, J., *A Lure of Knowledge. Lesbian Sexuality and Theory*. New York: Columbia University Press, 1991.

Root, J., 'Distributing *A Question of Silence*. A Cautionary Tale', in C. Brunsdon (ed.), *Films for Women*. London: British Film Institute Publishing, 1986: 213–23.

Rose, J., *Sexuality in the Field of Vision*. London: Verso, 1986.

Rosen, M., *Popcorn Venus. Women, Movies and the American Dream*. New York: Avon, 1973.

Ross, A. (ed.), *Universal Abandon? The Politics of Postmodernism*. Minneapolis: University of Minnesota Press, 1988.

Rubin, G., 'The Traffic in Women: Notes on the "Political Economy" of Sex', in R. R. Reiter (ed.), *Toward an Anthropology of Women*. New York: Monthly Review Press, 1975: 157–210.

Rubin, G., 'Thinking Sex: Notes for a Radical Theory of the Politics of Sexuality' in C. Vance (ed.), *Pleasure and Danger*, Boston, etc.: Routledge and Kegan Paul, 1984: 267–319.

Rubin, G., 'Sexual Traffic', in *Differences*, **6** (2–3), Summer-Fall, 1994: 62–99.

Russo, M., 'Female Grotesques: Carnival and Theory' (1986), reprinted in *The Female Grotesque. Risk, Excess and Modernity*. New York and London: Routledge, 1994: 53–73.

Sander, H., *Der subjektive Faktor, vertrackt*, Berlin: Basis-Film-Verleih GmbH, 1980.

Schlesinger P., Dobash, R. E., Dobash, R. P. and Weaver, C. K., *Women Viewing Violence*. London: BFI Publishing, 1992.

Schor, N., 'Dreaming Dissymmetry: Barthes, Foucault, and Sexual Difference' in A. Jardine and P. Smith (eds), *Men in Feminism*. New York and London: Methuen, 1987: 98–110.

Schor, N., 'This Essentialism Which Is Not One: Coming to Grips with Irigaray', in C. Burke, N. Schor and M. Whitford (eds), *Engaging with Irigaray. Feminist Philosophy and Modern European Thought*. New York: Columbia University Press, 1994: 57–78.

Shiach, M., *Hélène Cixous. A Politics of Writing*. London and New York: Routledge, 1991.

Silverman, K., 'Helke Sander and the Will to Change', *Discourse*, **6**, 1983a: 10–30.

Silverman, K., *The Subject of Semiotics*. New York and Oxford: Oxford University Press, 1983b.

Silverman, K., *The Acoustic Mirror. The Female Voice in Psychoanalysis and*

Cinema. Bloomington: Indiana University Press, 1988.

Silverman, K., *Male Subjectivity at the Margins*. New York and London: Routledge, 1992.

Silverman, K., *The Threshold of the Visible World*. New York and London: Routledge, 1996.

Simpson, M., *Male Impersonators. Men Performing Masculinity*. London: Cassell, 1994.

Snitow, A., Stansell, C. and Thompson, S. (eds), *Powers of Desire. The Politics of Sexuality*. New York: Monthly Review Press, 1983.

Sontag, S., *On Photography*. Harmondsworth: Penguin Books, 1979.

Spivak, G. C., 'Displacement and the Discourse of Woman', in M. Krupnick (ed.), *Displacement, Derrida and After*. Bloomington: Indiana University Press, 1983: 169–95.

Stacey, J., 'Desperately Seeking Difference', *Screen*, 28 (1) 1987: 48–61.

Stacey, J., *Star Gazing. Hollywood Cinema and Female Spectatorship*. London and New York: Routledge, 1994.

Stacey, J., '*Desert Hearts* and the Lesbian Romance Film' in T. Wilton (ed.), *Immortal Invisible. Lesbians and the Moving Image*, London and New York: Routledge, 1995: 92–130.

Stam, R., Burgoyne, R., Flitterman-Lewis, S., *New Vocabularies in Film Semiotics. Structuralism, Post-Structuralism and Beyond*. London and New York: Routledge, 1992.

Stanton, D. C., 'Language and Revolution: The Franco-American Disconnection', in H. Eisenstein and A. Jardine (eds), *The Future of Difference*. New Brunswick: Rutgers University Press, 1985: 73–87.

Stanton, D. C., 'Difference on Trial: A Critique of the Maternal Metaphor in Cixous, Irigaray, and Kristeva', in N. K. Miller (ed.), *The Poetics of Gender*. New York: Columbia University Press, 1986: 157–82.

Studlar, G., *In the Realm of Pleasure. Von Sternberg, Dietrich, and the Masochistic Aesthetic*. New York: Columbia University Press, 1988.

Suleiman, S. R., *The Female Body in Western Culture*. Cambridge, MA and London: Harvard University Press, 1986: 99–119.

Tasker, Y., *Spectacular Bodies. Gender, Genre and the Action Cinema*. London and New York, 1993.

Thompson, K., 'The Concept of Cinematic Excess', in P. Rosen (ed.), *Narrative, Apparatus, Ideology. A Film Theory Reader*. New York: Columbia University Press, 1986: 130–42.

Treut, M., 'Perverse Bilder', in K. Beinstein, *Obszöne Frauen*. Wien: Promedia Verlag, 1986: 5–19.

Treut, M., 'Female Misbehavior', in L. Pietropaolo and A. Testaferri (eds), *Feminism in the Cinema*. Bloomington: Indiana University Press: 1995: 106–21.

Vance, C. S. (ed.), *Pleasure and Danger. Exploring Female Sexuality*. Boston etc.: Routledge and Kegan Paul, 1984.

Wallace, M., *Invisibility Blues. From Pop to Theory*. London and New York: Verso, 1990.

Wallace, M., 'Race, Gender, and Psychoanalysis in Forties Film', in M. Diawara (ed.), *Black American Cinema*. New York and London: Routledge, 1993: 257–71.

Weiss, A., *Vampires and Violets. Lesbians in the Cinema.* London: Jonathan Cape, 1992.

White, P., 'Female Spectator, Lesbian Specter: The Haunting', in D. Fuss (ed.), *Inside/Out. Lesbian Theories, Gay Theories.* New York and London: Routledge, 1991: 142–72.

Whitford, M., *Luce Irigaray. Philosophy in the Feminine.* London and New York: Routledge, 1991.

Williams, L., 'A Jury of their Peers: Marleen Gorris' *A Question of Silence*', in E. A. Kaplan (ed.), *Postmodernism and its Discontents.* London and New York: Verso, 1988: 107–15.

Wilton, T., (ed.), *Immortal Invisible. Lesbians and the Moving Image.* London and New York: Routledge, 1995.

Wittig, M., *The Straight Mind and Other Essays.* New York etc.: Harvester Wheatsheaf, 1992.

Wollen, P., *Signs and Meanings in the Cinema.* Bloomington: Indiana University Press, 1972.

Woolf, V., *A Room of One's Own.* London: Panther Books, 1977 (1929).

Wright, E. (ed.), *Feminism and Psychoanalysis. A Critical Dictionary.* Oxford: Blackwell, 1992.

Young, L., *Fear of the Dark. 'Race', Gender and Sexuality in the Cinema.* London and New York: Routledge, 1996.

Filmography

(d. = director, s. = script, c. = camera, ed. = editor. Prod. = production)

Bagdad Café. Out of Rosenheim
Germany, 1988
d. Percy Adlon, s. Percy and Eleonore Adlon, c. Bernd Heinl, ed. Norbert Herzner
Prod. Pelemele Film GmbH/Project Filmproduction
With Marianne Sägebrecht (Jasmin), C. C. H. Pounder (Brenda), Jack Palance (Rudi Cox) and others
91 min., colour

Broken Mirrors (*Gebroken Spiegels*)
Netherlands, 1984
d. Marleen Gorris, s. Marleen Gorris, c. Frans Bromet, ed. Hans van Dongen
Prod. Matthijs van Heijningen/Sigma Filmsproductions BV
With Lineke Rijxman (Diane), Henriëtte Tol (Dora), Coby Stunnenberg (Madame), Edda Barends (nameless victim), Eddy Brugman (nameless murderer) and others
116 min., colour

Cruel Embrace (*Les Noces Barbares*)
Belgium/France, 1987
d. Marion Hänsel, s. Marion Hänsel, novel Yann Queffelec, c. Walter vanden Ende, ed. Susana Rossberg
Prod. Man's Films/Flach Film/TF1 Productions/RTL-TV1
With Thierry Fremont (Ludo), Marianne Basler (Nicole), André Penvern (husband) and others
100 min., colour

Dust
Belgium/France, 1983
d. Marion Hänsel, s. Marion Hänsel, novel J. M. Coetzee, c. Walter vanden Ende, ed. Susanna Rossberg
Prod. Man's Film/Daska Film/Flach Films/Fr 3 Production France
With Jane Birkin (Magda), Trevor Howard (Baas), John Matshikiza (Henrik), Nadine Uwampa (Anna) and others
87 min., colour

A Question of Silence (*De Stilte Rond Christine M.*)
Netherlands, 1982
d. Marleen Gorris, s. Marleen Gorris, c. Frans Bromet, ed. Hans van Dongen
Prod. Matthijs van Heijningen/Sigma Filmproductions BV
With Cox Habbema (Janine van den Bos), Henriëtte Tol (Andrea), Edda Barends (Christine), Nelly Frijda (An) and others
109 min., colour

211

The Subjective Factor (*Der subjektive Faktor*)
Germany, 1981
d. Helke Sander, s. Helke Sander, c. Martin Schäfer, ed. Ursula Hof
Prod. Filmproduktion/ZDF
With Angelika Rommel (Anni), Nikolaus Dutsch, Johanna Sophia, Lutz Weidlich
and others
138 min., colour

Sweetie
Australia, 1989
d. Jane Campion, s. Jane Campion, Gerard Lee, c. Sally Bongers, ed. Veronika
Haussler
Prod. Arena Film Pty Ltd
With Geneviève Lemon (Dawn/Sweetie), Karen Colston (Kay), Tom Lycos,
Jon Darling and others
97 min., colour

The Virgin Machine (*Die Jungfrauenmaschine*)
Germany, 1988
d. Monika Treut, s. Monika Treut, c. Elfi Mikesch, ed. Renate Merck
Prod. Hyäne Film I/II
With Ina Blum (Dorothée), Dominique Gaspar, Susie Sexpert and others
85 min., black and white

Index